To Bill,
Hope you enjoy the book
you helped write so...p
of it.
All the BEST.
Coli x·x

BELIEVING A MAN CAN FLY:
MEMORIES OF A LIFE
IN SPECIAL EFFECTS AND FILM

by Colin Chilvers and Aaron Lam

BearManor Media

Orlando, Florida

Believing a Man Can Fly: Memories of a Life in Special Effects and Film
Copyright © 2020 Colin Chilvers and Aaron Lam. All Rights Reserved.

No part of this book may be reproduced in any form or by any means, electronic, mechanical, digital, photocopying or recording, except for the inclusion in a review, without permission in writing from the the publisher.

Published in the USA by
BearManor Media
1317 Edgewater Dr. #110
Orlando, FL 32804
www.BearManorMedia.com

Hardcover Edition
ISBN-10: 1-62933-518-5
ISBN-13: 978-1-62933-518-6

Printed in the United States of America

Table of Contents

Foreword

Not every 16-year-old gets to see Superman fly. And I'm not talking about watching him on television or reading one of his adventures in a comic book. It was 1977, and I was in the Fortress of Solitude on the legendary 007 Stage at Pinewood Studios.

Standing at one end of the set was a soon-to-be-famous actor named Christopher Reeve, who was garbed in the famous blue, red and yellow costume of the world's most popular superhero. When director Richard Donner called for action, Chris defied gravity and took to the air with an effortlessness befitting a bird on the wind. This was *magic*. Pure and simple.

From that moment, I was hooked. I knew how I wanted to spend the rest of my life - I wanted to follow in my Uncle Colin's footsteps and create special effects for movies.

Working as a runner on *Superman: The Movie* was the best summer job a kid could have asked for. I did anything that was asked of me, from buying supplies for the workshop to making tea for the crew, all while trying to learn as much about the filmmaking craft as possible. As the Creative Supervisor and Director of Special Effects, Colin proved to be an excellent mentor as I took my first steps into a new world.

Despite my never-ending barrage of questions, Colin was happy to show me the ropes and pass on his knowledge. We worked together again on *Saturn 3, Superman II* and *Superman III*, and I was grateful for his boundless patience and support.

That's one of the great things about Colin - his openness. When he took me under his wing, he kept an open-door policy and was always available for a chat. He had a genuine passion for helping the next generation of filmmaking artists and technicians - something that lives on to this day.

My career continued to grow and develop over the years, and I found myself supervising special effects for such directors as Steven Spielberg, Ridley Scott and Roland Emmerich. In a field with so many remarkable peers, I consider myself extremely fortunate to have been awarded Oscars for my work on *Gladiator* and *Gravity*.

But Colin did it first. Along with five of his colleagues, he won an Academy Award for *Superman*. Long before the CGI revolution, the special effects they created made the world believe that a man could fly.

The book you are now reading is the story of how Colin got to that point - then continued soaring. After becoming an accomplished director himself, he went on to collaborate with Michael Jackson to create the most ambitious music video ever produced. He also helped the X-Men leap from the comic-book page to the big screen for the very first time.

Colin's life reads like a great adventure story. That's because it really *is* one. But I don't want to reveal too much and ruin it for you. As with all stories worth telling, getting there is half the fun.

Neil Corbould
November 2018

Acknowledgments

From Colin Chilvers:

I would like to acknowledge all of the people who helped me on my journey, who are too numerous to mention, but will have my undying appreciation. These people were my rocks.

I am grateful for the love and understanding of my wife Colleen and her large and generous family.

For my daughter Lucy, her husband Martin and her mother Josie.

For Mom, Dad, my sister Jean Corbould and my nephews Chris, Ian, Paul, Neil and my niece Gail, who have continued and improved upon what I started many years ago.

For Glen Robinson, my mentor and friend whose spirit still burns bright in my heart.

For the teachers who encouraged me, and my neighbours, family and friends from my early years who gave me so many good memories.

For my effects crews, film crews and fellow directors, who helped and inspired me.

For Michael Jackson, a man of the century who believed in me.

For Aaron Lam, who says that *Superman* was the movie that made him take flight.

The Chilvers of the world that I am proud to be a part of.

From Aaron Lam:

My sincere thanks to the amazing folks at BearManor Media, especially Ben Ohmart, for making the publication of this book such a pleasure.

Thank you to Allan Duffin of Duffin Creative for your patience and attention to detail.

Special thanks to Jim Bowers of CapedWonder.com for allowing us to use his rare behind-the-scenes photographs from the making of the Superman movies. Please visit his website, which is an incredible source of information and photos. Jim - your passion and dedication are a true inspiration!

Thank you to Kristine Krueger, Kristen Ray and Faye Thompson of the Academy of Motion Picture Arts and Sciences, Buddy Weiss and Todd Ifft of Photofest, Cathy Roy of the Niagara Falls Public Library, and Ruth Stoner and Jim Hill of Niagara Parks for their help with photography for the book.

Many thanks to Anita Pang Hrepic, Brad Moll, Celine Brideau and Brittany Strickland of the Skylon Tower for your help locating and photographing the menu used for the *Superman II* wrap party. Visiting the Skylon Tower is a must for any visitor to Niagara Falls!

A boatload of appreciation to Derek Fryer, Darren Lampson, Michael Cordeiro and Alyssa Lai for your support at the office. I couldn't have done it without your good humour and tolerance of my bad puns. And extra thanks to Derek for the amazing art he created for this book's cover.

Thank you to Neil Corbould for taking the time to chat about your early days in the film industry with Colin.

A big shout out to Owen Gifford for reading my first draft of the manuscript and providing feedback.

Thanks to Vivienne Mathers for always believing.

My love and appreciation to Ben and Anna Lam, Ryan and Franziska Lam, Moe and Shirley Murphy, Tina Murphy and the late Finley for your bottomless reserves of love and support.

A whole bunch of thanks to my wife Erin Murphy and our beautiful daughter Laura. Your love is at the core of everything I am and everything I do.

And of course, many thanks to Colin and Colleen Chilvers for your warmth, generosity and friendship. I am forever grateful.

Introduction by Aaron Lam

"Wanna see *Superman*?" Dad asked me on that fateful day in 1979.

I was out for a Sunday stroll with my family at Ontario Place in Toronto, when the poster for *Superman: The Movie* caught our attention. The Cinesphere, which was the golfball-shaped theatre that usually played IMAX documentaries about things like sharks and volcanoes, was playing *Superman* as part of a feature-film series.

The poster was pure magic. That unmistakable Superman "S" was framed against a moody sky, with a dramatic shaft of blue, yellow and red energy surging past the emblem and into the mysterious void beyond. Below the beautiful artwork was a simple tagline: "YOU'LL BELIEVE A MAN CAN FLY."

I was immediately hooked. I had to see this movie. Right away.

"Are you sure you want to watch it?" Dad asked. "Aren't you a little old for this sort of thing?"

"Nope," I replied. After all, I was only 5 years old.

"Okay. Let's get tickets."

For the next two and a half hours, we sat spellbound as the greatest comic book adventure of all time unfolded before us. From the very first note of John Williams' classic soundtrack, this movie kicked ass. Christopher Reeve *was* Superman. Margot Kidder *was* Lois Lane. *Superman: The Movie* was perfection.

It was the most exciting film I'd ever seen in a theatre. Come to think of it, *Superman* was the *first* film I'd ever seen in a theatre.

Even after the Man of Steel had finished saving the day, I sat spellbound as the end credits rolled to the heavenly sounds of the London Symphony Orchestra. Colin Chilvers. Derek Meddings. Les Bowie. And the list went on. These were the names of the magicians who'd made me believe that a man could fly. Those names would become quite familiar to me after my first dozen or so viewings of the film over the next several years. Thus began my obsession with *Superman: The Movie* that continues to this day.

By the time *Superman II* was released, my bedroom wall was plastered with posters of Superman, Lois Lane and General Zod (the best villain this side of the 28 known galaxies). I loved the second film almost as much as the first, and I applauded along with my fellow moviegoers when Superman saved that little boy from falling to his death in Niagara Falls. I was living in Dunnville, just down the road from Niagara, so it was thrilling to know that Superman had dropped by to perform some heroic deeds in my neighbourhood.

Little did I know that Colin Chilvers, the special-effects supervisor of the first three *Superman* films, was living just outside of Niagara Falls. It would take another thirty years or so before we'd actually meet.

"Colin Chilvers" was a name that I'd always respected. The guy won an Academy Award for *Superman*, which was impressive enough on its own, but it was much more than that. My brother Ryan was the world's biggest Michael Jackson fan, and I was totally blown away when he first showed me MJ's video for "Smooth Criminal." It wasn't just another music video - it was a 40-minute-long special-effects extravaganza with Michael Jackson morphing into a robot, fighting gangsters in a magical nightclub, and transforming into a spaceship to battle an evil warlord hellbent on selling drugs to the kids of the world. It had gun battles, a futuristic sports car, and a giant laser cannon that emerged from the side of a mountain. You couldn't fit more coolness into a single video. And who directed it? Colin Chilvers.

I was also a huge fan of the 1953 film *The War of the Worlds*. When it was announced that a new series based on H. G. Wells' classic story was scheduled to air in 1988, I knew I couldn't miss it. The two-hour series premiere was amazing, especially its explosive finale that featured Martian warships from the 1953 film blasting their way out of a top-secret government warehouse. Just awesome. And who directed it? Colin Chilvers.

On top of that, he also worked on *2001: A Space Odyssey*, *The Rocky Horror Picture Show* and *X-Men*. Not a bad track record.

Fast-forward to 2011. By this time, I was a documentary filmmaker and journalist working in Hamilton, Ontario. A friend of mine in the film industry was acquainted with Colin, and upon learning what a huge *Superman* fan I was, he told Colin about what a fanboy I was. My friend provided me with Colin's contact info and recommended that I reach out.

Picking up the phone to call Colin was one of the most nerve-wracking things I'd ever done. His work as a special-effects supervisor and director had meant the world to me growing up. When I finally mustered up enough courage, I dialed his number and left the rest to fate.

Colin answered the phone with a calm, friendly tone that immediately put my nerves at ease. That didn't stop me from gushing to him about how much *Superman* had always meant to me, but at least I didn't come across as hysterical. At least, I hope I didn't.

I asked Colin if we could meet for a coffee and discuss his career, which would be the equivalent of winning the lottery for a film historian like myself. To my delight, he invited me over to his house for a visit instead. It was surprising to discover that Colin had been living so close to me for all these years. If only I'd known about this back in the eighties - I would have been the happiest kid in the world! But now was better than never.

On my way to visit Colin, I blasted the *Superman* soundtrack through my car speakers. It felt like the right thing to do, as geeky as it was. Listening to John Williams' music during my drive made the day seem even more surreal. Was this really happening to me, or was it just a dream?

When I first pulled up to Colin's house, a handmade sign on his neighbour's fence caught my eye. A familiar name was etched across it: "The Kents." As it turns out, the neighbours weren't related to Clark Kent at all, but it was a suitable last name for the people living next to the man who'd made Superman fly.

When Colin answered his door, he greeted me with a relaxed smile that I've since gotten to know quite well.

"The Tour de France is just finishing up," he said. "Do you mind if we chat while we watch the end of it?"

We ended up chatting about his career for the next three and a half hours, first in front of the TV as the Tour de France came to its conclusion, and then in his backyard with its beautiful view of Lake Erie. Colin was happy to answer my questions about his career, especially his experiences making *Superman*, and he was generous enough to let me hold his Academy Award.

"Have you ever thought about writing a book about your life?" I asked.

"Sure," he said, "but I never got any further than jotting down some preliminary notes."

The afternoon went quickly, from my perspective anyway, and my visit came to an end because Colin had a business meeting booked for that evening. It was an unforgettable day and I was determined to remember his every word for posterity's sake.

The following day, I sent Colin an email to thank him for his hospitality. He sent a response back shortly, but it wasn't exactly what I was expecting.

"You know that book idea we were talking about?" he wrote. "Would you be interested in co-writing it with me?"

And so began the next two years of interviews and movie screenings at the Chilvers residence for the creation of the book you are now reading. I've had the pleasure of spending many afternoons shooting the shit with Colin, and I'm thankful to him and his wife Colleen for their kindness and friendship. And even though I'm more of a dog person, I like their cats too.

Collaborating with Colin on his autobiography has been a dream come true for me, and I feel honoured to help share his stories with a wider audience. Working on this book has never been a chore, largely thanks to his patience and good humour.

Colin has called me "the most obsessed *Superman* nut he's ever met." Whenever I share a new piece of obscure *Superman* trivia with him, he just shakes his head, grins quizzically and asks, "How do you know all this stuff?" I get a real kick out of seeing his reactions to my sheer geekiness, and I'm proud to report that he gave me that same head shake and bemused smile when I first did my General Zod impersonation for him, which, for the record, is spot on.

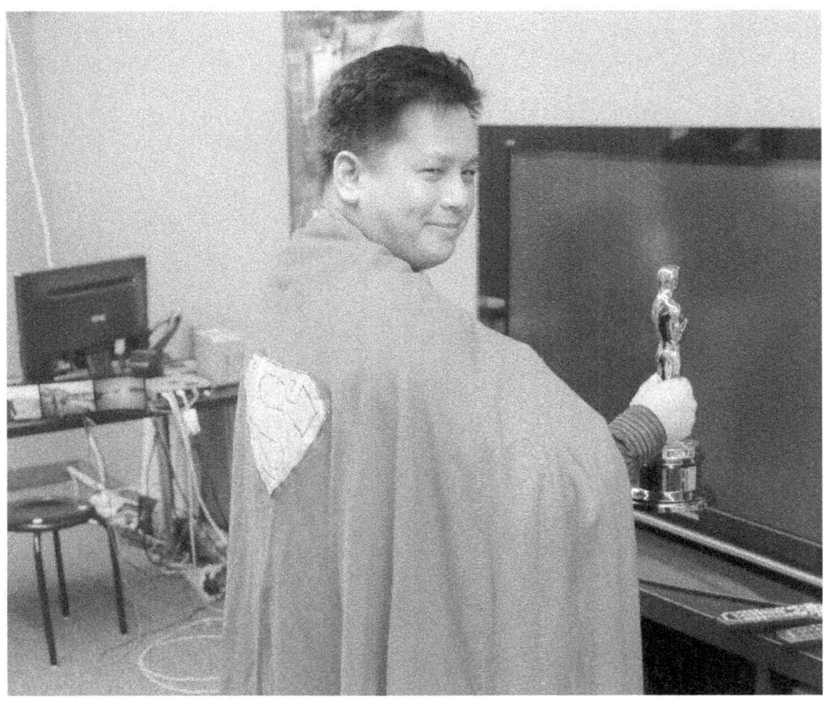

Me wearing a cape from *Superman II* while holding Colin's Academy Award.

In 2013, Colin attended his first ever Comic Con in Niagara Falls, and I joined him so I could gather more material for the book. Many fans approached Colin at his booth to ask for an autograph or share their fond memories of his work. Colin was always gracious when interacting with his fans, and he was happy to let people hold his Academy Award.

At one point, Colin needed to leave his booth for a washroom break. "I'll be back in a few minutes," he told me. "Make sure nobody walks off with Oscar, and if anybody asks, just say *you're* Colin Chilvers."

Colin has led an eventful life, full of remarkable accomplishments, crushing disappointments and unforgettable memories. After spending a little time in the life of Colin Chilvers through the pages of this book, I bet you'll agree that the journey was worth taking. And better yet, he'll make you believe that a man can fly.

CHAPTER 1
MAGIC IN BLACK & WHITE

Steve Martin had an arrow piercing his head. Not a real arrow, thank goodness, but one of those gag arrows that curves around the back of your head to create the illusion that it has tunneled through your brain. He also had a green hood covering his entire head. A strange sight, yes, but it all made sense.

The date was April 9, 1979, and I was backstage at the Dorothy Chandler Pavilion in Los Angeles for the 51st Academy Awards. Standing beside me (and the hooded, arrow-inflicted Steve Martin) were my fellow special-effects artists from *Superman: The Movie* - Denys Coop, Roy Field, Derek Meddings and Zoran Perisic. The sixth member of our team who was scheduled to be awarded that evening, Les Bowie, had recently passed away, so we would accept the Oscar on his behalf.

In retrospect, Les was the person responsible for starting Derek and I in the field of special effects, so it was especially sad that Les was not able to join us for such a prestigious honour.

On stage was the host of the evening, Johnny Carson, who introduced that "wild and crazy guy" Steve Martin to present us with Special Achievement Oscars for the effects we'd created for *Superman*.

Martin walked onto the stage with the hood and fake arrow, which got quite a laugh from the crowd. Thanks to special-effects magic, people watching the Oscars on TV saw Steve Martin without a head at all, and the arrow appeared to float in the air above his shoulders, following him wherever he went. His hood was removed from the shot as a live video effect, much like maps are added behind weather reporters during a news broadcast.

Also waiting in the wings backstage were Superman and Lois Lane themselves, Christopher Reeve and Margot Kidder, who would present the Oscar for Outstanding Achievement in Sound after the award for Best Visual Effects was presented.

It was a bit of an unusual year at the Oscars, as the Academy of Motion Picture Arts and Sciences had decided to give the visual-effects award to the *Superman* team without nominating any other films in the category. The Academy had felt that *Superman* was the clear winner without any other films at our competitive level. That doesn't happen very often and it's quite an honour when it does.

Soon, Steve Martin would be calling our names, and it would be our turn to make our grand appearance in front of the packed house and the millions of viewers watching around the world. Needless to say, I was scared shitless. All I had to do was walk onto stage when our names were called, pick up my statuette and look gracious, but I still couldn't keep my knees from buckling.

It all seemed so unreal. Of course I'd dreamed about winning an Academy Award someday, but part of me never thought the dream would come true. Yet here I was, about to be invited on stage by Steve Martin to accept an Oscar for a blockbuster film. We had also been awarded recently by the British Academy of Film and Television Arts, but being honoured by Hollywood was the icing on the cake.

My thoughts drifted back to my childhood growing up in Kentish Town.

My life had taken so many strange twists and turns since then. If only I'd known back then what the journey ahead would bring.

I started off with both feet planted firmly on the ground. Sort of. I was a happy child growing up in Kentish Town, a suburb of North London, England, with a loving household and a closely-knit community that made my formative years safe and nurturing.

But part of me was always stargazing, pondering fantastic worlds beyond the limitations of reality. I was craving adventure beyond the familiar trappings of my cozy little neighborhood. Little did I know that I would one day visit the planet Krypton and moonwalk with the Prince of Pop. But that would come later. First, I had the whole "growing up" thing to experience.

Feeding pigeons in London.

Kentish Town was a magical place for a kid in the forties and fifties. Neighbours were more than just nameless people who happened to live beside you. People really knew each other in the community and, more importantly, people actually took the time to care about each other.

We lived on a tiny street that was too narrow for any cars to squeeze down, so we could play outside without fear of being hit by traffic. With rows of terraced houses on both sides of the street, it looked a bit like *Coronation Street*. Kids would often tie ropes onto the lamp posts to make swings, secure in the knowledge that someone in the community was always on the lookout for their safety. It was a good time. A good childhood.

I was born at the end of the war in 1945 when my mother Kate was 44 years old, and I was an unexpected addition to the family 13 years after the birth of my sister Jean. When my mother became pregnant with me, she thought it was just a cold coming on. Boy was she mistaken. My parents weren't expecting to be changing diapers again any time soon. I was the sudden splash of water in their faces (quite literally, especially when diaper changes were involved). But despite my surprise arrival, they always treated me like an unexpected blessing.

My parents Kate and Cornelius.

I've always admired the strong work ethic of my parents. My father Cornelius, the youngest of thirteen children, worked for the local council in waste management. My mother joined the war effort at a local factory that manufactured aircraft parts and was employed there until her retirement at the age of 84.

Although my childhood memories of Kentish Town were full of happiness and security, it wasn't always the case for my parents. The Blitz transformed the face of London, reducing much of it to rubble and making life in the city one of fear, pain and death.

Sometimes my mother would sleep in the underground stations when the bombs started falling. It was the safest place to be and it was better to have an uncomfortable night if it meant living to see another day. Other times, she acted as fire-watcher on her factory's roof to ensure that none of the bombs were setting the building aflame.

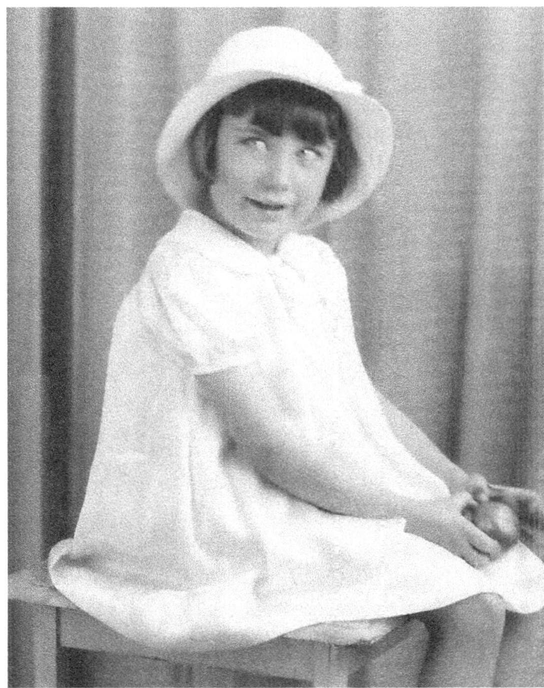

My sister Jean

Being too old to be called up for military service, my father volunteered and ended up fighting at the Siege of Malta. He was a Royal Marine who felt strongly about serving his country and making it a safer place for future generations.

My sister Jean was thirteen years older than me, and my parents decided that staying in London during the Blitz was too dangerous for a small girl like her, so Jean was evacuated to Guildford for two years.

Luckily for me, I came along too late to witness the horrors of World War II with my own eyes. With both parents working much of the time, Jean was like a mother to me and she played a major role in my upbringing. In fact, I was more scared of my sister than I was of my parents.

Our house was tiny, what we called a "two-up, two-down" because it had two main rooms downstairs and two small bedrooms on the second floor, as well as a cramped scullery kitchen, a loft or "boxing room" as we call it in England, and an outside toilet. The house may not have been a mansion, but it was a home that was always full of warmth from family and friends who would drop by for a cup of tea and a chat.

My parents in front of our home in Kentish Town.

As kind and sociable as my neighbours were, I had a naturally reserved temperament and I spent a lot of time alone in my youth. When I was four or five years old, I would go and hide under the table if we had visitors at the house, making up my own games to keep myself entertained.

My mother would call me "The Daydreamer" because I'd be lost in my own imagination all the time. I think it was good for my creativity because I didn't have the distraction of siblings or other kids. It allowed me to live inside of myself and create my own imaginative worlds.

Creativity didn't seem to have been passed down to me from my parents, who had practical jobs and lived very practical lives. My sister, however, demonstrated creative spark with her strong sense of fashion, and she channeled that into a job as a buyer for the children's department of a local store.

The creativity gene seems to have been passed on to the next generation, as two of my nephews, Chris and Neil Corbould, have already won Academy Awards for special effects. My nephews Ian and Paul, along with their sister Gail, also work in the field and continue to make the "Corbould" name synonymous with special effects in England.

Perhaps I inherited some of my creativity from my Uncle Toggy. We used to visit him in Stratford, not the one made famous by Shakespeare, but in the Docklands of London's East End. He was a talented carpenter who loved to make things out of wood. I would watch as he'd pull driftwood out of the local canal, the cheapest source of building materials. Uncle Toggy would dry out the wood and use it to build the most beautiful pieces of furniture. We both loved to get our hands dirty and create something out of nothing.

The only other relative in our immediate circle with a strong creative bent was Uncle Bill. He was a talented musician who could play pretty much any instrument with seemingly no effort. Maybe some of his creative spark also rubbed off on me.

Or maybe my creativity came to me via osmosis from the visitors who regularly packed our living room for the amazing parties thrown by my parents. Uncle Bill always played our piano and we'd have 50 or 60 people crammed into the place. After I was sent to bed, the whole house shook because of all the dancing downstairs. When I listened to the music and laughter coming up through the floor to my bedroom, I still felt a part of things because the whole house was alive with joy.

Gathering around the radio was another way that family and friends spent time together in the evenings. Some of the radio shows were amazing in those days, especially the ones that told tales of alien invaders and flying saucers like "Journey Into Space." This was probably my earliest introduction to the worlds of science fiction and fantasy.

I made a point of never missing one particular serial about a spaceman's intergalactic adventures. My imagination was forced into overdrive and I was on the edge of my seat the entire time. I can still hear the narrator's voice echoing in my head: "Will the heroic spaceman survive his encounter with the deadly lizard man from Mars? Find out next week!"

We didn't own a television until about 1955. The first time I ever watched TV was in 1953 when Queen Elizabeth was crowned. It was at a friend's house and he was the envy of the neighbourhood for having a state-of-the-art television set, which was the size of a refrigerator. It's amazing to think about how far technology has come.

I remember my sense of amazement at seeing images on a television screen for the first time. Pure magic. I was actually peering through someone else's eyes and participating in someone else's life through the magic of the broadcast image. My world suddenly became a whole lot bigger.

But as much as I was dazzled by TV in those days, it still couldn't hold a candle to a good old-fashioned book. It's magic when you read a compelling story with an exciting plot and engaging characters. The simple act of turning pages and feeling the paper under my fingers held a unique satisfaction that TV couldn't compete with.

My personal library continues growing to this day. The book collection at my summer cottage became so large that some creativity was required to find space for everything. I built a special bookshelf that can swing out from the wall to reveal even more room for books behind it. I guess being addicted to books isn't the worst thing in the world.

A Princess of Mars was the first book I'd ever read all the way through in one day, in a single sitting. Uncle Bill gave it to me when I was at home, sick in bed. I was only 10 years old at the time, but the memory of devouring that book is still fresh to this day.

Edgar Rice Burroughs' ability to tell a gripping story and breathe life into his characters was incredible. He was ahead of his time and the sheer level of imagination on display was astonishing. *A Princess of Mars* ended on a great cliffhanger, just like the radio serials, and it made me hungry to read the other books in the series that chronicled the adventures of John Carter. By this time, I was thoroughly hooked on science fiction and I could barely wait to get my next fix.

I always looked forward to reading the latest issue of Eagle Comics, which also featured the fantastic adventures of aliens, superheroes and detectives. Larger-than-life characters like Special Agent Harris Tweed and Navy Commander Storm Nelson came to life in bright primary colors, but it was Dan Dare, Pilot of the Future that always made the biggest splash with readers like me.

His adventures combined the intrigue of war stories with the high-tech gadgetry of science fiction. How could an impressionable young boy in England *not* fantasize about rocketing into action as Dan Dare and saving the gorgeous damsel in distress? These were the early days of the space race and the atomic age, so comic book adventures seemed all the more relevant and convincing to youngsters.

I eventually graduated to more sophisticated science fiction, including the works of Arthur C. Clarke. As fate would have it, I would eventually find myself working on the film version of his most famous novel, *2001: A Space Odyssey*.

I still love the genre for its ability to break free from reality to examine human existence from a fresh perspective. Still, nothing can take away the magic of those pulp novels and comics from my childhood. Sometimes you don't need to justify magic.

By the time I was ten years old, nobody was home after school because everyone was working, including Jean. My parents made arrangements with a friend in the neighborhood to take care of me after class. She was a nice lady who always had tea and cookies waiting. Her two daughters were four or five years older than me and they welcomed me as a surrogate brother. It was like having a second family.

Neither of my parents ever drove and we didn't have a car. If we wanted to visit Uncle Toggy and Aunt Mary in the East end of London, we'd take a couple of connecting buses and travel through the middle of London. The desolation left over from the Blitz was impossible to miss. Seeing bombed-out ruins of buildings everywhere was a regular reminder of the Second World War and its devastating death toll.

When I visited my cousin Allan in North London, I used to find shell casings and shrapnel from the war in the garden. I'd hold those bits of metal in my hand and imagine where they'd come from. The battles, tragedies and victories of the war came to life in my mind. I imagined myself as a great war hero, leading the British charge against the Nazis and striking a remarkable blow for freedom.

Any chance to get out of London was a welcome prospect for me and my family. I loved riding the big old steam trains that made the earth shake when they pulled into the station, and those monstrous engines just smelled wonderful. I know the fumes weren't the healthiest, but I always associated the smell of those trains with the carefree days of summer.

Our annual vacations took us to Canvey Island on the east coast of England. It took two or three hours by train to travel only 40 miles, but it felt like we were going to a different world. Every year, my family and I stayed in the same bungalow with Uncle Bill, Aunt Tich and cousin Allan.

The cottage didn't have enough space inside for all of us at night, so I slept on a bed they dragged out to the covered porch. It was an adventure sleeping outside with the sounds of nature and the shimmering stars to keep me company.

The next two or three weeks were always a refreshing break from the routines of Kentish Town. Uncle Bill and Allan both liked to have a good time and they always filled our vacations with great conversations. We loved to walk up and down the beach picking cockles and contemplating our futures.

The cottage was close to an estuary, where the tide changed dramatically, and we loved to race around the wet rocks and mud during low tide. An old torpedo boat had run aground in the estuary during the war and it still sat there. The things was in quite a state of decay and all of the guns had been stripped off. When the tide was out, you could actually walk out and play on the boat. It was the best playhouse a boy could've asked for.

During our vacations to Canvey Island, I enjoyed going on "Magical Mystery Tours," which involved booking a bus trip without knowing the exact route or destination. It was a great way to do some sightseeing in the area.

Inevitably, the trip would end up at a pub or two. Since we vacationed in the same area year after year, my uncle was quite well known at all of the local pubs. Before long, he was playing the piano and sharing pints with the locals. Because Allan and I were so young, we had to wait outside, but we loved to just sit and listen to the sounds of the piano and the good cheer as it spilled out into the street.

I loved going to the nearby fun fair when we were on vacation. My parents would give me some pocket money and I'd be allowed to go by myself. It was exciting to enjoy the rides and play the games without adult supervision. Ah, the taste of independence. I'd play bingo or ring toss, hoping desperately to come away with a prize of some sort. If I didn't win a prize, I'd often spend my pocket money on something cool like a penknife, which every self-respecting boy needed.

We always looked forward to visiting my parents' friends who lived on a Thames barge, a beautiful old sailing ship about eighty feet long and twenty feet wide. It had huge legs that would be dropped down its sides so it didn't tip over during low tide. What a strange but romantic place to make a home.

It was fun capturing crabs and holding our own version of the Kentucky Derby by racing them along the wooden decks of the ship. With my fanciful imagination and naturally inquisitive disposition, it was easy for a boy like me to find adventure wherever I went.

Sitting on that barge, with its red ochre sails flapping in the wind, I imagined myself as a pirate like Errol Flynn in those classic swashbucklers, sailing the seven seas in search of treasure. I couldn't picture myself living on an old boat like that in real life, but it was always great to visit and lose myself in make-believe escapades of derring-do.

A young man dreaming about adventure.

Given my tendency to daydream, maybe it was only natural that I'd gravitate toward films. In those days, you weren't allowed into the Saturday morning matinee if you were younger than eleven, but I couldn't let something like my age keep me from the movies. My neighbour's daughters used to sneak me into the cinema and we'd spend glorious afternoons living vicariously through the flickering black-and-white images before us. That was my first introduction to the magic of movies on the silver screen.

Jean often took me to the local cinema, which was the hotspot on Friday and Saturday nights. Sometimes I'd piss her off on purpose when they ran the newsreel before the feature. Just like MGM had a roaring lion, the newsreel company had a crowing chicken in its logo. I thought it was the funniest thing, so I would crow out loud in response to the chicken. This would embarrass Jean to no end and she'd sink low into her seat.

The first movies I remember seeing as a boy were the Superman, Flash Gordon and Tarzan serials that played during the kids' matinees. Every week brought a different serial that promised adventure and escape from reality. I also remember loving the 1940 version of *The Thief of Bagdad*, with its amazing special effects and memorable characters.

To actually see characters like Superman and Flash Gordon as "real" people in those serials was mindblowing. Those films are quite crude by today's standards, but they were more than adequate for the time.

In those days, before computer-generated imagery (CGI) was invented to help filmmakers bring the impossible to life onscreen, kids needed to use their imaginations to fill in the gaps when special-effects technology wasn't up to the task. With CGI making everything possible in movies, kids don't need to use their imaginations to the same degree anymore, which is unfortunate.

It's a shame that good storytelling has become secondary in a lot of modern blockbusters that rely too heavily on visual effects. Without a solid story to engage the mind and heart, effects for the sake of effects can be tedious. That being said, some wonderful stories could not have been told as effectively on film before the CGI revolution. Peter Jackson's *Lord of the Rings* films and the Harry Potter movies are prime examples - CGI was put in the service of storytelling that never sacrificed plot and character for the sake of spectacle.

I enjoyed watching those old black-and-white films on a couple of different levels. While I was totally engrossed in the stories themselves, my interest in the filmmaking process was also stimulated. I kept asking myself, "How did they do that?" I didn't know anything back then about double exposures or optical printing or what you could do with film effects, but from a mechanical perspective, I was able to figure out how they were achieving some of their physical effects, and that fascinated me.

As a kid, I was very apt to take things apart. If you gave me something mechanical, I would tear it to pieces in no time flat. I couldn't always put it back together again, but at least it was an educational experience. I was fascinated by how things worked, which set a good foundation for my future career.

The whole filmmaking process, especially when special effects are involved, is essentially problem-solving. Taking things apart and trying to rebuild them helped me to develop problem-solving skills, which came in handy years later when working on the team that figured out how to make Superman fly.

The process of taking a bunch of raw materials and using them to create something functional was always gratifying to me. I loved to gather odds and ends from around the house and construct soap-box carts that I could race around the neighbourhood.

Speeding around in my cart allowed me to have adventures that brought me one step closer to the square-jawed heroes of the comic books and serials - in my imagination, anyway. On top of that, I had the pride of knowing that I had assembled a one-of-a-kind creation using nothing more than my own resourcefulness, and maybe a few old baby-buggy wheels fastened to scraps of lumber. You can't get that kind of satisfaction by going to your local department store and buying something off a shelf.

I also discovered at an early age that I had some natural artistic leanings. I started drawing detailed diagrams to help me figure out the mechanics of things I'd disassembled.

Just taking something apart and learning about its guts wasn't enough for me anymore. It became apparent that a given machine might work a little better if I changed the shape of a part or completely redesigned the whole thing from the ground up. I wanted to be more than a mechanic - I wanted to be an inventor.

Even though I didn't realize it at the time, I was laying the groundwork for a long career in the field of motion-picture special effects. I was setting upon an unusual but seldom boring path that would take me to career heights I never dreamed possible.

CHAPTER 2
DRAWING UPON AN EDUCATION

I didn't feel very engaged during my primary school education. When I reflect back on those early years, I find it strange that the study of art never held any particular interest for me. I was good at math, especially when it came to its practical applications, and I enjoyed drawing diagrams to help me understand the inner workings of machinery, but the study of fine art was too abstract to grab my attention. I was far more interested in engineering real things for use in the real world.

Maybe it was the highly structured nature of schooling that never really appealed to me. Staying on task and retaining a sense of my immediate academic responsibilities was never my strong suit. Much to the chagrin of my teachers over the years, my head was always in the clouds.

Enthusiasm was never in short supply if my imagination was engaged, but that rarely seemed to happen in school. I didn't want to learn about the world second hand; I wanted to be out there in the thick of it all.

Many types of intelligence exist in the world. Being "smart" can mean so many different things to different people. It's a huge mistake to assume that someone who isn't an academic achiever is automatically lacking in intelligence. A bookworm who is extremely proficient in the theoretical teachings of academia can be completely clueless when it comes to the practical application of that theory in the real world.

In whatever field I'd end up working, I wanted to get my hands dirty and put my creative problem-solving abilities to work in a practical way. Maybe I wouldn't end up being a doctor or a professor, but I was determined to leave my mark on the world one way or another. I just wasn't sure how exactly.

If you were academically inclined as a young student in England, they put you into "grammar" school, which focused on academic excellence. Hopefully this would lead to a prestigious university and a career of high esteem (and pay). Somewhat less prestigious was "secondary" school, where students who were more technically inclined were placed for study.

Without the drive to be an academic, I was much better suited for study in secondary school and I soon found myself excelling in carpentry, woodworking, metalworking and technical drawing. I still had to take English, math and other basic subjects, but the emphasis was on studies that were practical and technical in nature.

Secondary school marked the beginning of my interest in art. After seeing the little sketches in the margins of my notebooks, my art teacher told me I had real potential and called me one of the best artists at the school. Nothing sparks enthusiasm more than being told how good you are.

My best friend Peter Proto and I were nurtured more than other students in art class because of our interest and ability, and I was soon fascinated by the use of line and colour in the expression of emotion. After all, that's what art is really about - stimulating the senses and engaging the viewer on an emotional level.

Thus began a lifelong passion for art. I fell in love with the infinite number of ways in which colours, lines and patterns could be combined to create a painting, a sculpture or a motion picture. That love of art still flourishes today, with bronze sculptures and paintings adorning my home.

Something was awakened inside of me when I started to put pencil to paper and brush to canvas. I found a sense of personal direction. Maybe I could be an artist — not just a hobbyist, but a professional. Creating art just felt right to me. If I could do something for a living that allowed me to hold on to that feeling, I would be a happy man indeed.

From secondary school, Peter and I went to the Hornsey College of Art together. I specialized in exhibition and industrial design, and Peter studied graphic design, which helped him become one of the top graphic designers in England. He would go on to design all of the packaging for the grocery store chain Sainsbury's in the sixties, starting a revolution in packaging design with his modernistic style for Sainsbury's Own products. Peter would also design the production office letterhead for *Superman: The Movie* years later.

Unfortunately, Peter's father was less than happy about his son's decision to attend arts college instead of joining the family trade as a plumber. I think his dad always blamed me for convincing Peter to study art instead of pursuing a plumbing apprenticeship.

The Hornsey College of Art was set up in a very strange fashion with a main building and a separate annex that had once been a primary school. Whenever we had classes in the annex, we would laugh every time we went to the washroom because the tiny toilet seats were only about nine inches off the ground - perfect if you're a six-year-old. Such was the life of an art student, where even the toilets were out of the ordinary.

The college had a wonderful photography department that soon became like a second home to me. I enjoyed the entire photographic process, from framing my compositions through the viewfinder to developing and printing the final images.

Photography allowed me to be a master of reality, which is what the motion picture business is ultimately about. That's even more true in the world of special effects, where new realities must be created from the ground up.

My interest in photography helped me develop an artist's eye. When viewing everything through the lens, whether trying to capture a perfect image from nature or a precious moment in a person's life, photography forced me to stop and notice the lines, shapes and colours in the world around me.

I always enjoyed opportunities to get away from the campus and venture out into the city. Our field trips often involved hopping on a bus and visiting a museum or a castle to sketch for the day. London was such a wonderful place to be an artist because inspiration was so easy to find everywhere you looked. The city has always been a curious mixture of tradition and trendsetting, full of proud history while also striving to be on the leading edge of culture.

We had two professors who enjoyed taking us on trips, and they had extremely different approaches to illustration. I was lucky to get both of their perspectives because they were both extremely influential in my development as an artist.

The one professor was an older gentleman with traditional views on the proper way to draw things, and he wanted us to create photorealistic illustrations by closely observing the environment around us. Our artistic interpretations of reality were of no interest to him - he wanted us to develop our skills capturing even the most subtle visual details of the people, places and objects that we take for granted every day.

That attention to detail ended up being very valuable in the film industry, especially when it came to designing equipment for special effects. I had always enjoyed drawing technical diagrams, so I appreciated this photorealistic approach to sketching.

The other professor who took us on field trips was interested in developing the "artist" in us, not just the "craftsperson." We each carried sketchbooks and the teacher made us divide a sheet into 40 rectangles of the same size. Coincidentally, they had a ratio of roughly 16:9, like a motion picture frame.

This professor wasn't interested in photorealism at all. He wanted us to spend the morning filling up the 40 rectangles with our artistic *interpretations* of things we saw. In his opinion, photorealism was for photographers and he wanted us to get in touch with our unique artistic voices through our sketches. I loved the freedom to interpret reality in my own way and I appreciated how he encouraged us to let our imaginations run wild.

"Composition is as important as the subject itself." That's something he taught us that always stuck with me. In both illustration and photography, your use of space and how things fit into that little frame is of primary importance. A hundred students might draw the same castle or take a photograph of the same museum, but the framing of the image and the use of space within the confines of that frame can determine whether that image is simply routine or is truly memorable.

We would come back at lunchtime and the professor looked at what we'd drawn in the morning. Then we went back out after lunch and we'd have to fill another 40 rectangles. This exercise forced us to look at the world with fresh eyes. I started to notice lines and forms that I hadn't noticed before, and how perspective and movement added interest and energy to images. It was amazing how much that exercise altered my perception and informed my artwork.

Gaining that kind of visual knowledge was probably the best thing that happened at art school. If anything came out of my time at college, it was the ability to *see*. The best artists are able to see what other people cannot. Whereas one person might see a boring old tree, an artist might see the most beautiful lines in the world.

I'd always had a high level of respect for artists, whether it was comic book illustrators or celebrated painters whose works hung on the walls of famous art galleries. However, I started to question my own level of artistic ability, and I came to realize that I wasn't good enough to be what I would call a fine artist. I could draw technical diagrams or do quick sketches, like the ones I had to do in the 40 rectangles. I loved to do those because I didn't need to draw perfectly, but I didn't have the level of control or technique to make it professionally as a fine artist.

Realizing I couldn't make a living painting landscapes or portraits, I started to think about other potential ways I could put my artistic skills to use professionally and actually get paid to do it. Maybe I could find an avenue to channel my artistic energies in the film industry.

Perhaps special effects in particular might be worth considering. I thought back to the days of my childhood when the amazing adventures of Superman and Flash Gordon took my breath away. Perhaps I could find a way to become a part of that movie magic myself.

To my dismay, economic reality kept rearing its ugly head. College wasn't cheap and the loftiest dreams in the world wouldn't mean a thing if I didn't have at least a little money in my pocket. Throughout college, I had to work when I wasn't in class to help pay for my education. Luckily, I also received a government grant to aid with tuition and expenses.

I found part-time work in a second-hand clothing store, a pawn shop and a grocery store. Anything to make a little extra money. I also worked at a fishing tackle shop, a fish-and-chips restaurant and a tea room. That's how I could afford to continue my education. It wasn't like I was resting on any laurels at the time because I didn't have any.

While I was in college, I met a girl named Josie Metson through my friend Terry, who was dating her sister. We hit it off right away and started dating. Our relationship continued throughout my three years of college and beyond. Both of us were just kids when we started dating, only about seventeen or eighteen years old, and we both did a lot of growing up together.

Looking back, I realize we had significantly different outlooks on life. Although we were both from working-class families, I had strong ambitions to pursue my dreams and make a living in a creative field, even if it meant taking risks and living an unconventional life.

On the other hand, Josie had no desire to attend college and she was satisfied with working a nine-to-five office job every day. There's certainly nothing wrong with that, but our different outlooks meant she never fully understood my passion for the arts, and therefore she was never completely supportive of my professional ambitions.

After art school was finished, the pressure was on to start working full-time and make real money. I knew I wanted to get into the movie business, but I didn't have a clue about how to do it. Nobody in my family had ever worked in the industry and I learned very quickly that it was nearly impossible to enter the biz unless you knew somebody in a position of influence (or you were extremely lucky).

Although I knocked on a lot of doors and made a lot of cold calls, I never seemed to make any progress. I didn't have any contacts in the business, and as the old riddle goes, I didn't know how to gain the experience I needed to find employment because I needed experience before anybody would hire me. It ended up taking me about three years before I landed a job in the film industry.

In England, if you weren't working and you were searching for a job, you would report to the labor exchange every week and they would help you find available employment. I was sent out briefly to be a rotary telephone engineer, which of course is a completely extinct occupation today. Another time, the labor exchange wanted to send me out to train as a typewriter engineer, which is another job that no longer exists.

Two years out of college, I still wasn't finding my entry point into the film business. Unemployed people would receive a certain amount of money from the government, but not very much. Money was what I needed at this point, as I had just proposed to Josie.

When we tied the knot, she was working as a filing clerk to help pay the bills. I hadn't found employment in the film industry yet and I was taking on any odd jobs I could find to tide us over. My sister was also married by this point and I went to work for her and her husband, who ran a successful wine-merchant business with a beautiful store in the fancy suburb of Blackheath and huge cellars in Greenwich. I used to deliver cases of expensive wine to people in wealthy neighbourhoods and I'd wash their cars on the weekend for a bit of extra cash.

Even though I wasn't working in my chosen field, I was thankful to be employed and I was earning something like six or seven pounds a week. My sister and brother-in-law were extremely generous, allowing Josie and me to live with them in their huge home. With several kids running around, it could be quite the rambunctious household.

All this time, I was trying to join the union ACTT, the Association of Cinematograph Television and Allied Technicians, so I could find steady work in the film industry. At first I couldn't figure out how to get past the dreaded catch-22 situation: I needed to be in the union if I wanted to find decent-paying employment in the film industry, but in order to gain admission into the union, I needed to log a certain number of working hours.

I learned that some film companies were willing to take on entry-level trainees for little or no pay. It didn't seem like the most attractive way to start in the industry, but few options were at my disposal. I had to get my foot in the door somehow, and if I could survive the ascent from the bottom level, I would eventually get into the union and be able to make a living working on films.

I was pretty fearless as a young man, not caring how hard I had to work to succeed in the film industry. At the time, the idea of "striking it rich" in the movies wasn't even on my radar. Since I'd never had money, I never missed it. I just wanted a career that would allow me to be creative. More than anything, I didn't want to be bored with my work, and filmmaking seemed like anything but boring to me. I would prove to be right about that.

My fearlessness proved to be my greatest asset when I was starting out in the business because I was never afraid to knock on doors and pursue my dreams full steam ahead. That sense of fearlessness starts to fade with age when you establish a certain lifestyle you want to maintain and you have increasingly more to lose. After you become married and have children, you begin to work for them as much as you do for yourself, so the best time to chase your dreams is when you don't have all those responsibilities.

One day, I thought of a possible entry point into the industry that could take advantage of my skills as an illustrator. When I was still in college, we had a lecturer whose daughter worked at an animation company in Borehamwood called Stewart Hardy Films. He had mentioned that they were on the lookout for trainee animation directors. They would train you for a year and see how you'd do, and if you had the right stuff, you could go on to direct film projects for the company. It sounded good to me. I didn't have anything to lose at this point.

I contacted Stewart Hardy Films and landed an interview for the position of trainee animation director. About 600 people applied and only four people were ultimately chosen for that year, and I was lucky enough to be one of them.

Because Stewart Hardy was a union shop, I was required to join the ACTT. My application was sent to the union through the film company because I was now officially one of their trainees. I'd finally found my way in, and being in the ACTT meant I now had access to the union's weekly employment postings.

Stewart Hardy was an amazing company with brilliant animators. I was lucky enough to be trained by the Stewart and Hardy of the company name, who shared their years of experience in animation with the trainees. The company produced instructional films for government agencies about how to use various pieces of equipment and machinery. With my interest in both engineering and art, it seemed like a match made in heaven.

My most memorable assignment was creating illustrations for a film about how a diving rebreather worked and animating it to break apart into its separate components. The images had to be more or less photorealistic, which involved a lot of detailed airbrush work. I did a fairly good job, but somehow my heart just wasn't in it.

After spending a year at Stewart Hardy, I started to look for work elsewhere because I simply didn't feel good enough to excel in animation. From reading the union job postings, I learned that a new film was being mounted at MGM Studios in Borehamwood called *2001: A Space Odyssey,* under the direction of someone named Stanley Kubrick. The production was looking for a trainee, a junior in the art department, so I gave them a call and arranged for an interview with one of the producers.

The interview went very well and the producer seemed to like me. My experience at Stewart Hardy Films no doubt helped me. I was hired on the spot and told to report first thing on Monday morning.

Being only in my early twenties, I was excited to hit the big time and work on a major motion picture, even if it was only in a junior position. At the time, I had no idea what the film was about. What mattered was that I'd finally gotten my foot in the door and my career in the film industry was finally underway.

Monday morning couldn't come soon enough. I reported bright and early to the art department, where I approached the film's production designer, Tony Masters. He greeted my arrival with a puzzled expression.

"Who are you?" he asked.

I introduced myself with more than a little confusion myself. "I'm the new assistant for the art department."

"Oh, really?"

Obviously, Tony had no idea who I was or why I was reporting for duty. He excused himself and left the office. A few minutes later, in walked the production manager, who apologetically sacked me. Apparently, the producer had hired me without conferring with Tony, who had been away on vacation, and Tony had already promised the position to a relative of his.

I didn't blame Tony for what happened, as it was a simple matter of miscommunication, but it was still a disappointment to be given my walking papers within minutes of starting work on a major movie at MGM Studios. Essentially I was given two weeks' notice of termination. The producer had been forced to give me notice right away, because they would have had to pay me for an extra week if I was given notice after midday.

Over the next two weeks, I helped to construct prototype spaceship models in the art department. They were still refining the look of the miniatures and we built rather crude maquettes out of cardboard for review by Stanley Kubrick. He would visit the shop to look at our prototypes through a small viewfinder and decide what angles worked best with the spaceship designs.

While I was still in college, I had worked at a company during the holidays designing various types of exhibitions. This experience proved invaluable when it came to working on the *2001* prototypes because it taught me the relationship between two-dimensional design and the three-dimensional reality at the end of the process. I was starting to realize how valuable all of my previous work experience was, no matter how trivial it seemed at the time.

When Stanley visited the art department, I was very frank with him about my ideas and I didn't hesitate to tell him how he should be doing things. Others thought it was amazing that someone like me was telling Stanley what to do. In truth, I had no clue who Stanley Kubrick was and I was too naive to know that I should have been showing more respect. By giving him my advice without being asked, I probably wasn't doing the right thing, but Stanley always took my thoughts into consideration and never seemed annoyed with my forthrightness.

Director Stanley Kubrick with actors Keir Dullea and Gary Lockwood on the "centrifuge" set of *2001: A Space Odyssey*. Photo courtesy of PHOTOFEST.

I actually did some work for Stanley again many years later, although he didn't remember me from *2001*. I was working for a friend named Martin Gutteridge at his company Effects Associates, and we were hired by Stanley to do some test shots of smoke and fog for the movie *Barry Lyndon* in Ireland. Ultimately, another company was engaged to do the effects for the production. By this time, I knew of Stanley's status as a legendary filmmaker and I didn't offer him any unsolicited advice.

On *2001*, I remember having access to the soundstages and seeing some of the enormous interiors they had built. The giant "centrifuge" set in particular was a wonder to behold. It was created for the gravity-defying scenes inside of the spaceship Discovery.

From the outside, the set looked like a rotating amusement park ride and it operated like an enormous hamster wheel. Because the camera was locked in sync with the movement of the wheel, some mind-bending illusions could be created that seemed to contradict the laws of gravity.

The film went to extreme lengths to create a disorienting environment where normal concepts of up and down didn't apply. We did a lot of tests with mirrors in an attempt to achieve shots of people standing upside down from ceilings. This was long before the digital age, and it was impressive what the filmmakers were able to achieve with in-camera effects and meticulous planning.

Even though I was on the film for only two weeks, I was lucky to be a part of *2001* and it was a real education meeting special-effects legends like Douglas Trumbull and Wally Veevers. Wally and I became friends and we ended up working together on a number of films, including *The Rocky Horror Picture Show* and *Saturn 3*.

People often ask me if I knew at the time that *2001* was destined to be a classic motion picture. The answer is no. It was my first job in the business and I didn't have any other film experiences for comparison. Sure, I was impressed with the scope of the production and the attention to detail in every department, but to me, it was just a job. I had no idea that I'd been blessed with an opportunity to watch an expert filmmaker at work as he created a masterpiece. If I knew at the time, I probably would have paid more attention.

It wasn't until I saw film years later that I fully appreciated the magnitude of Kubrick's vision. I was just a kid chasing his dream of making it in the movies and I was lucky enough to have a good first experience. Working with Stanley Kubrick on *2001: A Space Odyssey* wasn't the worst way to start out in the biz.

I enjoyed my time on the production, but two weeks went by quickly and then I was out of work once again.

CHAPTER 3
BREAKING THE WAVES

The hunt was on. Even though I'd become a union member and I'd had a great start by working on a soon-to-be-classic movie, finding more work in the film industry was proving far more difficult than I'd anticipated.

I was lucky that my parents were always supportive of my ambitions. First and foremost, they just wanted me to be happy in life and they didn't care if I wasn't a doctor or a lawyer. It was nice knowing they had my back.

Not everyone thought I was doing the right thing, however. My brother-in-law thought I was out of my mind for trying to make a living in the movie industry. With so many applicants for so few positions in such a specialized and small industry, the odds were against me.

He was paying me only 8 pounds a week, which worked out to be just over 400 pounds a year. Even though I was struggling to find work on a film set, I boasted to him that I'd soon be earning at least 1,000 pounds a year, which was a lot of money back in the mid-sixties. Unfortunately, it would end up being a while before I could make good on that boast.

It was almost a whole year before I found my next job in the industry, which involved working with the great Derek Meddings on the television show *Thunderbirds*. Created by Gerry and Sylvia Anderson, *Thunderbirds* was a unique program that made "Supermarionation" a household name with its elaborate use of marionettes and miniature work. Although I worked on the show for only five weeks, I count myself lucky for being involved with another project that has since garnered an ardent following around the world.

Derek was directing second unit on *Thunderbirds* and he was the one who interviewed me for the job. I was thrilled when Derek told me I'd gotten the job helping out in the workshop. Little did we know that we'd both end up winning Academy Awards for *Superman* a decade later.

I helped with the construction of the miniature sets for *Thunderbirds*, which were incredibly detailed. All of us in the workshop felt like big kids who were given the chance to play in the coolest toyland imaginable.

One of the scenes involved a big snowstorm and I was asked to help with the creation of a snowbound tabletop miniature. Derek handed me a big block of styrofoam that was about 8 feet by 4 feet by 2 feet, then he gave me a sanding disc and told me to start making snow. I spent the next two weeks grinding styrofoam to make the miniature set look sufficiently wintery.

After my time working on *Thunderbirds*, I received a call for an interview at Pinewood Studios to work on an upcoming war film called *Battle of Britain* in the special-effects department. The interview went smoothly with the production manager, Hugh Attwell, and he called the following day to offer me the job. He asked how soon I could start because they were beginning work on the film straight away. I told him I could start first thing Monday morning.

Next, he asked me how much I was earning with my brother-in-law's business. When I told him 8 pounds a week, he offered to start me off at 19 pounds. This allowed me to say a playful "fuck you" to my brother-in-law, which was quite satisfying indeed.

The thought of working at Pinewood Studios was thrilling, especially since so many classic motion pictures had been produced on its soundstages.

A Night to Remember, *Fahrenheit 451* and *Chitty Chitty Bang Bang* had been filmed there, and future productions would include *Alien*, *Batman* and *Mission: Impossible*. Pinewood Studios is probably most famous for being the home of the James Bond series.

The first time I arrived at Pinewood, I was in awe of its size and scope. The studio was its own self-contained community that had everything, including its own canteen, restaurant, bar, library and supply store. If you required tools, office supplies or reference books, you didn't need to leave the lot, and if they didn't have something in stock, they'd order it for you.

Pinewood had its own specialty departments for props, draperies, woodwork and costumes, and everybody knew everybody else, regardless of what department you came from. Many of the same crewmembers had worked together for years on picture after picture, learning how to make the best use of each other's skill sets.

When people weren't busy working, they were often found socializing at Pinewood's bar or restaurant. Even the security people were a part of the family and knew everybody on a first-name business. You rarely get that same level of camaraderie on film sets nowadays.

Pinewood was loosely based on the classic Hollywood studio system that existed before the "four-wall" system of renting space on a project-by-project basis. Standing sets on the Pinewood backlot could be redressed quickly according to the specific needs of a given production. Walking through the backlot, you could find yourself magically transported to Paris, a Victorian marketplace or a World War II battlefield. The craftsmanship on display made my jaw drop.

Battle of Britain was an epic war film directed by Guy Hamilton, who had hit the big time directing the James Bond picture *Goldfinger*. The all-star international cast included Sir Laurence Olivier, Trevor Howard, Christopher Plummer and Michael Caine. It was exciting to be involved with such a large-scale and highly anticipated production.

I made a couple of good friends on *Battle of Britain* who taught me a lot about the business. Maurice Carter was a top art director in the industry and a genuinely nice guy who brought every set to life with his meticulous attention to detail. Maurice was only about forty at the time, but he had an old-style classiness to him that befitted an older gentleman. No matter how hot or dirty the work was, he was always dressed to the nines in a suit and tie.

I also became good friends with special-effects supervisor Glen Robinson, who was already a legendary name in the business. Glen had done it all in the world of special effects and he was happy to share his wisdom with young people who were just starting their careers.

I worked with Glen for five weeks in the effects department at Pinewood, preparing for the start of principal photography. Then it all came to a screeching halt without any prior warning. The production was being shut down and we were told it might be months before production resumed. For reasons related to financing, all work on *Battle of Britain* was to cease immediately.

We were just gaining momentum in the effects department and the sudden turn of events completely took the wind out of our sails. However, I was grateful to have become good friends with both Maurice and Glen, who ended up being excellent mentors.

Maurice appreciated my enthusiasm and willingness to learn. He asked if I would be interested in working on his next film, which was called *A Challenge for Robin Hood*. My answer, of course, was an enthusiastic "yes."

The movie had a relatively modest budget, so the crew was small and everyone shared numerous responsibilities. I worked closely with him as a junior in the art department and it was a great opportunity to learn about designing sets, scouting locations and communicating with a director.

In addition to helping Maurice in the art department, I was given an invaluable opportunity to learn about the creation of physical effects for a period film. After telling Maurice about my interest in special effects, he put in a good word for me with special-effects supervisor Les Bowie, and soon I was helping out with his effects team.

Working on *Robin Hood* was like going back in time and playing make-belief with my cousin Allan when we were kids. With some ambitious action sequences, the film was a great initiation into the world of special effects, and it was our responsibility to make all the spectacle of the Robin Hood legend come to life without injuring anyone for real.

I was grateful to be learning about special effects under Les' guidance. He generously shared his years of experience creating every type of special effect imaginable, both large and small.

We did a lot of smoke effects on *Robin Hood* for the battle sequences, which taught me about the importance of subtle physical effects. Viewers often take effects like smoke and fog for granted because they aren't as spectacular as Superman flying or a car exploding, but they are vital to establishing mood and selling the story to an audience.

I also learned that the easiest way to do something was often the best way. Many characters were hit with arrows in the film and I helped to create the various arrow-hit effects. The simplest way was to pad the actor beneath his costume and then fire an actual arrow into him. The trick was to ensure the pad was thick enough to protect the performer without making him look like the Stay Puft Marshmallow Man.

When I was making the pads, I was acutely aware of how potentially dangerous special effects can be. With millions of dollars on the line with any given production, believability is paramount in terms of special effects, but nothing is more important than the safety of everyone on set. After all, it's only a movie, and nothing is worth a human life when making a film.

We also used flip-up arrows, which were remarkably simple but very effective on screen. You'd put half an arrow onto a spring clip and attach it to a performer's body so it was hidden from the camera's view. The actor would pretend to be hit by an arrow while simultaneously releasing a switch hidden in his hand. The arrow would then flip into view and give the illusion of a real arrow hitting its target.

The effectiveness of special effects like this are highly dependent upon the actor's performance and his ability to sell the illusion. The best technical effect in the world will fall flat if the actor is not convincing. This is more true nowadays than ever, when actors on big-budget blockbusters are asked to perform on empty soundstages against green screens, reacting to computer-generated monsters and environments that won't appear until months later in post-production. On-set effects give actors something real to play against, and nothing helps a performer more than making the experience feel as real as possible.

Les and I bonded quickly on the set of *Robin Hood*. I was eager to learn about the business and he was happy to take on an interested young student. After we finished *Robin Hood*, Les offered me a job at his company doing work on various film and television projects. I'd be sent out to work on different projects as needed, sometimes for only a day or two at a time. It was a great opportunity to gain practical experience on a number of productions and see how different directors worked.

Knowing about my background in art, Les started training me in the creation of matte paintings. He was a talented matte painter himself, able to create gorgeous vistas on panes of glass that would be combined with live-action optically to create the illusion of a single image.

For example, a film might require a shot of knights riding across a plain with a castle on the horizon. Rather than going through the expense of building a giant castle for the purposes of the shot, the filmmakers might hire a matte artist to paint the castle on a giant sheet of glass. The painting would then be lined up appropriately with the live-action footage of the knights and they would be exposed together on a single piece of film. The resulting shot would look knights were riding their horses in front of a real castle in the distance.

Matte painting is a very specific art form, one that requires a great deal of patience and technique. The paintings themselves must appear photorealistic if they are to blend convincingly with the live action in the final shot. A keen understanding of how light and shadow affect a subject is critical to the creation of a convincing matte painting.

Les taught me some of his painting techniques and allowed me to create some matte paintings for his company. I never felt particularly accomplished and I soon lost interest in pursuing work as a matte painter. Looking at the work done by Les and the other matte artists, it became clear that I'd never be as good as them, but it was still a valuable part of my ongoing education in special effects.

When my interest in matte painting waned, Les suggested training me to do optical effects work. Bowie Films did a lot of optical compositing, or the combining of separate pieces of film into a single shot. Optical work might involve the use of a blue screen or the combination of animation with live action.

Nowadays, various elements of an effects shot are combined in the digital realm for greater control, but that technology didn't exist during my time at Bowie Films. Everything had to be combined using an optical printer, which could expose images from various sources onto a single piece of film for a finished shot.

Optical effects didn't feel like my calling either. I didn't want to be trapped indoors all the time running strips of film through an optical printer. I wanted to get my hands dirty with the production crew, making use of my ingenuity and problem-solving abilities on the front lines.

Thank goodness I didn't pursue matte painting or optical printing as a career. Both crafts have become extinct in the face of digital filmmaking technologies, which can do a better job more quickly and less expensively. That's not to say that computers do all the work though. Talented artists are still needed to create convincing visual effects in the digital realm. After all, computers are just an extension of the artist. However, I'm glad that I specialized in practical effects, which are still an important part of filmmaking today.

After we finished on *Robin Hood*, I worked at Bowie Films for four or five months on various smaller projects. Two weeks into my time working with Les, he told me about an independent special-effects supervisor he'd hired who needed help on a movie called *Inspector Clouseau*. Les' effects supervisors at that time, Kit West, Nick Allder and Brian Johnson, were all busy on other projects, which necessitated the hiring of this gentleman. Kit, Nick and Brian would go on to work on such classic movies as *Raiders of the Lost Ark, Alien* and *The Empire Strikes Back*.

The next day, I went to work on the special effects of *Inspector Clouseau*. We shot that film at Borehamwood, which was where I'd gotten my start in the industry with my two-week stint on *2001*. *Inspector Clouseau* was a bit of a strange entry in the *Pink Panther* film series. Blake Edwards, who had already directed two *Pink Panther* films prior to this one, was not involved with the production of *Inspector Clouseau*, and the clumsy French police inspector made famous by Peter Sellers was now played by Alan Arkin. Bud Yorkin was hired to direct when Edwards proved unavailable.

Under the leadership of the special-effects supervisor, our team prepared for a scene that required a simple sight gag. Clouseau had all these James Bond-type gadgets, one of which was a laser lighter. In the scene, Superintendent Weaver asks Inspector Clouseau for a light so he can smoke his pipe. Clouseau pulls out the lighter and accidentally cuts the pipe in two with his laser. The end of the pipe then falls off. A simple gag, right?

The supervisor had rigged the pipe and we were ready to roll. I was there just to aid him as his assistant, to pass him tools or run errands as required. We made at least four attempts to execute the gag as the camera rolled, but each time the end of the pipe failed to fall off. It was the end of a long day and frustration was setting in.

Bud, who could be a brash personality but was a very good director, grew increasingly irate when we couldn't make this one simple gag work. He was under a lot of pressure because he had big shoes to fill as the director and some big-time producers on the movie were looking over his shoulder, including Lewis J. Rachmil, who had produced such hits as *Gidget* and *633 Squadron*.

By the end of the day, the supervisor still couldn't make the gag work, so we all went back to the workshop. Les and the producers expressed their disappointment and he promised to make the gag work the next morning.

I had nothing to do with the conversation and I was in another part of the workshop. Les came over to me while the others continued talking and he asked my opinion, which I was stupid enough to give. I told him the truth - that I thought the supervisor was totally wrong in his approach. He asked me how I would accomplish the effect, so I explained how I would do it.

Les walked over and proceeded to tell the producers about my idea. Lewis told the supervisor that he had one more chance to make the effect work, with shooting of the scene to resume first thing in the morning. Then I was told to be ready too as backup.

After the supervisor left the workshop, Lewis explained how he wanted the supervisor to go before me in the morning so he'd have an opportunity to save face. If he couldn't make the gag work, then I would be given a chance to try it my way. That was fine with me. It was never my intention to make the supervisor look bad - I was just being honest with Les and I didn't think he'd tell Lewis about it the way he did.

The supervisor went first the next morning. Twice. And it didn't work. Everyone was disappointed again, especially the supervisor himself. I felt terrible for him, but now it was up to me. I'd been in the business for only a short period and my stint on *Inspector Clouseau* was scheduled for only a couple of days working as the supervisor's assistant. I was terrified because dozens of crew members and actors were looking on, waiting for me to get on with it.

With hands shaking, I explained how I thought the gag should work. When actor Frank Finlay would bite down on the stem of the pipe, it would ignite a little fuse head inside. We had fuses that worked the same way as striking a match, but they were ignited electrically. I precut the pipe and then stuck it back together with wax. When the fuse ignited, a small flame would melt the wax. The battery for the fuse was hidden in the bulb of the pipe, which gave it weight, so the bulb would fall right off when the wax melted. Simple.

I readied the pipe and Bud rolled camera, anxious to move ahead in the shooting schedule. The gag worked perfectly, with a puff of smoke and the end of the pipe falling off. Unfortunately, the actors ruined the take because they were so surprised that it actually worked. They broke character after the pipe fell apart and started cheering. We set up the pipe for another take and it worked perfectly again. The actors were happy and everyone applauded. That was the end of it as far as I was concerned.

Then lunchtime came and Les visited the workshop to tell me that the supervisor had been dismissed from the production. They wanted me to take over as the special-effects supervisor on the movie. I was quick to say yes - even though I didn't have a clue what I was doing, being only 22 years old at the time and barely having any special-effects experience on a movie set.

I don't think the supervisor ever forgave me, even though it wasn't my fault and I didn't purposely take over his job. After the pipe gag failed so many times, it was a matter of trying to salvage the reputation of Bowie Films in the eyes of the cast and crew.

The supervisor tended to oversell himself and he couldn't always deliver. Wasted time on a film set is extremely expensive when large crews are standing around waiting. To the supervisor's credit, he was quite talented when it came to electronics, and I worked with him again on future projects that could make use of his expertise.

Location shooting in Germany was scheduled to begin soon and I needed to prepare for many different physical effects in a relatively short period of time. For example, the script called for an arrow to be flown along a wire during an action sequence. Another scene required a gun hidden in an actor's belt to flip out and fire. Clouseau also needed a special suit that inflated like a balloon when it became wet. I had a pile of stuff to do and I didn't know where to start.

I had little choice but to learn on the job quickly. Luckily, Borehamwood was a hotbed of talented industry veterans who could share their wisdom and help me survive this ordeal. I had instant access to technicians in the special-effects, prop and camera departments to help me whenever I didn't know how to tackle a specific challenge. As we prepared for shooting in Germany, I wanted to make the best possible use of their knowledge because most of them would not be joining us on location. Once we went to Germany, I'd have to figure things out for myself.

The location shooting was stressful because I lacked confidence, but the people around me were understanding about the way I'd been thrust into this position. Somehow or another, I managed to survive the experience and successfully pulled off the physical effects that were asked of me. The producers were happy, and that's all that mattered at the end of the day.

It was an educational experience to be sure, but I honestly wouldn't wish it on anyone. I simply wasn't ready. Sure, I learned a lot by being thrown into the deep end, but it was a nightmare trying to stay afloat.

After shooting wrapped on that picture, I went to Les and said, "*I'll* tell *you* when I'm ready to be a supervisor because I don't want to go through that hell again." My time working on *Inspector Clouseau* convinced me that I required more experience before taking on that post again. That's when I started working for other effects supervisors to gain the knowledge and confidence I needed.

After a few months at Bowie Films, we received word that the behind-the-scenes problems on *Battle of Britain* had been sorted out and production was gearing up again. It was exciting to reunite with many of our colleagues and pick up where we'd left off. Glen Robinson was also back on *Battle of Britain* as head of the special-effects second unit and I worked as his assistant. He was a smart and generous man who was happy to be my mentor. Glen had won five Academy Awards during his long career, which started with *The Wizard of Oz* and included such classic films as *Forbidden Planet* and *Earthquake*. The world lost a true genius when he passed away in 2002.

We became good friends both on and off the set, which made our experience on *Battle of Britain* a lot of fun. Although we were stationed at Pinewood Studios, we often traveled to other parts of England like Duxford or Dover to shoot scenes or scout locations. It was often late by the time we were finished, so Glen would invite me to stay the night with him and his wife Beverley. They were renting a beautiful mansion just down the road from Pinewood with a spare bedroom I could use on the top floor.

On one such evening, we had eaten dinner at Glen's house and were watching some TV to help unwind. Beverley started talking about how the house had been built back in the 1500s and how she was sure it was haunted. Some of the locals had told them stories about strange supernatural events occurring at the house and scaring away some of the previous inhabitants. Sometimes in the middle of the night, Beverley would hear slow, creeping footsteps coming up the stairs when no one else was home.

Glen told me about a time they were sitting in the living room, having a conversation with the owners of the house. A cat that was relaxing on the couch suddenly jumped into the air with his hairs standing on end. His back was arched in fear and his eyes seemed to follow something invisble that was moving across the room. But nobody could see anything unusual in the room that would account for this strange behavior.

As though locked on target, the cat continued to watch his invisible quarry until it reached the corner of the room, then he suddenly lost interest and went back to relaxing on the couch. According to Glen, it was as though the cat was able to see a spirit that floated across the living room and passed right through the wall. I'm a pretty rational person, not caught up in superstitious beliefs, but I was definitely getting wound up by the stories being told.

Glen and Beverley headed for bed, so I made my way up the creaky old staircase to the tiny spare bedroom in the attic. With their stories still fresh in my head, I tucked myself into bed and tried to sleep.

Then the window flung open with a bang and startled me. It must have been a sudden gust of wind. A few seconds later, one of the doors on the cupboard squeaked open all by itself. Things were getting mighty creepy. I lay under the heavy duvet on the bed, using it as a shield against whatever evil forces lurked just beyond my sight. Suddenly, the duvet pulled itself off my body and down to the floor. I was practically shitting myself at this point.

Then I heard the laughter from outside my door. It was Glen, the practical joker extraordinaire, laughing his ass off at the success of his "special effects." He had set up the window, cupboard door and duvet with invisible fishing line so he could control them from outside the room, and he'd done a convincing job. I tried the same trick on someone many years later and I almost gave that person a heart attack, so I never did it again.

Once production got rolling on *Battle of Britain* again, it kept us busy for the next year and a half. We handled all of the second-unit physical effects, including explosions, fires, bullet hits and crashing airplanes, and we also shot second-unit action sequences under Glen's leadership.

It was a hell of a crew working on *Battle of Britain* and we all bonded as though we were brothers in a real war. Come to think of it, filmmaking is like fighting a war against fatigue, budgets, schedules and egos. Victory comes in the form of a good picture at the end of it all. Considering the countless obstacles that must be overcome, it's a miracle that so many good movies are made. The crew members on the special-effects team were so hardworking and skillful that I ended up hiring many of them to work with me on future productions.

The Spanish Air Force was nice enough to lend us some working planes for use in the film. We weren't allowed to damage any of them for real, so we had to rely on our special-effects ingenuity to create the illusion that dozens of aircraft were destroyed over the course of the film.

Using the Spanish planes for reference, the amazing artists at Pinewood built numerous full-sized replica Spitfires and Hurricanes that lacked the heavy guts of the real ones. These light-weight dummies could be towed around easily and blown up in spectacular fashion. The script called for planes to be bombed or strafed in an airfield by the Luftwaffe and the dummies worked beautifully for these shots.

One shot called for a plane to roll down an airfield, turn a corner and explode after hitting a fuel tank. Glen showed me how to rig the shot so the plane would be towed by a powerful truck off camera. A guide wire was attached to the plane's front end, which was threaded through a couple of off-camera pulleys and attached to a tow truck on the other end. The plane was pulled along the guide wire by the truck and the pulley system could be set so the truck-to-airplane speed ratio was two to one. In other words, if the truck was moving at 30 miles an hour, the plane would move at 60.

The plane was made to turn a corner by a pulley out of the camera's view. When we wanted the plane to move in one direction without wavering side to side, the tow line was kept straight by a web of crossing guide wires anchored on both sides. On the front of the plane was a small box with mounted cutters that severed the guide wires as the plane moved forward. The wires were thin enough to be invisible on camera.

The plane's ultimate destination was a big fuel tank, which would explode upon impact. Behind the tank, we set up an explosive switch with a sandbag beside it to act as the trigger. When the plane hit the tank, it nudged the sandbag forward and activated the switch, detonating the explosives.

Glen avoided using remote-controlled detonators whenever possible because he was afraid that stray radio signals might accidentally set off a blast. He was a wonderful creative thinker who often came up with simple and inexpensive ways to create spectacular effect shots.

We wanted to have some planes explode midair and have others crash into the ocean, and Glen came up with practical ways to achieve those shots without resorting to expensive optical-effects work. By staying in the realm of practical effects as much as possible, we were also able to keep a high level of realism that can be lost with opticals. Shooting miniatures on a practical set allowed for real interaction between the model and the environment.

We flew and destroyed numerous remote-controlled aircraft on *Battle of Britain*. Photo copyright Andrew Oxley | Dreamstime.com.

Quarter- and half-sized models of aircraft were constructed and used to make molds. Then we cast the molds in urethane foam, which meant the final miniatures would be relatively light but still sturdy enough for the rigors of filming. We ended up constructing a whole fleet of radio-controlled planes that were packed with explosives so they could be detonated with the flick of a switch.

The model planes were taken over the ocean by helicopter and then released from hundreds of feet up in the air for the cameras filming below. Using our joysticks, we could send them into spinning dives or make them bank dramatically as the shots required. In order to get the COG (centre of gravity) correct on the miniatures, we had to weigh down the noses for our diving and crashing shots.

We could control when the plane began smoking, caught fire or exploded. Some of our most dramatic shots had the planes disintegrating into bursts of flame as they hit the ocean. Because the miniature planes were quite large, we didn't have scale problems with the flames, smoke or water, which often look unconvincing in miniature shots if the models are too small.

Glen was really smart about avoiding unnecessary work, which was important to helping us stay sane in the face of our workload. If one side of a model wouldn't appear on camera, it wasn't necessary to paint it just for the sake of painting it. Because many of the aircraft models in our crashing shots would be seen only in wide takes, it wasn't necessary to paint the fine details. Glen was extremely conscious about getting a shot right and achieving a high level of quality, but he also knew when to save money and effort for better things.

One of the most memorable sequences in *Battle of Britain* involved the destruction of a radar station. The station's buildings and radar towers were pulverized under enemy fire, which was achieved through a combination of full-sized sets and miniatures built by the special-effects department.

In order to be cost effective, only the first 30 feet or so of the radar towers were built full-scale so the actors could be filmed in front of them. For shots in which the towers are seen all the way to the top, miniatures were constructed and filmed on the coast so the appropriate vista of the ocean was seen in the background.

For shots of the buildings blowing apart, the special-effects department precut parts of the set so the walls were practically collapsing on their own, then they wired everything with explosives. When the charges were detonated, the resulting eruption of debris was even more spectacular.

Glen was an explosives expert for the American navy during the Second World War, so he knew how to blow things up. He taught me that creating explosions for the movies was an art form in itself. More explosives doesn't necessarily make for a better explosion on screen and the goal shouldn't be to completely destroy something. You could easily pack a car with enough explosives to vaporize it instantly, but that usually isn't what we want to do because it lacks drama.

When blowing something apart, Glen used staggered charges to detonate different parts of an object in rapid succession, building up to the final fireball. It's similar to the showmanship behind fireworks; if you have one big bang after another, each of the exact same intensity, the show quickly becomes monotonous. It's all about building up to the climax.

If we needed to stagger our explosions with precise timing, we would use delay detonators that allowed us to control the blasts so they could be milliseconds apart. If we wanted to control a sequence of blasts manually, we would use a series of switches, with each one triggering an individual blast.

I've still got a firing box in my garage that I used on *Battle of Britain* for bullet hits. It has forty switches that can each be triggered manually, as well as a ratchet switch that sets off all forty detonations sequentially in rapid succession. It's an amazing toy.

Different explosives were used for different situations, and Glen was an expert at knowing what to use in order to achieve a particular effect. Some explosives would give a more spectacular light show, whereas others would be less showy but more effective at quickly obliterating an object.

Whenever he built a prop or a set piece to be destroyed on film, he used different construction materials depending on how he wanted the final effect to look. Certain materials will break apart into large pieces while others will shatter into tiny particles of dust. Glen knew how to do it all.

One scene called for a car to become airborne thanks to the force of an explosion. We used what we called boiler ends, which were large metal plates that measured two or three feet across. The boiler end was packed with explosives and attached to the bottom of the car. When the explosives were detonated, it created such an enormous downward force that the car rose a good 40 feet into the air during the explosion. We used to giggle all the time when we did the tests. Boys with toys.

Glen also showed me how to make a car skid and flip end over end. A metal pipe was installed inside the car, off to one side of the vehicle. An explosive charge was placed in the pipe, then a section of a wooden post like a telephone pole was placed into the top of the pipe.

When the cameras were rolling, the car was pulled down the road with a tow line to create the illusion that a driver was inside. The car was made to skid, then the explosives were ignited. The metal pipe essential worked as a plunger and the wooden post shot down into the ground, which sent the car flipping. In order to properly sell the effect, it was important to position the camera so the wooden post wasn't visible beneath the car as it started to flip.

Some of the battle scenes required large chunks of earth to blow up around the actors. For each explosion, we dug a hole six or eight feet deep and we put a thick metal plate on the bottom. We took a stick of dynamite and wrapped it with primer cord, then we'd lower it into the hole surrounded by other sticks of dynamite.

The free end of the primer cord could now be run out of the hole to a safe distance from the explosion site. Since the detonator wouldn't be connected to the end of the primer cord until it was time to shoot, you could safely work with the primer cord without fear of a premature detonation.

We filled the hole with a mixture of earth and cork and then smoothed over the top of the hole so it would be invisible. Cork was used because it was lightweight and it made for a more spectacular shower of debris.

Everybody, especially the actors and stunt people, should always know where the explosives are going to be set off. Directors always want performers to be close enough to create a sense of danger on screen, but that desire for "the perfect shot" should always be tempered by the need for safety. Effective communication between all departments is essential to keeping things as safe as possible, especially with large-scale action sequences that could involve dozens of performers in front of the camera. It can be easy to get swept away by the excitement of it all, but it's important to stay alert.

On *Battle of Britain,* I worked once again with the effects supervisor who had been dismissed on *Inspector Clouseau.* Glen Robinson liked him and made use of his expertise in electronics, which resulted in the creation of some special firing boxes based on old rotary-telephone selectors. It was quite an ingenious design for the time and it helped us with the epic battle sequences.

A beautiful interior of a Heinkel bomber was constructed for *Battle of Britain.* One scene required an explosion inside of the plane, and the director wanted the actors and the explosion to be shot together for maximum realism. Glen came up with an approach that made for a dazzling effect without compromising the performers' safety.

We used a powder called lycopodium, which is actually a type of pollen. Once the pollen is liberated into the air and a spark is put to it, the lycopodium flashes brilliantly. You could actually put your hand in it and it won't hurt because it burns up so quickly.

As safe as it was, we separated the actors from the blast with a clear sheet of plexiglass just to be extra cautious. The plexiglass wasn't visible through the camera, so when we detonated the flash charge, it looked like the actors were unprotected right next to the explosion.

The first- and second-unit effects crews had a fun rivalry throughout production. One day, we were ambushed by the first unit with an impressive barrage of water balloons. Not to be outdone, a technician from our unit named Jimmy Harris plotted a bit of mischievous retaliation. Someone in the first-unit effects crew had recently purchased a BMW and had kept the windows down because it was so hot. Jimmy fed a fire hose into one of the open windows and proceeded to fill it with water.

On *Battle of Britain*, not only was I receiving the education of a lifetime working alongside Glen, but I was also starting to make money the likes of which I'd never seen before. When I first started working on the movie before production went on hiatus, I was earning a nice 20 pounds a week. When we resumed production months later, I was earning 20 pounds a week again for the first few weeks. Then I was given a raise to 40 pounds.

One day we were in Dover prepping for our shoot. It was a Thursday, meaning we had to fill out our timesheets so they could be sent to Pinewood. I was sitting with other crew members at lunchtime, completing my timesheet, when one of the grips asked me how many hours I was putting down for the week. I told him it was 40.

"Only 40?" he asked.

"Well, that's what I worked," I told him.

"Give me your timesheet," he replied.

The grip totally rewrote my timesheet so it included extra pay I didn't know I was eligible for. The union had a deal that required us to receive extra pay for working on location as opposed to shooting at the studio, extra pay for our time spent traveling, extra pay for overtime, etc.

My paycheque the following week was a staggering 140 pounds and I was paid that amount for the next year and a half until finishing the movie. I suddenly found myself making a small fortune. It was ironic that my brother-in-law thought I'd never earn a decent living in the movie business, and here I was earning four times as much as he was. Now he works in the film industry for one of my nephews!

Pinewood Studios had a wonderful corporate culture that mixed hard work with a relaxed and highly social sensibility. No matter how tight our shooting schedules were, we always made time to eat well and enjoy our tea. It wasn't just a perk; it was the unwritten law of the place.

We arrived at 8:30 every morning, ready to tackle the day's work. Then halfway through the morning, a trolley was rolled in with bacon sandwiches, tea and scones. Work came to a complete stop for 15 minutes so everybody could enjoy the break.

Sometimes when North-American directors came over to shoot a film in England, they were puzzled by the seemingly religious need for a tea break every morning. Directors like James Cameron, who shot *Aliens* in England, were reportedly frustrated that productivity and momentum were compromised just as the day was gearing up. But English traditions are hard to break, and a happy crew is a more productive crew.

We returned to work after the tea break, then we took an hour for lunch and had another tea break with sandwiches in the afternoon. If the producers wanted us to work past eight hours, they needed to ask the crew for permission, and we were paid bonus for our overtime if we agreed to keep working. This prevented us from working those insane 14-hour days that are so common nowadays and it allowed us to see our families in the evening.

Working on *Battle of Britain* was a fulfilling but exhausting experience, and I was glad when production wrapped so I could move on to other projects. The film opened to rave reviews and big business in 1969. I am proud to have been a part of such a successful film and I learned a tremendous amount working with Glen Robinson.

I had come a long way in a relatively short period of time, breaking the waves and establishing myself in the world of special effects. I had also made good friends at Pinewood, many of whom I would work with again on future productions. After a rough and sometimes stressful beginning to my career, I had finally arrived.

CHAPTER 4
THE BIG BANG

After *Battle of Britain*, I was lucky to find work on some high-profile and large-scale productions that taught me how things were done by the big studios. One such production was 1971's *Murphy's War*, an ambitious World War II film directed by Peter Yates, who had also helmed the classic *Bullitt*. Peter O'Toole plays the survivor of a merchant ship that is sunk by a German U-boat off the coast of Venezuela. Using a surviving floatplane from his merchant ship, he plots revenge against the U-boat that cost the lives of his crewmembers.

We filmed along the Orinoco River in Venezuela, which was an adventure in itself. This was my first time filming in such a remote location and I didn't know what I was getting myself into. I spent four months in the jungle in stifling heat and humidity without many of the creature comforts I would have expected working on a big-budget film. When we looked at our main shooting locations on a map, they were in the middle of nowhere. The producers explained that our accommodations along the Orinoco would be aboard a so-called "luxury liner," allowing us to live in comfort in close proximity to our shooting locations.

An Aer Lingus aircraft was chartered to take us from London to the airport in Jamaica, where we'd pick up our luxury liner and cruise it up the Orinoco to our first location. Unfortunately, the plane was overloaded and couldn't take off properly. Everything deemed "unessential" was unloaded and would be shipped to us later on a separate flight. Then we had to make an emergency landing in Shannon for some technical reason, which was fine for us because it allowed us to top up on beer at the duty-free shop for the rest of the adventure.

When we landed in Jamaica and unloaded the plane, we discovered that our film stock and wardrobe had been offloaded in England to reduce weight. It would take an additional ten days before they arrived and we could actually begin shooting.

The accommodations in Jamaica ended up being anything but the "luxury liner" we'd been promised. Ten tiny cabins shared one shower on the boat, which was overcrowded with a predominantly Greek crew who had difficulty communicating with the anglophones. Talk about working outside of your comfort zone. At times it felt like a refugee camp.

Three women stayed with us on the boat: two members of the production crew and someone to take care of our laundry. With only three women to 110 men, the ladies were extremely popular with our male crew for the duration of our shoot in the middle of the jungle.

Our journey to the first shooting location was hardly a smooth one. At one point we had to pay off members of the Venezuelan navy who came threatening us with a gunboat. We also had difficulty navigating our way because our charts were from the Second World War and were extremely outdated. Parts of the river had dried up and were extremely shallow, so we had trouble getting the boat through at certain points and we found ourselves stuck more than once.

A settlement along the Orinoco River. Photo copyright Bayazed | Dreamstime.com.

When we neared our first shooting location, our boat was anchored and we took 40-foot tenders to the set on shore. At 5:00 every morning, we took the hour-and-a-half journey to the shoot, then we jumped back into the tenders at the end of the day and returned to our floating hotel, the "big boat" as we called it. Even that proved treacherous at times, since the waters of the Orinoco could be rather turbulent. If the river and the tide were opposing one another, waves could reach as high as 20 or 30 feet, making for an unpleasant and dangerous commute.

Once I couldn't even make it back to the big boat. I'd been flown out to a local town in a Cessna to get some supplies and I was on my way back in a tender. As we approached the big boat, the waves were getting crazy. The captain of the tender, who could speak only Spanish, got on the radio with the captain of the liner, who could speak only Greek. They couldn't understand one another and it was a frustrating comedy of errors trying to get both boats to manoeuvre in the rough waters so we could dock alongside.

Luckily, the production was keeping a small houseboat docked on shore near the set in case of emergencies. I was tired and fed up by that point.

"Forget it!" I yelled. "Just take me back to shore!" They took me back and I slept on the houseboat until the following day's shooting.

The script called for a rickety crane barge that was barely seaworthy, having rotted from years of exposure to the elements. It was constructed in Jamaica and the plan was to bring it by river to our shooting location. Unfortunately the barge was made a little *too* rickety and it sank en route. The whole thing had to be rebuilt in Jamaica, adding stress to a production that was already struggling to keep its sanity.

Peter O'Toole and the other lead actors didn't stay on the big boat with the crew. They stayed at a hotel in the nearest town, which was quite modern and prosperous because an American iron-ore operation was based there. The mountain close to this town was reportedly 60-percent iron ore, so it was an enormous operation to take the mountain apart and ship the ore out piece by piece. Huge trainloads of ore were leaving the town on a regular basis.

Because the Americans lived there, the restaurant at the hotel served some decent food, including some surprisingly good steak and eggs, and they had a nightclub in town where everyone could blow off some steam when they weren't working.

Peter, who was a notorious party animal and drinker, was extremely well-behaved on *Murphy's War* as far as I could tell. This might have been due to the casting of Peter's then-wife, Siân Phillips, as his co-star on the film. He was far more likely to stay on the straight-and-narrow path with her on set.

Everybody, cast and crew, ate together in the dining room of the big boat. The food was less than adequate, but just about edible. At least the bar onboard was well stocked. After each day's shooting, we took the tenders back to the big boat and settled in for the night. As we approached the boat, the barman hung over the railing and took our drink orders. By the time we were onboard and in the bar, he had our drinks waiting for us. We couldn't complain about that part of the experience.

I worked six days a week with the special-effects department creating explosions, bullet hits and smoke effects for the battle sequences. We could buy basic supplies at the nearest town, but we had to bring all of our specialized equipment and supplies with us from England.

After we'd finished the week's shooting on a Saturday, the big boat traveled up a tributary of the Orinoko and took us to another town, where we could spend Saturday night and most of Sunday unwinding or preparing for the next week's filming. We could go to the local stores and buy supplies and food, and we visited the local bars for drinks and dinner. It was nice to get away from our "luxury liner" once in a while. Some of the crew members *really* liked to unwind by visiting the local brothels for an evening's entertainment. The boat took us back to our shooting location on Sunday night and we'd be ready for work first thing Monday morning.

We eventually moved shooting to another location where the natives lived on a river bank that rose more than 40 feet above the river. Even though the Orinoko was 2 miles wide at this point, the rainy season would bring so much precipitation so quickly that the water level would quickly rise forty feet, which explained why all the native structures were built so high.

The villagers welcomed us and they didn't seem to mind our intrusion into their community. We were told not to let any of the villagers eat our food because it would kill them. Apparently their digestive systems had become extremely specialized from centuries of eating a specific diet and their bodies would not react well to any of our foreign food.

On top of one hill was a beautiful old castle that was left behind from the time of the Conquistadors, which we used as a shooting location. Children from the village often tried to sell us doubloons they'd found in the area to make some extra money for their families.

The production had secured a German submarine for use in *Murphy's War* and it was brought to Venezuela for filming. One scene required the sub to attack a local village, so a detailed set was constructed on shore for us to blow away. Natives were brought in to populate the village for the scene, and we had a hard time explaining how it was only a set. They became irate upon learning that it would be destroyed - they thought it was such a waste and they couldn't understand our reckless ways.

After obliterating the village, the sub was supposed to go into a deep dive. During the first take, the sub began to sink below the water's surface as expected. Then we saw a small human figure on the back of the sub waving his arms frantically to get our attention. Due to our ongoing communication problems, first assistant director Dusty Symonds had accidentally been left on the back of the sub! Luckily we managed to stop the take and rescue Dusty before he drowned.

Miscommunication wasn't the only danger we faced in the jungle. We set up our special-effects workshop in an abandoned old building made out of breeze blocks. It took some work to get it into shape for our use, including the addition of a roof and a door. One day we discovered an unexpected visitor in the workshop - a 7-foot long anaconda that didn't seem to appreciate our presence there. We had a local doctor on our crew, so we told him about our reptilian encounter.

"If you get bitten by a snake," he said, "make sure you kill it and bring it to me so I know which antidote to give you."

It was a relief to know we had an expert with us.

"Do you have a lot of antidote handy?" we asked.

"Not yet," he replied. "But it's coming."

The antidote didn't arrive until three or four weeks into the shoot. Luckily nobody was bitten.

Our time in the jungle was difficult and exhausting. In addition to the hardships of shooting in the middle of nowhere without the comforts of home, I had to deal with developing stresses in my personal life as well. As a married young man at this point, it didn't help my marriage that I was only able to phone home and speak to Josie once every week or so. She wasn't happy that I was taking off for months at a time and leaving her all alone back in England.

I was more than happy when our time in Venezuela came to an end and we were back in England to finish shooting *Murphy's War*. Compared to our jungle adventures, shooting inserts at Pinewood Studios was like heaven. It was nice to eat decent food again and sleep in a comfy bed. I could have a real shower and I didn't have to worry about being killed by giant snakes.

In the film, Murphy takes to the air in a seaplane and starts bombing the German submarine. We built a replica of the plane on a gimbal at Pinewood so we could shoot close-ups of Peter for the sequence. Stage hands gently rocked the plane back and forth to help sell the illusion of flight.

Next, we were off to Malta for four months to shoot in the "big tank." An English special-effects man named Benjamin "Jim" Hole had worked with the government to build an enormous water tank there for movie productions. Measuring 300 by 400 feet, the tank was 4 feet deep and featured a small area at the centre that was an additional 7 feet deeper.

It was a "horizon" tank, meaning it was built on a promontory, so if the camera was lined up properly, the end of the tank would blend in perfectly with the Mediterranean Sea in the distance. It was perfect for shooting, except for the occasional stench from a nearby sewer outlet.

The tank gave us a lot more control of the elements than we had when we were shooting on the Orinoco. We didn't have to worry about changing tides or unwanted currents. Wavemakers and wind machines were used in a controlled fashion without putting any of the performers at undue risk.

We shot some major sequences in the tank. The first was the scene at the beginning of the movie when the submarine attacks Murphy's boat. Explosions and bullet hits were all shot in the tank, as were the shots of the men jumping overboard. The footage shot in the tank blended perfectly with the shots taken in Venezuela.

For the finale of the film, Murphy commandeers the aforementioned crane barge in his final confrontation with the Germans. He uses the crane to drop a torpedo on top of the German submarine, but he ends up trapped under the fallen crane after the resulting explosion. The whole crane barge then sinks below the water, taking our trapped hero along with it.

Shots of the barge had already been filmed on the Orinoco, and an exact duplicate of the barge was constructed and brought to Malta. It was placed at the top of a ramp in the tank and it was slowly towed down into deeper water, creating the illusion of the barge descending below the waves. Divers were standing by who could swim in and supply Peter with oxygen after he became submerged for the shot. It was easy to do multiple takes - all we had to do was winch up the barge and we were ready for the next take.

At the film's climax, the submarine is destroyed by the torpedo dropped from the crane. We couldn't bring the real sub from Venezuela to the tank in Malta, so we built a model replica to blow up. Since this was the big payoff for the story, the destruction of the sub had to be suitably spectacular, and I think we succeeded in spades. We blew the shit out of the sub in a wonderful display of underwater fireworks.

Josie came with me to Malta, where we spent four months shooting. I was also a father at this point and my daughter Lucy was less than a year old. She was colicky, which made Josie's experience in Malta particularly challenging. Beyond sunbathing, there wasn't anything for her to do. She was far from family and alone during the day, taking care of a baby who wouldn't stop crying.

With my daughter Lucy.

Luckily, Martin Gutteridge's wife Evelyn and their two kids joined him in Malta for the remainder of the shoot. We moved into the same apartment block together, which gave Josie a friend who could help out with Lucy. That took some of the pressure off, considering how little time I was able to spend with them. We were working twelve to fourteen hour days, sometimes on weekends, but that's how we earned our money.

If you're supervising the special effects of a major motion picture, your team could be as large as 40 people and they're all counting on you for direction. On top of that, your team is part of an overall production of 200 or more people, all of whom are working hard to stay on schedule and bring the director's vision to life. Millions of dollars are at stake and every day counts.

I don't think Josie understood how much responsibility was resting on my shoulders. If you're not ready to give it your all when making a movie, you might not be the right person for the job. If my team wasn't prepared whenever the director was ready to roll, then dozens of cast and crew members would be waiting on us and wondering what the hell was going on. You have to deliver in the movie business or you won't be asked back the next time.

Nurturing personal relationships can be difficult when you're working in the film industry. You have to really work on it and your partner needs to realize how consuming your work can be. Unfortunately, Josie just wasn't able to embrace my career.

After my work on *Murphy's War* was finished, I returned to England and began work on the oddball film *200 Motels* at Pinewood Studios. Over the years, I was lucky to work on many film projects with top talent from the music industry. This included directing music videos and contributing to the special effects of musicals. *200 Motels* was my first stop on that road, working with Frank Zappa, the Mothers of Invention, Keith Moon and Ringo Starr.

Trying to describe *200 Motels* to someone who hasn't seen it doesn't do the film justice. You just have to dive in headfirst and experience the insanity for yourself. It's a truly unique motion picture experience, but I guess you couldn't expect anything less from the creative mind of Frank Zappa, who is often credited with inventing the music video.

Co-directed by Tony Palmer and Frank, the film explores the surrealistic mayhem that ensues when Frank's band visits the town of Centerville. To give you an idea of how unusual the film is, Keith Moon is credited as playing "The Hot Nun" and Ringo Starr is "Larry the Dwarf."

The movie was shot on videotape and then transferred to 35mm film, and it was decided to shoot it like a live television production with multiple cameras rolling at the same time. During each take, Tony monitored the camera feeds and gave direction from a control van as though he was shooting a live sporting event.

The entire film was shot on one giant set for the town of Centreville. At the end of production, the assistant director contacted me by headset and told me that Tony wanted to blow up the set for a spectacular finale. I hadn't been told about this previously, so I said I'd need an hour or so to lay the charges. However, I wouldn't be able to start until the set was cleared.

Tony wasn't satisfied with my response. He didn't want to lose time while I set up the explosives and he wanted to keep shooting with the actors on set while I lay the charges.

I refused to do that. It's a simple safety rule in special effects - you never lay charges until the set is cleared. It's just too dangerous if you have cast and crew shooting at the same time. My explanation didn't change Tony's mind. I could hear him yelling at the AD over the headset. He sent the AD from the control van to speak with me in person.

"He wants you to do it now," said the poor AD, who was just the messenger and was unfortunate to be caught in the crossfire.

"I won't do it," I replied. "You're still shooting. I'm not going to lay explosives with actors around. It's too dangerous."

The AD conveyed my response over the radio before getting another earful from the van. I was given the AD's headset, then Tony proceeded to scream at me directly for not following orders. I promptly told him to fuck off. Tony stormed onto the set from the van and he continued yelling at me, but I wouldn't budge. Safety always comes first.

One of the producers had been there listening to the entire thing transpire. I didn't know at the time that he was an ex-stuntman who was quite familiar with safety protocols on a set, especially when potentially dangerous explosives are involved. He joined the conversation and came to my defense.

"This is ridiculous," the producer told Tony. "If he'd started to lay explosives like you told him to, I would've shut down the set because you don't do shit like that. You don't lay explosives when actors are around."

Tony grudgingly backed off and we waited until the set was cleared before the charges were set.

Throughout my years in the film industry, my favourite directors have been ones who plan everything in detail well in advance of shooting so the special-effects department has adequate time to prepare and deliver exactly what the filmmaker is looking for.

Other directors, as I experienced with *200 Motels*, liked to work on the fly. Sure, a certain level of spontaneity is expected on set and can create a nice energy for the actors in a scene, but what I experienced on *200 Motels* was an extreme example. I think this was reflected in the final product - audiences and critics didn't know what to make of this confusing film when it was released in 1971.

After my experience on *200 Motels*, a lot of fantasy films came my way that allowed me to further develop my skills as a special-effects technician. In 1972, I worked on *Alice's Adventures in Wonderland* under special-effects supervisor Roy Whybrow, with whom I'd worked on *Battle of Britain* and *Murphy's War*. Because this was long before the dawn of the CGI revolution, the special effects in the film had to be done practically on set. Instead of creating the strange inhabitants of Wonderland with computer animation, we relied on animatronics used on set with the actors.

Alice involved some wonderfully talented crew members, including cinematographer Geoffrey Unsworth and special-effects makeup designer Stuart Freeborn, both of whom I ended up working with again on *Superman: The Movie* years later.

One of my favourite scenes in *Alice* is the humorous croquet game. The Queen of Hearts is in the garden playing croquet and she's using a flamingo instead of a mallet. We created an animatronic flamingo that could move its head like a live bird. Much to the Queen's chagrin, the flamingo pulls up its head every time she takes a swing at the ball.

The art department came up with an interesting way to make Alice shrink that wouldn't require any optical effects. It would be done completely in-camera using simple mechanics and forced perspective. When you looked through the camera during shooting, it really looked like Alice was shrinking, but if you looked at the set from any other angle, the workings of the illusion were revealed. The effect was achieved by properly positioning the camera so all the elements aligned exactly through the lens.

In the final shot, the floor of the room was covered in checkerboarded tiles, which created a sense of perspective as they receded into the distance. Positioned close to the camera was a life-sized section of the floor and a table. This part of the set was built up on a platform so the rest of the room beyond was considerably lower in elevation. On the table was the bottle of shrinking liquid for Alice to use.

Thirty feet beyond the table was a another section of set that was five times bigger than real life, consisting of an oversized floor, wall, door and light switch. When this giant section of set was properly lined up behind the life-sized section of set, they both blended together when viewed through the camera lens and appeared to be one continuous room of normal size. This is known as forced perspective.

To better understand this principle, hold a penny an inch from your eye. The penny looks giant compared to a person standing twenty feet away from you. It's all a matter of how the eye perceives relative sizes. With two-dimensional film, it's easy to trick the eye into thinking that something closer to the camera is comparatively larger and vice versa.

Fiona Fullerton, who played Alice, stood on a platform that was attached to a track hidden from the camera's view. After she took a drink of the shrinking potion, we slowly moved the platform down a ramp and away from the camera toward the giant-sized section of set. When all the elements were perfectly lined up, she appeared to shrink in one continuous shot.

We also made extensive use of foreground miniatures on the film, a classic technique that had been used since the silent-film era. It was a relatively inexpensive but effective way of adding extra scope to a film's sets. Foreground miniatures utilized forced perspective much in the same way as the shrinking effect.

For example, if we wanted a giant castle wall to appear along the top of the frame above the actors' heads, it wasn't necessary to build the entire full-sized wall. Only the bottom portion of the castle wall behind the actors would be needed as a practical set.

A miniature wall could be built and hung a few feet in front of the camera while the rest of the scene was shot live with the actors off in the distance. As long as the miniature matched the appearance of the real wall through the camera lens and everything was lined up properly, the audience would be fooled into thinking the entire wall was real.

Since the effect can be achieved in-camera, the director is able to see how the shot looks on location instead of needing to wait for post-production. Also, the lighting on the foreground miniature matches the lighting of the live action, which can be difficult to reproduce exactly with process photography.

Alice required the use of several special-effects techniques and Roy Whybrow always rose to the challenge with ingenuity and resourcefulness. Roy was another great mentor to have in the business as my practical education continued. I worked with Roy again on my next movie, *The Legend of Hell House*, which was a horror film about a medium's investigation into the afterlife. Once again, he came up with amazing solutions to special-effects challenges that were simple but effective.

One scene involved a character who walks into her bedroom and sees the shape of a person sleeping underneath her sheets. When she pulls the sheets back, the bed is completely empty. The person under the sheets was actually laying on a spring-loaded trap door. When the actress started grabbing the sheets, we triggered the trap door so the "ghost" person fell beneath the bed and the door sprung shut. It was a matter of getting the timing just right and it worked perfectly.

Another scene involved a poltergeist going berserk as several people sat around a dining room table that was beautifully dressed with fancy plates and crystal glassware. We built the table with air cylinders embedded in each of the six legs, which allowed us to make the table bounce up and down on cue.

In the scene, the table suddenly jumps and startles the characters with the rattling china. Soon, it's shaking so violently that all of the plates and glasses are flying about. The malevolence of the ghostly presence was perfectly conveyed using the simplest of practical effects.

Another effective gag we rigged for the film was a pen that could write by itself. We achieved the shot using a pantograph, which is a mechanical linkage device like a complex drafting compass that allows you to write something on one surface and duplicate it exactly on another surface simultaneously.

We used tungsten wire that was only one- or two-thousandths of an inch thick. Tungsten wire didn't have a shine like piano wire, so it was less likely to be visible in the final shot if it ever caught the light at the wrong angle. The wire was attached to the back of the ghost pen, which was connected to the pantograph. The final shot was quite convincing and dramatic.

After *Hell House*, I worked with Roy on another horror film, this time a TV movie called *Frankenstein: The True Story*. In the film, Dr. Frankenstein creates a female companion for the monster in his laboratory. The companion, named Prima, was played by the lovely Jane Seymour.

The script called for Prima's naked form to hang unconscious in a giant test tube. Jane didn't want to do a nude scene, so a cast was made of her body and a dummy of her was used instead. The art department fabricated the test tube, which was about 30 inches wide and 6 feet high. To simulate a sort of amnionic fluid used by Frankenstein to bring Prima to life, the scene called for the test tube to fill slowly with water.

We realized this would cause some unforeseen problems. If you fill a rounded glass with water, whatever is inside will appear magnified in the rounded portions of the glass. Suddenly this beautiful dummy of Jane Seymour looked like a stocky American football player.

Everyone was in a panic over this. We put our heads together and came up with a solution that blended practical effects with optical effects. Another dummy was quickly built that was the same height as the original but only half the thickness. We locked off the camera and shot the original dummy in the test tube without any water. Then we shot the second, skinnier dummy in the test tube and slowly filled it with water. The optical department then did a "travelling matte," using the top of the rising water as their matte line and following the water as it filled the tube.

Essentially, they did an optical wipe from the original dummy to the second dummy in the water. Because the second dummy was much thinner, it appeared to have the proper human proportions when the test tube was filled with liquid. Most viewers probably wouldn't even recognize the final shot as a special effect, but it took quite a bit of work to make the shot convincing.

Roy Whybrow, Lord love him. He was such a character, great at getting work because he was always lucky enough to be at the right place at the right time. We had an understanding that if one of us got work on a film, we'd bring the other person onboard the project whenever possible.

He worked his way through the industry from the old school of special effects, working on huge movies like *Lord Jim* with Cliff Richardson, which earned him a reputation for being able to blow up stuff real good. But Roy wasn't really a strong technical guy - he was much more of a supervisor-type personality. However, he was such a good talker and he could convince producers that anything was possible with him on the job.

The monster dies at the end of *Frankenstein* when an ice cave in the Arctic collapses on top of him. I designed the set for the avalanche effect, which involved building a fake cave on the backlot of Pinewood Studios that was about 60 feet wide and 30 feet high, complete with walkways for rigging and lighting.

We carved giant styrofoam blocks, some as large as 6 feet across, to look like blocks of ice. They were lifted on wires to the top of the cave, where they hung in place until it was time for the avalanche. Then we dressed the whole set with fake snow and sprayed everything down with hot wax. Using melted wax in a flocking gun, we gave the cave a texture and sparkle like you'd find in a freezer that hadn't been defrosted very often.

On cue, we would cut the wires holding up the styrofoam ice blocks and they would come crashing down. Actor Michael Sarrazin, who played the monster, would be positioned inside of the cave as the blocks fell between him and the camera, creating the illusion that he was buried under tons of rubble. For extra safety, we made sure there was a catchment area at the back of the cave so he could always exit the set from the rear if needed.

It had taken a week to set it all up and Roy hadn't been involved at all. He was busy working on other parts of the production, so he didn't even know what was happening there on the backlot.

We'd just completed the finishing touches on the set and the scene was scheduled for the following day's shooting. While we were cleaning up, Roy arrived to see what we were doing. He was admiring our handiwork when a limo pulled up with the director and the producers, who were returning from location. Extremely happy with the look of the ice set, they started shaking Roy's hand and patting his back.

"This looks amazing!" they told him. "You did a great job! How's this going to work?"

Roy didn't have the slightest clue, but he wasn't going to let them know that. Talk about being at the right place at the right time. Roy called me over and I explained how it was all going to work for the cameras. He was happy to take the accolades even though he hadn't even seen the set two minutes before, but it didn't really matter to the rest of us and we found it quite amusing. Honestly, we were just happy to be working. This happened to me on more than one occasion with Roy, but I never had any hard feelings because he was such a nice guy.

After *Frankenstein*, I returned to the world of rock musicals with the film version of *Tommy*, again starring Keith Moon, and this time I worked as a special-effects supervisor. After working on a number of pictures as a special-effects technician, including *The Ruling Class* and *Alice's Adventures in Wonderland*, I felt I had enough experience to take on the mantle of supervisor again.

Tommy was a musical based on The Who's rock opera album of the same name and the film was directed by the famously eccentric director Ken Russell. The cast was filled with luminaries from the worlds of cinema and music, including Ann-Margret, Oliver Reed, Roger Daltrey, Elton John, Eric Clapton, Jack Nicholson, Pete Townshend and Tina Turner.

By this point in time, I was working at Effects Associates, which was run by my friend Martin Gutteridge. He had a similar setup to Bowie Films, where his company would work on several different films at the same time and he'd send his people to work on various projects as needed. Nobby Clark was the effects supervisor on *Tommy*, but the script involved a number of effects sequences that he couldn't oversee because he had so much on his plate, so I was called in to help as an additional supervisor.

Like *200 Motels*, *Tommy* is also filled with surrealistic imagery straight out of a dreamworld. One sequence required Keith Moon to play a large organ that was also a motor vehicle. We built the organ on a modified Mini chassis and one of my effects guys was inside driving it while Keith played his music. We had to cut down the chassis so it was small enough to look right with the organ on top.

Keith and the driver learned that the rig could brake on a dime and the whole thing would tip forward precariously if you applied the brakes too hard. They thought it was hilarious to drive around the set like maniacs and brake hard at the last minute, sending the back end into the air.

Tina Turner plays the Acid Queen, who places Roger Daltrey's Tommy into a metal cabinet that looks like a futuristic iron maiden crossed with a knight's suit of armour. The inside of the thing is lined with hypodermic needles, with the plungers of the syringes extending to the outside of the cabinet. In the scene, Tommy enters the casket so he can be injected with enough hallucinogenic drugs to experience the ultimate trip.

I built 40 or 50 syringes for the sequence. The needle points on the inside of the cabinet needed to look sharp and dangerous without actually poking into Roger once the doors of the cabinet were shut to trap him inside. When the doors were shut, the needle points were rigged to retract into the syringes before they could hurt him, but the illusion is given that the needles are piercing his skin.

Once Tommy was closed in, the plungers of the syringes needed to move automatically to deliver the drugs and extract his blood into a network of transparent tubes that lined the outside of the cabinet. It was fun rigging the plungers to work by themselves and pumping the fake blood through the tubes. The effect worked out nicely, with the movement of the plungers and the flowing blood creating a nice visual rhythm to accompany Tina Turner's musical performance.

When we were rigging it all on stage before the cameras rolled, Ken Russell and Oliver Reed stopped by to see how things were progressing. We were going to give them a demonstration of how the cabinet and syringes would work for the sequence.

I had an older gentleman working on my effects team named Frank George, who always wore a white lab coat while he was working. Frank was fixing the hypodermic needles into the side of the cabinet for me. Upon seeing Frank, Oliver immediately dropped his pants, mooned us, and said, "I'm ready for my injection now, doctor!"

Oliver was an amazing actor who was full of life, but he never seemed to take anything seriously outside of acting. He would go out with Keith Moon and get absolutely blasted once shooting was done for the day. They'd been thrown out of all the major hotels in the south of England for completely trashing their rooms. It was all a part of what made them legends in their time.

Ken Russell had a remarkable imagination and it was always interesting to see what he'd come up with. The imagery in his movies was often bizarre and provocative, which made him the perfect director for films like *Tommy* that called for a surrealistic edge. He was also an extremely intense personality who demanded perfection from everyone around him. Ken's temperament could be quite fiery if he didn't get his way, but we got along well. I respected him as an artist, so I didn't mind if he acted a bit eccentric.

I don't think that Ken's off-the-wall creativity was drug-fueled, even though drug use was featured prominently in *Tommy*. I think Ken saw filmmaking as a big game that he enjoyed playing. He wanted to see how far he could push the envelope of "normal" filmmaking and bring his own fresh vision to the world of cinematic storytelling.

I had the opportunity to work with him on a couple of projects, and the experience of working on a Ken Russell film was always unpredictable and exciting. He was often spontaneous and you never knew what strange ideas he was concocting in the back of his mind.

One particularly memorable day made headlines when we were shooting on the South Parade Pier in Southsea. A fire broke out that spread quickly and soon engulfed the entire pier. Ken decided to keep the cameras rolling and he included the blaze in the final film. All of the emergency vehicles and firefighters were real. The fire started when some of the arc lights that were aimed through the ballroom windows set the curtains aflame. Apparently, it was the biggest fire seen in Portsmouth since World War II and the flames were visible for miles.

I also remember when my nephew Chris Corbould was visiting the set for *Tommy* and he almost killed himself. Chris, who has since been recognized with an Academy Award for his work on the visual effects of *Inception*, was still in school at the time and was visiting during his vacation. When he found out I was working on *Tommy*, he begged me to bring him to the set because he was obsessed with The Who.

Chris came with me when I went to speak with Ken on set about some upcoming scenes. When Pete Townshend arrived for shooting, Chris's jaw hit the ground with awe. Pete was Chris's hero, and Chris was more than happy to oblige when Pete asked him to hold his newspaper during filming. I think Chris still has it to this day.

Still floating on cloud nine, Chris went wandering around the set and he came upon a bank of 24-volt batteries all linked together. For reasons still unknown, Chris ran a screwdriver across this bank of batteries to see what would happen. After a huge bang and flash, the screwdriver was melted. Chris managed to survive, but was scared shitless. He still had a few safety lessons to learn before becoming a successful special-effects supervisor himself.

The same year as *Tommy*, I had the opportunity to work on another musical that ended up being a cult favourite - *The Rocky Horror Picture Show*. Directed by Jim Sharman and based on the play *The Rocky Horror Show* by Richard O'Brien, the film was similar to *Tommy* in its sheer level of strangeness. Starring Tim Curry, Susan Sarandon and Barry Bostwick, the film followed the oddball adventures of two young lovers who stumble into sexual misadventure with a transvestite at a Transylvanian castle.

Tim Curry and Richard O'Brien in *The Rocky Horror Picture Show*. Photo courtesy of PHOTOFEST.

Musicals like *Tommy* and *The Rocky Horror Picture Show* were full of over-the-top theatrics and required a great deal of imaginative problem-solving on the part of the special-effects department. One of the fun effects we created was Dr. Scott's wheelchair being dragged throughout the castle and up the stairs when Frank N. Furter turns on a giant magnet in his lab. I used the same principles that Glen had taught me for towing aircraft on *Battle of Britain*. The speeding wheelchair was achieved the same way, with a vehicle out of frame towing the wheelchair with a simple pulley system, sending the poor doctor down hallways and around corners.

If you look carefully, you can see the wires pulling him along as the wheelchair is dragged up the stairs. These days the wires could be erased by a computer in post-production, but we didn't have that sort of technology available to us back then.

In another scene, Meatloaf's character drives a motorcycle out of a freezer and through a wall of ice. I had learned how to use hot wax to simulate ice during the production of *Frankenstein: The True Story*, and I was able to reuse the same technique to make Meatloaf and his motorcycle appear frozen. Simple effects like this can be subtle and sometimes barely noticeable, but they are important to establishing a sense of reality within the context of the story.

Because of the movie's inherent zaniness, it was okay if some of the special effects had a cartoony feel to them. For the scene in which Rocky is born in his tank, Jim wanted liquids of different colours to enshroud the floating body. He asked us to find a way to make the liquids separate into distinct layers of colour to create the effect of a watery rainbow.

We weren't able to get that to work with real liquids, so we simply suspended Rocky on wires and stuck panels of rainbow-painted plexiglass on the side of the tank. A simple solution, but the stylized look of it satisfied Jim.

For Frank N. Furter's performance of the song "Don't Dream It," we filled the room with a blanket of mist to hide the fact that he was actually on a diving board. Seen from a dramatic overhead shot, he then jumps into the mist and disappears from sight. Suddenly the mist separates in all directions to reveal Frank N. Furter floating in a swimming pool. Painted at the bottom of the pool is *The Creation of Adam* from the ceiling of the Sistine Chapel.

Jim wanted the reveal of the pool to be spectacular, so I came up with the idea of using dry-ice smoke to completely cover the diving board and the pool. This way, Frank N. Furter appeared to fall through a bank of clouds like an angel falling from heaven. We used a fan that was strong enough to part the smoke like a perfectly drawn curtain to reveal the pool below.

I used the same idea for a Budweiser commercial I directed in 1990 called

"Ladies Night," in which two guys throw some magic paint across the floor of an empty bar. The floor becomes blanketed with a mysterious fog, and a number of beautiful women rise up through the mist to begin partying. The final shot of the commercial echoes the big reveal from *The Rocky Horror Picture Show*, with the fog parting in every direction until the Budweiser logo can be seen printed on the floor.

My nephew Chris visited me again when I was working on *The Rocky Horror Picture Show*. One night, we were walking along the River Thames by the house we used for the movie, where we had a huge fire hose standing by to pump water from the river to create rain.

Chris was wandering around the set when the camera started rolling. He came upon the hose, which was flat because the pump had just been activated and the water hadn't arrived at his end yet. Hearing a strange hissing sound, Chris decided to pick up the end of the hose and look into it. Suddenly he was blasted by the full force of the spray.

I didn't know much about *The Rocky Horror Show* before I worked on the film version, but a friend of mine loved the original stage production and he predicted that the movie would be a hit. Boy, was he right. I never expected it to become such a cult classic around the world. In fact, it wasn't until several months after the film was released that it caught on with audiences and began to make money on the midnight circuit.

After completing my work on *The Rocky Horror Picture Show*, I returned to the world of rock opera with Ken Russell's insane *Lisztomania*. It was an erotically charged film about the life of Romantic composer and piano virtuoso Franz Liszt, who was played by Roger Daltrey. The cast included Ringo Starr as the Pope, as well as Paul Nicholas as Richard Wagner and Oliver Reed as Princess Carolyn's servant, both of whom had also appeared in *Tommy*.

Lisztomania is full of surrealistic sexual imagery like nothing ever depicted on film before. One scene involves a lavish song-and-dance sequence that takes place around a giant cock. The plaster department created a seven-foot penis with two huge testicles, and the special-effects department built a trolley inside of it so a group of chorus girls could tow it like a sled. The penis was counterweighted so it could bob up and down during the sequence, and Roger straddled it while he performed with a crinoline dress on.

The day we shot that scene, two of us from the effects department carried the cock to the set on our shoulders. We got some really strange looks as we walked through the halls of Shepperton Studios.

At another point in the film, Liszt visits an antechamber where the walls are covered in molded plastic assholes. The effects team had to shoot smoke out of these assholes to simulate drugs being pumped into the air. Liszt then proceeds to Princess Carolyn's decadent bedroom, which was designed to look like something out of Sigmund Freud's subconscious. Even her four-post bed is adorned with sexual imagery - each of the bedposts was molded in the shape of a giant penis with testicles.

For the scene in which Liszt is "born again," we built a giant vinyl womb that Roger could enter from the back. Then he slid down an adjoining chute that we designed to look like a vagina. Seemingly everything is Liszt's life had a sexual connotation to it, at least according to Ken Russell's interpretation.

A lot of artistic license was taken in portraying the lives of various historical figures. For example, the film shows Richard Wagner (resurrected in a Nazi ceremony as a zombified Adolph Hitler) wielding a steel guitar that doubles as a deadly firearm. We constructed the guitar so it could belch flames out of one end to simulate machine gun fire. That probably never happened with the real Wagner.

When Liszt plays a piano in an effort to exorcise Wagner (don't even try to make sense of that), the entire piano starts to spin like a carousel. We placed the piano on a giant turntable that rotated at great speed - so fast in fact that poor Roger had to hang on for dear life. We also rigged the piano so it could shoot fire like a flamethrower during the exorcism. In case you haven't noticed yet, this film is completely bonkers.

Compromise was not a part of Ken Russell's genetic makeup and he wasn't afraid to get his hands dirty if it meant achieving his goals. Ken was someone who would always go all the way and he expected his actors and crew to give it their all too. While some people thought Ken was an overbearing dictator on set, I was inspired by his conviction and desire to explore the limits of his imagination.

Lisztomania was a really fun project because every day was so unique and creative. If we weren't making a seven-foot penis or a machine-gun guitar, we were sending smoke through assholes or blowing shit up. It could be stressful trying to keep up with Ken, who changed his mind about things nonstop, but it forced the best out of the effects team and it definitely kept things from becoming routine.

For one scene, we used two radial-engine fans with 8-foot blades to blow open the doors of a set. Ken was complaining to Jimmy Harris that we weren't giving him enough wind. What he didn't realize was that these fans will start to spit oil if you turn them up too high.

"More wind! I need more wind!"

Jimmy just looked at me and shrugged. If that's what the director wanted, that's what he was going to get. Jimmy cranked up the fans and blew the hell out of those doors. Ken, who had been wearing a spotless white suit, ended up looking like a Dalmatian.

If Ken didn't like you for one reason or another, you were totally fucked. Luckily, he liked me and we always got on well, which is one reason he asked me to work on *Lisztomania* after our experience together on *Tommy*. In fact, Ken wanted me to work with him on *Altered States*, but I was unavailable at the time.

If he didn't like the way something was being done on set, he'd go berzerk and yell violently. He never did that to me, fortunately, but he did shout at some of my effects guys. For example, we were filming the rotating piano when Ken went crazy and started laying into someone. Another one of my crew, Roy, was thirty feet up in the air working on the lighting grid. After Ken finished his verbal assault, you could have heard a pin hit the ground. Nobody dared to breathe lest they be the next target of Ken's wild rage.

Then Roy giggled from above. That just infuriated Ken further, and he proceeded to yell something rude in response. Roy replied with a curt "fuck off"! We all braced for yet another eruption from Mount St. Russell. Instead, Ken found it quite amusing and we were all safe from another fit of anger. Ken could be a bit of a bully, but he respected people who stood up to him.

Lisztomania never became the cult classic that *Tommy* or *The Rocky Horror Picture Show* did, but it cemented my love of rock and pop music. Although I never had a chance to work on another one of Ken's films, I'm proud to have worked with such a visionary filmmaker on two occasions.

The mid-seventies were a very busy time in my career. While at Effects Associates with Martin Gutteridge, I was sent throughout Europe to work on different projects as needed. Martin sent me to Germany for a short period to work on a little-known film called *Lady Dracula*, for which I built a bat that was flown on wires. It wasn't a particularly challenging film after something like *Lisztomania*, but it allowed me to visit the beautiful city of Munich on someone else's dime.

I also worked on a movie in Holland called *Katie Tippel*, which was the most expensive production in Dutch history at the time. The film was a huge critical and commercial success and it helped to propel director Paul Verhoeven into the international limelight. Years later, he moved to the United States and directed blockbusters like *RoboCop*, *Total Recall* and *Basic Instinct*.

Starring Rutger Hauer, *Katie Tippel* was the story of a Dutch family's struggle with poverty during the late 1800s. Parts of the film took place in a large factory and it was my job to create the steam and smoke effects that would bring the factory to life on screen.

The production was budgeted for a very small special-effects team, which ended up being just myself and Jimmy Harris. We worked on *Katie Tippel* for only a week, but we were immediately swept up by the strong sense of family amongst cast and crew. Everybody helped everybody else no matter which department they belonged to, and we all went out for a nice dinner every night and socialized well into the evening. The entire crew consisted of only about 18 people, so it was much more intimate than working on something like *Battle of Britain*, which had a crew of hundreds.

Back in England, I did a short stint on a thriller called *11 Harrowhouse*, which starred such great actors as Charles Grodin, Candice Bergen, James Mason, Trevor Howard and John Gielgud. I wasn't that heavily involved with the production, but I did get to work with legendary stuntman Yakima Canutt and crash a bunch of cars using techniques I'd learned while working on *Battle of Britain*.

Yakima was born in 1895, so he was already quite old by the time I met him. Best known for being John Wayne's stunt double on *Stagecoach*, Yakima also worked on such classic films as *Old Yeller*, *Ben-Hur* and *Spartacus* as a second-unit director. I felt privileged to hear so many great stories about his career.

Sometimes projects are invigorating to work on because they make you feel like a kid again. One example was the 1974 version of *Great Expectations*, which starred Michael York and James Mason. We filmed in a water tank at Shepperton Studios with a beautiful three-masted ship that was right out of my boyhood fantasies.

The ship was built upon a powerful hydraulic rocker that simulated the vessel's movement on the sea. Using wave machines and giant fans, we blasted the ship with water and wind to simulate stormy conditions. It was like getting to play in my own private water park, drenching the hell out of the poor actors and making the biggest mess possible.

So much of my work over the years was fun because I could play with expensive toys I didn't have to pay for. I got to blow up planes, sink submarines and crash cars for a living, and no two days were exactly alike. I'm glad I didn't choose an office job.

In 1977, I worked on *Sinbad and the Eye of the Tiger*, the last of the big-screen Sinbad adventures from legendary stop-motion animator Ray Harryhausen and producer Charles H. Schneer. It was a joy working with Ray, Charlie and director Sam Wanamaker at Shepperton Studios and on location in Malta.

Ray was a true gentleman, very soft-spoken and easygoing. He was remarkably patient with everything, which wasn't surprising considering how much patience was required for him to accomplish his frame-by-frame animation. Impressively, Ray never used any assistants on *Sinbad* and he did all of the animation by himself, locked away in the solitude of his studio.

Even though Sam Wanamaker was officially the director, it was clear that Ray was a strong creative force on the project. My guess is that Ray never directed any of his movies because he was more comfortable animating miniatures than he was dealing with actors. He tended to avoid confrontation whenever possible, and I think he was just too reserved to be a director.

Charlie Schneer was a different story altogether. He was loud and brash, like a stereotypical mogul of Hollywood's Golden Age. I loved him all the same, though, as he was always full of energy and fun to work with.

The contrast between the two men's personalities was most apparent when screening dailies. Charlie was always concerned about money first and foremost, whereas Ray was more creatively driven. With his boisterous voice ringing throughout the screening room, Charlie always complained about how much money was being spent.

"Why the fuck did we need that shot?" he'd yell as the rushes unfolded on the screen. "We could've done without that shot too. Do you know how expensive that was?"

Ray would respond calmly with his soft voice and explain why a particular shot was important in the grand scheme of things or why it was necessary to spend money in certain areas. Charlie often backed off once Ray explained the situation, then the whole thing would happen all over again the next day.

Sinbad made extensive use of miniatures to bring the mythical land of Hyperborea to life on the big screen. I worked in the model shop at Shepperton, helping to build a number of miniature boats for the production. This included Zenobia's ship, which we outfitted with a battery of motorized oars that rowed in unison to give the illusion of great power in the water. Building full-sized ships for the required shots was out of the question given the film's tight budget.

Many shots of the pyramid and the Shrine of the Four Elements were created using miniatures as well, with the actors matted in later during post-production. Unfortunately much of the matte work in the film is less than convincing, with noticeable matte lines fringing the actors.

Practical effects also played an important role in the film. The first big stop-motion sequence is Sinbad's encounter with a trio of ghouls who try to kill him in Rafi's tent. During their battle with Sinbad, the ghouls' weapons knock things astray during the ensuing mayhem.

While we were filming the sequence, actor Patrick Wayne was actually fighting thin air, since the animated ghouls wouldn't be added to the shots until later. I rigged the tent to collapse, which helped to sell the illusion of a ghoul slicing through a tent pole with his axe. Adding to the excitement, I rigged barrels to tumble and vendors' stalls to overturn when the fight spills out into the street. Simple effects like these helped to make Ray's amazing animation even more believable.

Another memorable character in the movie was the Minoton, a mechanical bronze giant with the body of a man and the head of a bull. While Ray built and animated a miniature Minoton for the action scenes, a full-sized prop was also constructed for the scene in which Zenobia and Rafi install a newly built heart into his chest and bring him to life.

I built the mechanical heart for the scene, complete with visible gears that spun around like the innards of a large clock. Everyone was impressed with how the mechanical heart turned out, and Ray kept that in mind when he was looking for someone to build a mechanical owl a few years later for *Clash of the Titans*.

In the frozen wastelands of Hyperborea, Sinbad and his friends encounter a giant walrus during a snowstorm. Ray would add the animated walrus later during post-production, and the effects department was required to create a blizzard for the shooting of the live-action plates. The sequence was shot on the runway of an airport in Malta, where it was a sweltering 104 degrees. I felt terrible for the actors, who had to dress in heavy winter clothing and pretend to be freezing in the midst of the overwhelming heat.

We covered the ground with styrofoam snow and blasted the performers with giant fans to simulate the blizzard. More blowing snow was added optically to some shots after Ray had completed his animation. Much like we did with the sequence involving the ghouls, I had to rig some boxes to fall over on cue. In the final film, it appears as though the giant walrus is responsible for knocking them over.

I also worked on practical effects for the climax of the film, which takes place at a magical shrine. The temple had to start crumbling in on itself, which we accomplished by dropping styrofoam boulders and bits of lightweight debris from the rafters of the soundstage. Simple but effective.

The set also required dressing to make it look like parts of the temple were frozen in sheets of ice. We ended up making the ice out of clear cellophane paper. Ultimately, I don't think it was very convincing and I wish we'd had more time and resources to make it look right.

I recently watched *Sinbad and the Eye of the Tiger* again for the first time in years, and I don't think it holds up as well as some of Ray's earlier films like *Jason and the Argonauts*. Some of the acting and dialogue aren't up to snuff, and long stretches of the film are rather dull.

Looking back, it's hard to believe the film was released during the same summer as *Star Wars*, which was light years ahead of *Sinbad* in terms of its special effects. *Sindbad and the Eye of Tiger* was less successful critically and commercially than the previous films in the series, possibly because it was considered too "old fashioned" in the face of the dawning special-effects revolution. Maybe it was just as well that Ray and Charlie didn't produce any additional Sinbad adventures.

After *Sinbad and the Eye of the Tiger*, the next project really kicked my career into high gear. I got to play in the biggest cinematic sandbox yet, working on one of the most expensive epics ever produced. It was time to take flight.

CHAPTER 5
VERISIMILITUDE

1977 was a year of major change for science-fiction and fantasy cinema. A film called *Star Wars* was scheduled to open later in the year and it was already gaining a lot of pre-release buzz from genre fans. *Close Encounters of the Third Kind* was also set to open, the much-anticipated new film about extraterrestrials from *Jaws* director Steven Spielberg. And I was about to begin work on a fantasy film that would take up the next year and a half of my life and be hailed as another classic of that era.

Of course we didn't know at the time that *Superman: The Movie* would become such a critical and financial hit. Nor did we know what a torturous path lay ahead of us in bringing this comic book legend to the silver screen.

I had befriended a production designer named Michael Stringer on the films *Alice's Adventures in Wonderland* and *Inspector Clouseau*, and we'd kept in touch over the years. Knowing I was between projects at the time, Michael called and said he was working in the art department of *Superman*, which was in pre-production at Cinecittà Studios in Rome.

Michael recommended me to the producers and I soon found myself heading up the physical-effects department in Italy. To be honest, I think I was the only experienced effects supervisor who wasn't already booked for the other big films in production, so the job went to me by default.

Superman: The Movie was the brainchild of producers Alexander Salkind, his son Ilya Salkind and Pierre Spengler, a close friend of the family. They had produced *The Three Musketeers* and *The Four Musketeers*, which were hits at the box office, and they were now looking for another well-known property that could be the basis of a motion-picture franchise.

The Man of Steel was at the top of the list and they quickly bought the movie rights to the character. Realizing that big names were needed if their comic-book film was to be taken seriously, they signed major stars like Marlon Brando and Gene Hackman for astronomical sums of money.

Director Guy Hamilton, who had directed *Battle of Britain* as well as four of the James Bond pictures, was set to helm the new *Superman*. I remember the first time I met Guy in his office to discuss the project. He was a larger-than-life personality, full of bravado and eager to establish himself as boss.

With his feet resting atop an enormous desk that dwarfed him, he asked me to take a seat in a considerably smaller chair facing him. I couldn't even see his face past the soles of his shoes. His feet parted when he addressed me, then he'd close the gap whenever I responded. Guy was definitely an old-school showman and the meeting was meant to be intimidating, but it would have taken a lot more than that to shake me up.

Josie and Lucy stayed with me in Rome during pre-production, which I thought might be good for our relationship, but I found myself fighting with Josie again on a regular basis. It was like the time she stayed with me in Malta, when she didn't have anyone to keep her company and she felt trapped looking after the baby all day. As is expected on a large-scale production like *Superman*, I worked long and often irregular hours that left me little time to spend with them.

Aside from her growing discontentment, my experience in Italy was an enjoyable one with lots of fantastic food. Eating and drinking well was an important part of the culture, and once you got a taste of the local cuisine, it was easy to see why. Every morning on my way to Cinecittà Studios, I stopped at this wonderful cafe that had outstanding espresso and paninis for breakfast.

Early poster concept for *Superman: The Movie*. © Warner Bros. From the personal collection of Colin Chilvers.

The good eating and drinking continued throughout the day. Our two-hour lunches were virtual feasts. The ten guys on my Italian special-effects crew were much more relaxed than you'd find in Hollywood or England, and we formed a strong sense of family over those extended lunches. The Italians greatly valued their social time during meals.

One of my carpenters always left the studio an hour before lunch on his little three-wheeled truck and he returned with a big jug of local wine that was still cloudy because it was so fresh. The freshly baked buns, ham, tomatoes and mozzarella cheese were to die for. Once in a while, we'd have some nice champagne to go along with our meal.

Josie's parents came over for a visit, which was a nice change of pace for her. One day, her father joined us for lunch at the studio and he was shocked at how well we were eating and drinking. He especially enjoyed the local wine, which had a really high alcohol content, and soon he was drunk to the gills. His nap lasted for the entire afternoon.

I'd been working on the pre-production of *Superman* in Rome for about four months when I learned that the production would be leaving Italy in the near future. Apparently, the Salkinds' latest budget showed that filming in Italy would be considerably more expensive than they'd originally expected, so they'd been exploring other potential countries with available studio space.

Logo design for the *Superman* movie poster. © Warner Bros.
From the personal collection of Colin Chilvers.

At the time, other European countries were emerging as film-production centres where expenses could be kept low. However, many of these countries also lacked the necessary facilities and infrastructure, so the Salkinds moved the production to England.

Superman resumed pre-production at Pinewood Studios, which caused some unforeseen difficulties for the director. Guy Hamilton was a tax exile from England, so he couldn't enter the country to work or he'd be forced to pay a lot of income tax. The Salkinds briefly considered having Guy direct the entire film via video link from France, but the idea was scrapped when everyone realized how impractical it would be.

Guy left the project and the search was on for a new director. As the story goes, the Salkinds looked at the box-office charts to see what movie was making the most money that week. The biggest hit in theatres at the time was *The Omen*, directed by Richard Donner, so the Salkinds called him up and offered him the job of directing *Superman*.

Once Dick accepted, he flew to England from the States to meet everyone involved with the film. Dick and I got on well from the moment we first met to discuss the project. He was full of great ideas and his booming voice made his enthusiasm contagious to those around him.

Shortly afterward, I was approached by production supervisor Bob Simmonds, who had been speaking with Dick about the special-effects team for *Superman*.

"Dick used John Richardson as head of effects on *The Omen*," Bob explained. "No offense to you, but Dick would like John to head up the effects on *Superman* because they worked together so well last time. Would you be willing to stay on *Superman* and work under him?"

I'd worked with John before on *Battle of Britain* and our personalities didn't necessarily gel. It's not that we were bitter enemies or anything like that, but I just couldn't see myself working under him. Also, I'd been working on *Superman* for six months by the time Dick was hired as director, so I didn't have a big desire to keep working on the film if I was demoted from supervisor to technician.

"It's entirely up to Dick who he wants to supervise the effects," I told Bob, "but if Dick wants to work with John, then I'll move on. I completely respect Dick's decision and wish John the best of luck if he takes the job."

For whatever reason, John ultimately didn't accept the post and I stayed on as special-effects supervisor. My title on the film ended up being "creative supervisor and director of special effects."

A top-notch effects crew was assembled to tackle the eclectic challenges we'd be facing. Roy Field oversaw optical effects, Zoran Perisic supervised flying effects that involved his specialized "Zoptic System" of front projection, Denys Coop supervised special-effects photography, Les Bowie created the matte paintings, Derek Meddings headed up the miniatures department, and I was in charge of mechanical and floor effects. Once we began to refine the wire-flying for Superman, Wally Veevers joined the production and helped with the wire team.

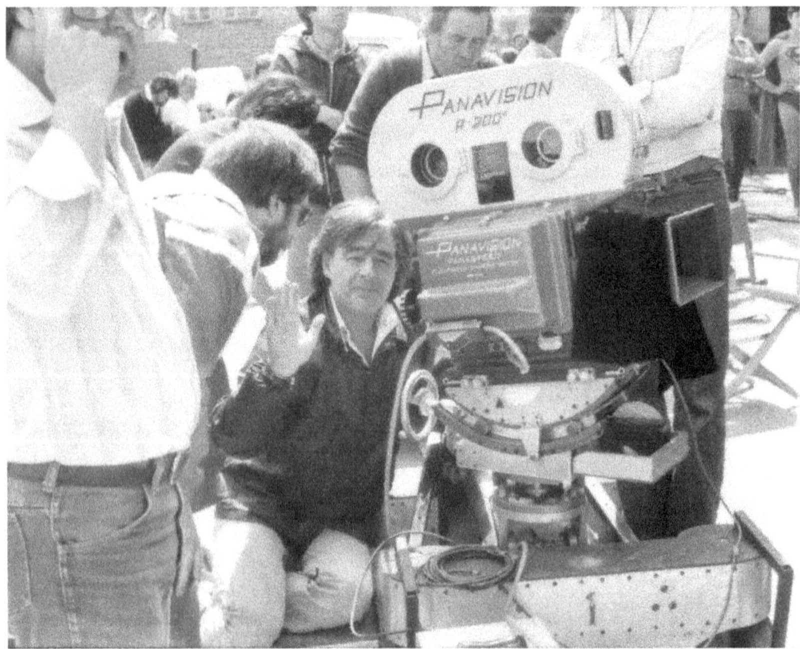

Conferring with *Superman* director Dick Donner. Christopher Reeve can be seen in the distance dressed as the Man of Steel. Photo courtesy of Jim Bowers at CapedWonder.com.

Mario Puzo, David Newman, Leslie Newman and Robert Benton wrote the original screenplay, which Dick thought was too jokey in tone, so he brought in his friend Tom Mankiewicz to do a rewrite. Tom and Dick were a riot together and they brought a lot of fun to a stressful production that was often beset by technical problems and creative disagreements.

Superman would not have been the success it was without the vision of Dick Donner. He knew exactly what he wanted to do with the movie and he had great respect for the Superman legend. In fact, he hung up a huge banner in the production office that read "Verisimilitude" - a reminder to everyone working on the movie that we needed to take the Superman universe seriously and find the truth in every detail. We knew that comedy would be an important aspect of the film, but we were determined to avoid the self-conscious camp of the old *Batman* series at all cost.

Dick kept a completely "open-office" policy on the production. Anytime you wanted to speak with him, you could just walk into his office and have a discussion about any aspect of the movie. If you had ideas about how to improve something, he was open to considering your thoughts. If you did a particularly good job, he'd buy you a case of wine to show his appreciation. Dick was such a huge positive force on that movie and he inspired all of us to give it our all. He saw *Superman* as an important part of American mythology, and he'd be damned if he wasn't going to do it justice with his film.

Being such a strong personality with his own unique vision, Dick was soon bumping heads with the Salkinds and Pierre Spengler. The main bone of contention was money. The producers wanted to keep costs down as much as possible, but Dick refused to cut corners or settle for second best. If he wasn't happy with a take, he kept doing more takes until he was happy with the result. The Salkinds got increasingly fidgety as the expenses kept adding up.

Both Dick and Tom grew up loving the comics and they were driven by their passion for the Superman legend. On the other hand, I don't think the Salkinds really cared who Superman was. They saw him as just another silly character from the funnies who would attract kids to cinemas.

Reportedly, the Salkinds had chosen to make a film version of *The Three Musketeers* for purely financial reasons. After hearing that the *The Three Musketeers* was the second-most read book after the Bible, they thought they could make a tidy profit by bringing the Alexandre Dumas novel to the big screen. After they hit it big with that movie and its sequel, they decided to buy the film rights to Superman because it seemed like a good financial investment.

Things got so bad between Dick and the producers that they refused to speak with one another. This made Warner Bros. quite nervous and they decided to send in Charlie Greenlaw as an associate producer to keep an eye on things. Originally, he was supposed to be on *Superman* for only ten days, but he ended up staying for ten months. Charlie acted as a buffer between Dick and the Salkinds, although Charlie was a huge supporter of Dick and could appreciate the director's grand vision for the film.

To act as their representative on set, the Salkinds hired Richard Lester, who had directed the Musketeer movies for them. This way, the Salkinds could communicate with Dick through Richard and avoid any ugly confrontations in front of the cast and crew. It's also possible that the Salkinds were sending Richard to the set each day as a backup in case Dick quit or had to be sacked. Although Richard was always very cordial and professional, he was the Salkinds' constant reminder to Dick that a new director could be brought in at a moment's notice.

Personally, I got along well with the Salkinds and Pierre Spengler. Alexander wasn't that involved with the day-to-day production of *Superman*. He concentrated on the fundraising side of things, so my contact with him was more limited. His son Ilya was mostly a "big-picture" guy who knew how to sell and market the film, and Pierre was the line producer who dealt with Dick on a daily basis.

Dick and Pierre in particular fought a lot, and Ilya backed up Pierre because they were childhood friends. The bad blood between Dick and the producers was common knowledge, and we all trudged onward with our heads down trying not to get caught in the crossfire.

Pierre and I remained on friendly terms even after the Superman films were finished, and I came to realize what a difficult job he had trying to keep the production on track with so much in-fighting.

The original plan was to shoot *Superman: The Movie* and *Superman II* back-to-back and release them in theatres a year or so apart. To make the most efficient use of sets, Dick actually shot some scenes for the second movie during filming of the first. When production continued to go over schedule and over budget, the Salkinds abandoned the idea of shooting two movies and put all of their effort into completing part one. Production on the sequel would resume only if the first film was successful at the box office.

Dick and the producers continued to fight on many fronts, but at least they could agree that the film was exceptionally well cast. With big stars like Marlon Brando as Jor-El and Gene Hackman as Lex Luthor, Dick decided to go with an unknown in the lead role. Rather than going for a macho man, a soft-spoken young actor named Christopher Reeve was chosen to fill the blue and red suit.

When he first came in to read for the part, he was a string bean who didn't look much like a superhero. At one point, there was discussion of building a muscle suit for him to wear under the spandex, but that was abandoned after Chris built up his body with months of weight training.

The special-effects team was extremely lucky to have an actor as patient as Chris Reeve as the Man of Steel. He was totally dedicated to the role and was willing to do whatever it took to make the best movie possible. Whether that meant being dangled from wires dozens of feet in the air or spending hours in an uncomfortable flying harness under hot studio lights, Chris was always game.

Throughout pre-production, one of our top priorities was figuring out how to make Superman fly convincingly on film. When I'd first arrived at Cinecittà Studios in Rome, the art department had started their own R & D team to come up with ideas, but they ultimately lacked the practical experience and engineering expertise to come up with solutions. What works on paper doesn't always work in reality. By the time production had been moved to

Pinewood and Dick Donner had replaced Guy Hamilton as director, we still hadn't completely nailed down the effects.

We experimented with a number of ways to make Superman fly and most of them failed miserably. Screen tests were done with radio-controlled models, but they didn't look natural unless they were filmed in extremely wide shots. Using traditional hand-drawn animation wasn't successful either.

We talked about dressing a skydiver in a Superman costume and hiding his parachute under his cape somehow, but that didn't seem practical for the number and variety of shots we'd need. At one point, we put a Superman costume on a dummy and shot him out of an air cannon, but that looked like shit. We were crashing and burning with astonishing regularity, but we had to go through all of that to see which ideas weren't going to work.

Ultimately, we came up with several different methods of making Superman fly. Some of the shots would be achieved live in front of the camera, while others would rely on optical-effects processing during post-production. Our methods ranged from the downright simple to the state of the art.

Wally Veevers came on board to work on the flying systems for *Superman* and it was nice being reunited with him after working together on *The Rocky Horror Picture Show*. We designed an overhead track system in the studio that allowed us to lift Superman into the air, fly him around and land him with considerable grace. It was a sophisticated system that allowed us a great deal of control in manipulating Chris, but it was also extremely noisy and would occasionally cause nuts and bolts to rain from the heavens.

The system was like an upside-down skateboard dolly, with two sets of wheels running along a network of tubing mounted from the ceiling. Chris was hung on wires attached to the dolly. We built curves into the track and had drop-down spindles on the wires, which allowed Chris to pivot his body as the dolly was pulled around a corner, giving the illusion that Superman was changing course mid-flight.

One of the flying-rig guys sat in a little pod above Chris controlling the wires with a little steering handle. That's how we accomplished the first flying shot in the film, in which Superman takes off from his perch in the Fortress of Solitude, flies directly toward the camera, and banks sharply at the last moment.

The track system was counterweighted, which helped us return Chris to the starting position easily and quickly for subsequent takes. Counterweights on the wires also helped to eliminate any jerkiness when he took off or landed.

We used one-strand piano wire, which had to be thick enough for safety, but thin enough so it wouldn't be visible on film. The wires were reasonably strong, but we had to keep them nice and straight because they had a tendency to break when bent. To make the wires less visible under the lights, we had them black-anodized to make them less shiny.

Working with the cinematographer Geoffrey Unsworth, we did everything possible to make the wires invisible on film to avoid the need to paint them out frame by frame. Wire removal was considerably more challenging to do before the days of digital effects. Roy Field, who was in charge of optical effects on *Superman*, had to paint out some wires as a last resort for certain shots.

Les Bowie came up with the idea of vibrating the wires, which helped to make them less visible on camera. Nowadays, considerably thicker wires can be used for extra safety because it's relatively simple for an effects artist to remove wires on the computer during post-production.

Bob Harman supervised the wire team on all of the Superman films. Chris put a great deal of trust in Bob, who had to balance the dramatic needs of the shot with the actor's safety. Bob didn't believe in using motors for the wire system because he felt it wouldn't be as safe. He insisted that all the wires be maneuvered completely by hand for the flying shots. If something got jammed in a pulley or something wasn't working right with the track system, the guys handling the wires would feel it with their hands and they could stop a take before an accident occurred.

The wires were attached to special harnesses that was hidden under the Superman costume. We imported them from a company in the States that specialized in making harnesses that were relatively small and lightweight. Although the harnesses worked wonderfully from a technical point of view, they had a tendency to put pressure on the groin area. Long days of being hoisted up and down on wires became uncomfortable very quickly, but Chris never complained. No power-tripping from this young actor.

Chris had trained extensively before shooting began and he was in amazing shape by the time we started the wire shots. He needed strong core muscles to stay properly balanced on the wires and look convincing as the Man of Steel in flight. It was decided early on that the flying would be done by Chris himself as opposed to a stunt performer. A stuntman is a stuntman and an actor is an actor.

Superman's flights had to be *acted*, so the challenge of giving the character wings became another extension of Christopher Reeve's performance. Once he was in that suit, he *was* Superman and he believed he could fly. That level of dedication and verisimilitude clearly shows on screen and helped to bring Superman to life.

In order to make the wire work convincing on screen, Chris had to be in total sync with the flying team. Whenever Superman had a vertical liftoff, Chris would bend his knees first to give the illusion that he was pushing himself off the ground. The person handling the wires on the other end of the pulley had to give Chris enough slack to do that and then time the liftoff perfectly with Chris' actions.

Superman's running takeoffs required even more coordination because considerably more movement was involved. Chris and the wire team became well coordinated and they operated like one collective mind.

Computerized motion-control wouldn't have worked with the wire-flying because so much of the subtlety in Superman's flight is in the coordination between Chris and the guys controlling the wires. Whenever Superman lifted off or landed, it was slightly different each time because he was being controlled by human beings. Films like *Star Wars* could use motion-control rigs to achieve shots of spaceships gliding across the screen in perfectly geometric courses, but that works only for inanimate objects. Relying on manually controlled pulleys added character and subtlety to Superman's aerial acrobatics.

One of the most complex sequences using the track system was Superman's romantic flight above the clouds with Lois Lane. It was particularly challenging because it involved the coordinated flying of two characters instead of just one. In addition to flying alongside one another, they were also required to make complex movements in the air independently of one another.

Concept art of Lois Lane's flight with Superman. © Warner Bros.
From the personal collection of Colin Chilvers.

Margot Kidder was another example of perfect casting for the film. She captured the spirit of Lois Lane beautifully and had a magnetic chemistry with Chris on screen. Despite many hours hanging from uncomfortable wires in a hot studio, they made their flying look so effortless on screen. It was easy for viewers to forget they were watching special effects because the performances were so strong.

Another method of making Superman fly was used whenever we were on location, since we couldn't bring our overhead track system with us. We used an 80-ton crane that could extend up to 240 feet. Bob and his team rigged Chris with wires attached to the crane so he could take off and land. Sometimes Chris would be 60 feet in the air on wires, but it didn't seem to bother him.

"It doesn't matter if I fall from 10 feet or 60 feet," I remember Chris telling me. "I'd probably die in either case!"

Making Chris take flight. I'm watching the magic unfold in the background.
Photo courtesy of Jim Bowers at CapedWonder.com.

The flying shots accomplished with the crane are among the most convincing in the film. When Superman descends from the air with the jewel thief and turns him over to the police, you can clearly see it's Chris doing the stunt.

His takeoff after rescuing Lois from the helicopter was also accomplished with the crane, as was the shot of him taking flight after rescuing the kitten from the tree. Because no process photography was needed, Chris was able to interact with the other actors as he took to the air.

Some of Superman's liftoffs were done with a simple teeter totter that Chris would stand on. The shot was framed so you couldn't see his feet as his body was lifted into the air. Once his arms were out of the shot, he grabbed onto a bar above and hoisted his entire body out of frame.

We also used a platform on a camera crane that Chris could stand on. The crane began in the air and descended gently to the ground, at which point Chris simply walked off the platform. As long as the shot was framed so his feet couldn't be seen, the illusion of a soft landing was achieved.

Sometimes we couldn't avoid process photography and had to film Chris hanging in front of a blue screen. Shots of Superman flying among the skyscrapers were accomplished this way because we had no way to rig him with wires at such a height for real, plus the shots required complex movement that could be accomplished most easily with optical effects.

For these "traveling-matte" shots, the blue backing was removed optically and replaced with a different background, like a cityscape or a sky. That was Roy Field's specialty - taking separate images and printing them onto a single piece of film so they appeared to have been photographed at the same time.

Roy faced an unusual challenge in that Superman's suit was largely blue itself, causing potential headaches when it came to combining the various photographic elements in the optical printer. The camera must be able to discern between the color of the blue screen and the color of objects in front of the screen for the effect to be successful. That's why people who are filmed in front of a blue screen are usually dressed in colors other than blue. With Superman's blue suit, we risked having portions of the background image ghosting through him in the final shot.

We worked around this potential problem by having the costume department create a new suit specifically for blue-screen work. Chris wore this special costume, which was more turquoise than pure blue, whenever he hung in front of the blue screen. This way, we avoided any problems with the backgrounds ghosting through. During optical processing, the suit was color-corrected so it appeared its normal blue hue.

Another way of making Superman fly was the use of front-screen projection. Essentially, Chris was filmed in front of a large screen onto which film footage, also known as a background plate, was projected. The background plate, which was often footage of clouds or landscapes rushing by, helped to create the illusion that he was really flying high above the earth.

Chris was held in front of the screen with a pole arm that was hidden from the camera's view by his own body. The pole went through a hole in the screen and was attached to a hydraulic rig that could roll him, move him from side to side or tilt him up and down. My design for the hydraulic rig and pole arm was inspired by Glen Robinson, who had built something similar for filming miniature aircraft on *Battle of Britain*.

We took a mold of Chris' body to create a perfectly fitting rig for him. The rig was essentially a fibreglass tray holding him up by the stomach and thighs, with a matching piece that sandwiched him from the top. The body suit and cape were put on over the rig, which was connected to the pole arm.

This was even more uncomfortable that the wire harness, but Chris still never complained and he remained in character during shooting. Even with the worst discomfort, he had to keep his energy up for the camera and exude sheer confidence as Superman.

Sometimes he'd be on the pole arm for three or four hours straight. The rig was particularly uncomfortable for his stomach, since there weren't any bones down there to help support his weight. His arms also became tired after hours of keeping his body straight as an arrow, so we wheeled in a platform that he could rest his arms on between takes.

In order to create the illusion that Superman was flying toward the camera when Chris was mounted on the front-projection pole arm, Zorin Perisic created what he called the Zoptic System. This involved tying two zoom lenses together, one on the camera and the other on the projector for the background plate. When the camera zoomed in, the front-screen projector was synchronized to zoom out correspondingly. If you looked through the camera lens, the front-projected image of the clouds in the background appeared to stay the same size, but Superman appeared to zoom straight toward the camera.

To make the flying scenes even more dynamic, the whole projector was counterweighted so it could be maneuvered up and down in front of the screen. The camera was synchronized with those movements too, so it looked like Chris was the one moving in the final shots. The projector must have weighed six or seven hundred pounds, and it required a great deal of power to shoot an extremely bright image onto the screen that was still visible under the strong lights trained on Chris.

Using the Zoptic System was an effective way to fly Superman because it had a softer, more natural look than some of the blue-screen shots, which sometimes had harsh matte lines around Superman that were difficult to hide. We filmed some wonderful background plates from helicopters and planes that really sold the illusion of flight for these shots.

One of the most exciting sequences in the film involved Superman chasing a rocket through the Grand Canyon. The spectacular background plates were shot by Learjet and then sped up considerably to give the impression of dangerously high speed. This chase sequence involved a mixture of blue-screen work and shots done with the Zoptic System.

For the shots of Superman catching up with the rocket, we mounted both Chris and a life-sized mockup of the rocket in front of the projection screen. With the use of steam and lights in the rear of the rocket, we were able to create the illusion of great power and heat. You can almost feel the force of the rocket's exhaust fighting off Superman's desperately reaching fingers.

One Zoptic shot in particular never fails to give audiences a wonderful sense of vertigo and weightlessness, especially when seen on the big screen. Superman flies into the shot with the glittering skyline of Metropolis behind him, only the buildings are upside down! He goes into a barrel roll and does a complete 360 degree rotation as the cityscape behind him proceeds to do its own barrel roll in the opposite direction.

This shot perfectly captures Superman's sense of playfulness in flying. It required a great deal of coordination between the rotating background plate, the projector, the camera, and the pole arm that held Chris in front of the screen.

Just making Superman's cape flap properly was a huge ordeal. When we first put a cape on Chris and aimed a wind machine at him, the cape just wrapped around him like a wet towel. We were trying to recreate that classic image from the comic books of the cape dancing gracefully in the wind.

Les Bowie designed a motorized rig that went on Chris's back underneath the cape. The rig had cams that controlled thin poles running down the length of the cape, kind of like the wiry bones that help a bat control its wings. The cams were offset so the poles would flick up and down to create a wave-like motion for the cape, making it look like it was flapping behind him in natural fashion.

Back in the seventies, we couldn't just "fix it in post" as the cliché goes. If we encountered a problem with a physical effect on set, we had to work it out then and there using our ingenuity and whatever resources we had available. Again, it was really the problem-solving aspect of special effects that I found the most engaging. Those pre-CGI days were the most fun for me personally.

One of the funniest sequences in *Superman* was achieved using an old-fashioned technique that was commonly used in the sixties' *Batman* television show whenever Batman and Robin were seen scaling the side of a building. In *Superman*, a burglar clumsily scales the side of an office building with suction cups attached to his hands and knees.

The side of the building was actually constructed on the studio floor and the actor playing the burglar simply climbed across the floor while pretending to struggle against gravity. When the camera was turned on its side, it effectively created the illusion that the criminal was climbing straight up.

He eventually encounters Superman, who appears to defy gravity by standing sideways on the wall. In shock and panic, the burglar loses his grip and tumbles toward the pavement below. Luckily, Superman is able to fly past the falling man and catch him before the sidewalk does. These shots were accomplished in studio using the overhead-track system.

It always gets a big laugh when the scene cuts to the interior of an office with a man working at his desk. Outside of the window behind him,

Superman can be seen standing on the side of the building, defying gravity once more as he casually catches the falling burglar in his arms.

This shot was achieved with clever camera placement. The desk was actually facing straight down with the camera shooting up toward the office worker. This allowed Chris to stand on the window behind him, and from the camera's point of view, Superman appeared to defy gravity. The office guy was actually strapped into his chair so he wouldn't fall and everything on his desk was securely fastened. Even the man's hair was slicked back so it wouldn't fall down and ruin the illusion.

The helicopter sequence in *Superman* has become one of the most famous scenes in cinematic history. We dubbed it the "Double Jeopardy" sequence because it introduced an extra, unexpected element of danger at the end. In the scene, Lois waits on the rooftop landing pad of the *Daily Planet*, where a helicopter will fly her to Metropolis Airport for an important assignment.

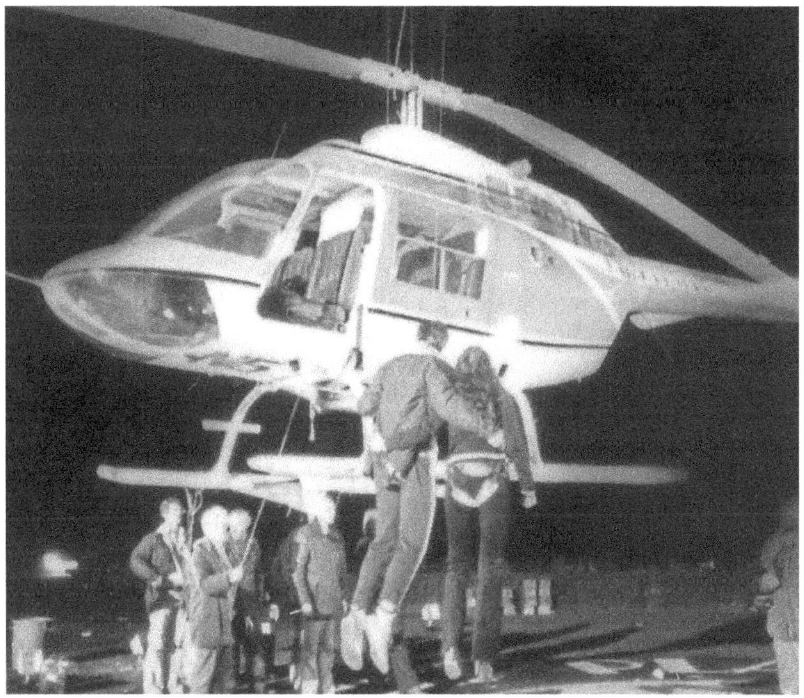

Hanging around on the rooftop set. Photo courtesy of Jim Bowers at CapedWonder.com.

While lifting off, the helicopter hooks a loose cable on its skid and spins out of control, crashing precariously on the edge of the roof. Lois tries to climb free from the helicopter, but she loses her grip and falls from the edge of the building. Superman catches Lois midair, much to the disbelief of everyone watching from the ground.

The danger was originally supposed to end there, but Dick thought it would be more exciting if the helicopter then slid off the edge of the roof and fell toward Superman and Lois below. Hence the "Double Jeopardy" nickname. Without even breaking a sweat, Superman catches the falling helicopter and lands safely on the roof of the *Daily Planet* with the copter in one hand and Lois in the other.

This was an extremely complex sequence because it involved so many different kinds of special effects, including wirework, Zoptic System shots, matte paintings, miniatures and practical effects. It was important that the special-effects techniques blended together seamlessly to make the sequence convincing.

The production bought a helicopter that was no longer in use because it had crashed in real life. It was missing several parts, including the cockpit windshield, so we tracked down and purchased these parts to make it look completely operational for the camera.

We removed the helicopter's heavy engine so it would be lightweight enough to maneuver on wires suspended from a crane. At the same time, the helicopter needed a motor powerful enough to make the blades rotate quickly enough. Instead of using real helicopter blades, we constructed special lightweight versions that could run on a much smaller and lighter car motor.

Geoffrey Unsworth and I studied footage of helicopters in action. We noticed that the outside two thirds of the blades were virtually invisible because they were moving so fast, so we decided to build only the inner third of the blades, which allowed us to further reduce the weight of the helicopter. This also made for a safer set because the blades didn't have as much reach. At Geoffrey's suggestion, we painted the blades with a high gloss paint so they would reflect light and be more visible on camera.

Working with Margot Kidder and Chris Reeve on the helicopter sequence.
Photo courtesy of Jim Bowers at CapedWonder.com.

In order to move the helicopter around by crane, we needed to lift it from a point directly above its centre of gravity, which was over the rotor blades. The rotor was built hollow so we could feed a wire all the way down the shaft and into the helicopter where we could secure it. We were then able to use the crane to make the helicopter take off, land and spin out of control as needed.

During the helicopter's wild spin, its tail crashes through the office module beside the landing pad. The module was constructed with breakaway glass and balsa wood so the tail could plow through easily, and we rigged pyrotechnics for shots of the helicopter crashing on the roof's edge in a flash of flame and smoke. Stuart Baird's lightning-quick editing, coupled with dramatic sound effects and John Williams' suspenseful score, effectively conveyed the runaway helicopter's destructive power.

For shots that looked upward at the helicopter perched over the edge of the building, we built a set that was 20 feet off the ground so we could position the camera low enough to get the proper perspective. A hydraulic rig was used to control the helicopter so it could be rocked dramatically without

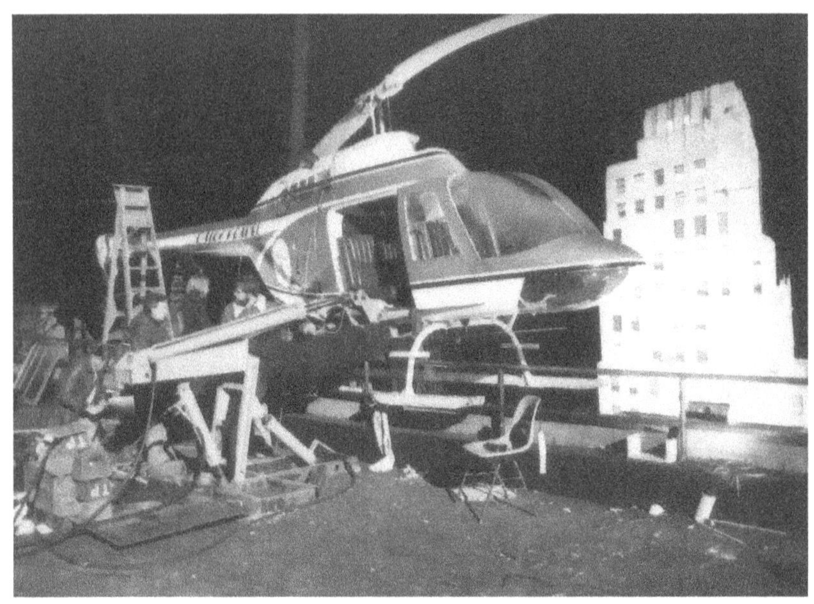

Filming the helicopter sequence at Pinewood Studios.
Photo courtesy of Jim Bowers at CapedWonder.com.

A 60-foot section of the building was constructed for the shot of the helicopter falling directly toward the viewer. The copter was lowered toward the camera by crane to give the impression of a free fall. This shot lasts only about a second, but it really puts the audience in the middle of the danger.

A miniature set of the building and a model helicopter were also constructed for a wide shot of the smoking helicopter perched precariously on the roof's edge, as well as a wide shot of Superman flying the helicopter back up the side of the building to the landing pad.

Although the Double Jeopardy sequence amounts to only a few minutes of screen time, it required an exhausting three weeks of shooting. It seemed like a major pain in the ass at the time, but it was all worth it when we saw how well the final sequence turned out.

I'd been working on *Superman* for about nine months when *Star Wars* opened in theatres and quickly became an international phenomenon. Dick had George Lucas send a print of *Star Wars* over to us in England and the whole crew watched it in Theatre 7 at Pinewood Studios. To say we were blown away would be an understatement. *Star Wars* changed everything. It showed that fantasy movies could find major success with mainstream audiences, and that genre films didn't need to be B-movies of dubious quality.

It also set a new benchmark for special-effects. Even though a lot of older effects techniques were used in *Star Wars*, like matte paintings, animation and miniatures, nobody had ever put so much care into the effects before or had ever presented them in such a visually extravagant package. *Star Wars* inspired everybody working on *Superman* because we now saw what was possible. Lucas had set the bar high, but we were more determined than ever to reach or even surpass it.

Dick was always great at keeping his cast and crew inspired. Partway through production, he had Stuart Baird edit together a 5-minute promo of footage we'd shot. The score for *Superman* hadn't been composed yet, so he used John Williams' stirring music from *Star Wars*.

At this point, nobody on the production was feeling particularly confident about the flying effects achieved so far. We'd been working for several months trying to make Superman soar on screen, but we'd had many more failures than successes.

The crew gathered in the theatre to watch the promo Stuart had assembled. Included was the shot of Chris wearing the Superman outfit for the first time in the film. He takes off from a ledge in the Fortress of Solitude, flies toward the camera and veers off screen gracefully. Beautiful. It made the hairs on the back of my neck stand up. Chris Reeve *was* Superman, and we had made him fly. It was pure movie magic and the seams didn't show. Everybody in the theatre erupted into applause. At that point we knew our hard work over the past nine months had been worth it. It gave everybody a new lease on life.

One of the great things about the film industry is working with screen legends like Marlon Brando, who played Superman's Kryptonian father, Jor-El. I remember hearing about Dick's visit with Marlon in the States to discuss the film. After Dick returned to England, he told us about the crazy ideas Marlon was suggesting. Apparently, Marlon wanted to play Jor-El as "a suitcase," whatever that meant. Not afraid to speak his mind, Dick came right out and said the magic word - "no." That wasn't going to happen. Dick would not allow Marlon to play the character as a suitcase or any other piece of luggage for that matter. I think Marlon liked to test people to see if they would push back or let him walk all over them. Dick was cordial but he wouldn't be pushed around, so Marlon respected him from that point on.

Marlon was a really nice guy to work with. He was on set for only ten days and had a horrendous cold the entire time. I had limited contact with him, mainly to tell him which parts of the set to avoid walking on. Parts of the floor on the Krypton set were constructed with breakaway panels so giant crystals could be thrust up through them during the planet's destruction. Anybody who tried walking on those parts of the floor would be sure to fall through. I didn't want to see the world's most expensive movie star taking a tumble into a deep pit.

On Krypton with *Superman* director Dick Donner.
Photo courtesy of Jim Bowers at CapedWonder.com.

Every time we built a breakaway section of the floor, we quickly put up a safety barrier so nobody would fall in. One time we were doing a survey with Dick to explain how the destruction of Krypton would be achieved. Assistant director Dusty Symonds was in a rush to get across the set, so he ducked beneath one of the barriers and promptly fell right through the floor. Luckily he wasn't hurt, but it goes to show how seriously safety should be taken on a film set.

For each of Marlon's scenes, I helped to place his cue cards around the set strategically so they wouldn't appear on camera. Marlon explained that he didn't like to memorize his lines because it helped him stay fresh take after take. He knew exactly where each cue card should be placed for different parts of the scene. For example, he'd take a few steps, look up with a thoughtful expression and read from a cue card posted high on a wall behind the camera, take another few steps, look down pensively, then read from the cue card stuck on the floor. That's why he'd pause now and then.

I think Marlon respected Dick's strong vision for the film and his commitment to quality. Once Marlon arrived at Pinewood and saw the ambitious scope of the sets, he realized this wasn't just a kiddie movie - it was a full-blown epic. *Superman* was a major motion picture like *The Godfather* and Marlon was happy to be involved with another high-profile production.

Concept art for the *Superman* movie poster featuring Marlon Brando as Jor-El.
© Warner Bros. From the personal collection of Colin Chilvers.

When he first signed on for *Superman*, Marlon originally stipulated that he didn't want any press on set and he didn't want to do any interviews. As filming progressed, he became so comfortable under Dick's leadership that he agreed to let the press visit and interview him. That level of comfort was largely due to the strong family environment Dick created.

The wardrobe, hair and makeup people came to know Marlon well over the ten days of shooting and he was always appreciative of their efforts to make him look good on screen. At the end of his shooting, he gave them all a solid gold Dunhill lighter as a token of his appreciation. A very nice gesture indeed.

For the scene in which Jor-El pleads with the Kryptonian council to evacuate the planet, the actors' costumes were covered with small strips of Scotchlite, which is a highly reflective material created by 3M that's also used for making movie screens. When bright lights were trained on the costumes, they glowed as though they were white hot.

Throughout production, Geoffrey Unsworth used Scotchlight in another interesting way to give the film a unique visual style. He shot the movie through a one-way mirror positioned in front of the camera lens. A lightbox was mounted beside the lens, and it was aimed at small piece of mounted Scotchlite. The light was reflected off the Scotchlite onto the front of the one-way mirror to create a slight haze in-camera. He adjusted the lightbox according to how much softness he wanted for each shot. This unusual approach gave *Superman* a dreamlike quality suitable for a fairy tale.

Watching Geoffrey work was like getting a master class in cinematography. He took the time to light each scene to perfection and his meticulousness matched Dick Donner's, so they were a great pair to work together. It must have driven Pierre Spengler and the Salkinds crazy when Geoffrey spent so much time getting the light just right, but the results were undeniable worth the effort.

One of the most spectacular sets was the Fortress of Solitude, which looked spectacular on film thanks to John Barry's wonderful production design and Geoffrey's stunning cinematography. Getting the Fortress to look just right on film wasn't an easy task, however.

The idea was to make the Fortress feel like a truly alien environment - one possessed by the benevolent spirits of the extinct Kryptonian race. The lighting had to be soft, as though emanating from the snowy walls themselves. The lights also had to be hidden from the camera's view, which was made extra challenging by the fact that the Fortress's ceiling would be visible for numerous shots.

Geoffrey's approach to lighting the set was really quite clever. He put all of his effort into lighting a small patch of the Fortress to his satisfaction, then he gave his crew one simple instruction - "Please light the entire set the exact same way." Thanks to all of their efforts, the Fortress of Solitude remains one of the most memorable and iconic locations in motion picture history.

On *Superman*, I never had the chance to visit any of the shooting locations in Canada for the Smallville sequences. John Richardson, who had turned down the opportunity to be the effects supervisor on the film, joined the production to supervise the special effects scheduled for filming on location in Alberta. One of the sequences was designed to showcase Clark's ability to run at extraordinary speed alongside a rushing locomotive.

Actor Jeff East, who played the teenaged Clark, was suspended by wires hanging from a crane on a camera truck. He made running motions with his legs, but his feet never actually touched the ground. The camera was undercranked, so when the film was played back at 24 frames per second, it appeared as though he was chugging along at high speed.

I don't think the final shots are particularly convincing, and in retrospect, I probably would have done the shots differently if I hadn't been so busy at Pinewood Studios. In my opinion, it would have been more convincing if Clark was running so fast that he appeared as nothing more than a blur.

The sequence starts working for me once he's shown running in the distance, leaving a long trail of dust from moving so fast. They simply drove a motorcycle down the road with an open sack of dust trailing behind it, but it looked convincing and left a lot to the imagination. Sometimes it's better to show less.

A couple of shots in the film have really captured the imaginations of *Superman* fans and I'm often asked about how we achieved them. One of these shots takes place during the balcony scene, after Superman takes Lois on a romantic flight above Metropolis. In a single uninterrupted take, Superman and Lois wish each other a good night. Then Superman takes off from the balcony and flies out of frame. Lois hears a knock at the front door and the camera follows her into the apartment. Without cutting away, Lois unlocks the door and in walks Chris Reeve dressed as Clark Kent.

Many people have wondered how that shot could have been achieved without any edits. Was Chris a quick-change artist? Was Superman actually played by a double for the takeoff? Was a perfect edit somehow hidden amongst all the action?

In reality, it was none of these things. Dick Donner came up with the solution, which was elegant in its simplicity. When Superman wishes Lois a good night and flies off, Chris Reeve isn't physically there on set with Margot. She's actually looking at film footage of him on a front-projection screen. Chris is already dressed as Clark Kent and he's standing outside the front door at this point. After the projected image of Superman flies out of frame, Chris knocks on the door and Lois lets him into the apartment.

The shot was designed to sell the illusion that Superman could move at inhumanly fast speeds, and the final effect is pretty seamless. Even when the producers were breathing down his back to move faster and simplify shooting, he was clever at finding new and interesting ways to film scenes.

The other shot I'm often asked about shows Superman spinning like a top and drilling his way through the sidewalk. We filmed that on a set made to look like downtown Metropolis, and the busy city street behind Superman was actually footage on a front-projection screen.

Chris stood on a special rig that we built into the sidewalk that could lower him like an elevator and rotate like a merry-go-round. The film was sped up so it appeared as though he drilled into the ground at high speed. Then Roy Field added some blurring optical effects for added impact.

In the theatrical release of the film, Superman is next seen arriving at the front door of Lex Luthor's underground lair. However, we actually created a number of effects for a sequence that was supposed to occur before he arrived at Luthor's hideout. In this deleted scene, Superman faces a gauntlet of booby traps set by Luthor in the tunnels beneath the city.

The first trap Superman encounters is a hail of gunfire from automatic rifles that spring from the tunnel walls. The flashes from the bullets bouncing off his body are sparks that Roy Field superimposed over the image of Superman during optical printing.

The second trap is a trial by fire, with flames shooting from vents in the walls and floor. Geoffrey Unsworth filmed the flames from such an angle that they appeared much closer to Chris than they actually were. Chris was a comfortable distance from the fire and was never in any danger.

The final trap involves a freezing chamber that encases the Man of Steel in ice and snow. We used the hot wax method I'd used previously on *The Rocky Horror Picture Show* and *Frankenstein: The True Story*. We also used a toxic urea-formaldehyde foam that's banned now but was commonly used for insulation back then. The whole set was covered in it.

In 2013, I was a guest at Niagara Falls Comic Con, where I had the pleasure of attending a screening of *Superman* alongside fans. The special edition of the film was shown that included previously deleted scenes reinstated at the behest of Dick Donner. To my delight, the restored footage included the long-lost booby-trap sequence.

Unfortunately, another major effect that was deleted from the theatrical cut of the film wasn't included in Dick's restored version. The script called for a row of townhouses in San Francisco to jiggle precariously during the earthquake sequence. We built lightweight townhouses that had a lot of give between the parts so they could shake dramatically with the earthquake. The pieces of the houses were hung on wires and they were made to shake on a platform.

The effect was quite convincing, especially with people running in panic on the street in front of the houses, which helped to establish that miniatures weren't used. These shots were included when *Superman* first aired on broadcast television in an extended version specially prepared for ABC, but they haven't seen the light of day in any other release.

Concept art for the movie poster showing Superman in action. © Warner Bros.
From the personal collection of Colin Chilvers.

It was great working with Derek Meddings again on *Superman* after our time together on *Thunderbirds*. As usual, he did an amazing job with the miniatures on the film. To make them more convincing, Derek built extraordinarily large models so he could get the camera right in to capture all the details.

The model of the Golden Gate Bridge was a good 20 feet tall and 70 feet wide, and it was filmed outdoors to take advantage of natural lighting and a real sky in the background. It can be difficult to simulate outdoor lighting convincingly on a soundstage, so Derek decided to go with the real thing.

I was in charge of filming the sequence in which Superman sends an avalanche of rock down a cliff to protect a neighborhood from a flash flood. When I first saw the model houses on set, I thought they appeared far too clean to be convincing on screen. Miniatures rarely look convincing if they lack the minor imperfections that you'd find in real life, so I worked with the model team to dirty down the houses and add more detail so they didn't appear too "perfect."

I asked the crew to imagine the personalities of the people living in each house, then I requested that the houses be customized accordingly. As a result, some of the houses ended up dirtier because the inhabitants were messier by nature, while other houses ended up with extremely cluttered backyards because the people didn't have any other place to put their junk. This extra attention to detail can really help to sell a special-effects shot, even if it's on screen for only an instant.

At Pinewood, we built a rig to crush Lois Lane's car after it sinks into the ground during the earthquake. The rig was about 25 feet long, 12 feet high and 10 feet wide so we could fit a real car inside. We had to create the effect of the car being scrunched under the weight of the shifting earth and falling debris without hurting Margot, who was seated inside.

This was a major dramatic moment in the film, so the audience had to see that it was really Margot inside and not a stunt performer. The rig used hydraulic cylinders to implode the car, and we did numerous tests in the shop to establish the right degree of pressure that would achieve the desired effect without endangering Margot. We ended up destroying a few cars before we got it just right.

Margot was a real trouper when it came to shooting the scene. Not only did she put her life in our hands with the car-crushing rig, but she also let us pour all kinds of dirt on top of her to simulate Lois being buried alive. Anything we dropped on her was clean material like peat moss, insulation material and clay. For extra safety, we built escape routes into the car so she could always escape if things got too dicey. Margot certainly looked terrified in that scene. I wonder how much was acting and how much was reality!

During filming of the movie's final scene, in which Superman delivers the villains to a prison courtyard, I was standing on the set with Dick Donner and screenwriter Tom Mankiewicz. As originally written, Superman flies into the scene, drops off the villains, wishes the warden a good night, then flies off. Roll credits. Luthor and Otis didn't have any lines. I leaned over to Dick and Tom to make a suggestion.

"Luthor has been so verbal throughout the film," I said. "Isn't it a bit strange that he has nothing to say here at the end of the film?"

They agreed with my observation and quickly wrote some lines for the villains. Now Luthor proclaims himself to be a criminal mastermind and Otis echoes his sentiments before they're both dragged away. I think this was more consistent with their characters as they were established earlier in the film.

After an intense year and a half of experimentation, failure and triumph in bringing Superman to the big screen, our job was done and Stuart Baird continued working with Dick in fine-tuning the edit. Then it was time to sit back and watch the finished film for the first time from beginning to end.

Concept art for the movie poster. © Warner Bros.
From the personal collection of Colin Chilvers.

I remember the first time I heard John Williams' epic music during the opening credits. I got chills as the names of the cast and crew appeared on screen to the backing of a truly great film score. *Superman: The Movie* was exciting from the first scene and it didn't let up. It was also moving, funny and clever - a movie we could all be proud of. Despite all of the political infighting that had occurred between the director and the producers, Dick Donner had succeeded in bringing his vision of Superman to the masses.

When I look back now, I regret that I didn't keep some souvenirs from the shoot, like a miniature or perhaps a piece of the Fortress set. While making the film, none of us knew it would become such a classic. It was just another production and we were happy to have work for such a long stretch of time.

If I'd kept even a crystal or two from the production, I could have made a fortune years later on eBay. Of course eBay didn't exist in the seventies and the market for movie props wasn't like it is today. I didn't even take any photos on set because I was too busy actually making the film.

Superman: The Movie became a smash hit all over the world and it received several positive notices for its special effects. "You'll believe a man can fly" read the tagline on the movie posters, and audiences did indeed. The cast and crew of *Superman* had done their job well enough to suspend disbelief for moviegoers, who were eager to escape the grim political climate of the seventies and be swept away by a modern-day fairy tale.

While we were knee-deep making the film, we never even considered that we might win an Academy Award for our work on the special effects. Now that the movie was released and people were talking about how exciting and ambitious the effects were, it began to dawn on us that we actually had a shot at winning.

In order to be considered for an Oscar, we needed to submit an application to the Academy of Motion Picture Arts and Sciences that explained how we'd been innovative with technology and how we'd pushed the art of special effects. Then we had to put together a 15-minute reel of our best work on the film. I still have that original effects reel somewhere in the attic. Next, all of the special-effects heads on *Superman*, myself included, were invited to Los Angeles in January for what they called the "bake-off."

All of the special-effects teams being considered for the Oscar screened their film reel for Academy members and then answered the panel's questions. After that, were asked to wait outside while they deliberated. Eight or ten other effects teams also attended the bake-off and they were all as nervous as we were.

Any given year, the visual-effects members of the Academy had the option to decide that no films were worthy of receiving the Oscar for special effects, they could vote to determine five nominees and the actual winner, or they could award the Oscar to a specific movie outright.

The final option is what happened to us because of the outstanding level of technical innovation and excellence we had achieved. Richard Edlund, who had won an Oscar himself for the special effects of *Star Wars*, came out to tell us that we would be receiving the Academy Award for *Superman*. We were pleasantly shocked to receive the news. The possibility that we'd be handed the Oscar straight away hadn't even occurred to us, but we were deeply honoured. I was only 34 years old at the time, which I believe made me the youngest person to ever receive the Oscar for special effects.

Myself, Les Bowie, Denys Coop, Roy Field, Derek Meddings and Zoran Perisic won the Special Achievement Award for Visual Effects in 1979 and all of our names appeared on all the statuettes. Unfortunately, Les passed away shortly after *Superman* was released and he was never able to accept his Oscar with the rest of us.

The Academy Awards ceremony took place in April and we went to L.A. a bit earlier to do some visiting and sightseeing. We toured some of the big Hollywood studios, including Disney, where they were shooting miniature effects for *The Black Hole*. Using a state-of-the-art motion control rig far more advanced than anything we had on *Superman*, they were filming a impressive glass and metal ship that must have been sixty feet long.

It was interesting to see how a different team of effects artists approached their work, especially with the latest in computerized technology at their disposal. The following year, *The Black Hole* would be nominated for its outstanding visual effects work.

I also remember touring a company that had a Cray supercomputer, the most advanced computer of its day. The thing was enormous and it took up much of the room. I was already interested in computers at the time and it was fascinating to ponder the possibilities that digital technology would open up for special-effects artists in the years to come.

The whole trip to L.A. felt like a fairy tale come true. We were put up at the Beverly Hills Hilton and treated like royalty. I'd come a long way since sleeping on a boat in the middle of the Venezuelan jungle. I had to buy a suit and tie, which was far from my usual style of dress. Dressing for comfort and practicality was the norm, especially for work, but it was nice to get fancied up like James Bond for a special occasion like the Oscars.

Denys, Roy, Derek, Zoran and myself were asked to attend the rehearsal at the Dorothy Chandler Pavilion the day before the actual ceremony. The director did a run-through of the show so camera shots could be worked out for the broadcast. Since we already knew we were receiving the Oscar for visual effects, we rehearsed our acceptance of the award on stage.

From behind the podium, it was strange looking out at all the seats that would be filled with Hollywood's finest the following evening. In fact, the seats *were* filled for the rehearsal, not with stars, but with life-sized cardboard cutouts of the stars to give the camera people an idea of who would be sitting where.

The 51st Academy Awards were held on April 9, 1979. Josie didn't want to attend the ceremony because she wasn't a fan of the glitzy Hollywood lifestyle, so she decided to stay at the hotel instead. As for the actual ceremony, I barely remember any of the details and it all went by in a dreamy haze. Even though we knew we would be receiving the Oscar that night, our nerves were still frazzled.

I do remember being treated like a dignitary by everyone. We were shown to our seats and told to relax. Relaxing was definitely easier said than done, and it was difficult to concentrate on the show knowing what was ahead for us.

Then they told us it was time. We slipped out of our seats and headed backstage. I took a deep breath. This was really happening to me.

Steve Martin presented the Special Achievement Award for Visual Effects and we all walked onto the stage as the audience applauded. "One apiece," Martin said jokingly as we took turns picking up our statuettes. Since there were five of us and there wasn't enough time for all of us to speak, we elected Denys Coop to speak on our behalf because he was the oldest. Relieved that I didn't have to do any of the talking, I just stood there in a state of shock and fear. Here's what Denys said at the podium:

> Ladies and gentlemen, on behalf of my colleagues and myself, I'd like to thank the Board of Governors of the Academy for these magnificent awards. Sadly, our other associate, Les Bowie, recently passed away. It's a great loss to us and to the industry. We'd like to thank our producer; Richard Donner, our friend and director; and particularly our British crews who, without whose support we wouldn't be here this evening. And finally a thank you to Margot Kidder and Christopher Reeve. What a "Superman." Thank you.

The music started playing from the orchestra pit and the audience applauded again. We were led backstage where the press was waiting to take our photos and interview us. The whole experience was a whirlwind and I was too overwhelmed at the time to take it all in at once.

After our time with the press backstage, we were shown back to our seats. I was surprised and somewhat put out by the fact that somebody else was occupying my seat. What I didn't understand is that shows like the Oscars employ seat-fillers to take your place when you're gone so the seats aren't empty for the cameras.

Denys Coop, Roy Field, Derek Meddings, me, Zoran Perisic and Steve Martin. Copyright ©
Academy of Motion Picture Arts and Sciences.

My mother was so excited for me and she planned to watch the awards ceremony on television in England. Due to the time difference though, she ended up falling asleep in her chair and missing my big moment.

We attended a big Oscar party after the broadcast, where we were treated to first-class food and drink into the night. It was the Hollywood dream come true. The five of us sat together and it was surreal seeing five Oscars lined up on our table. We all wished that Les could have partaken in the celebrations with his own statuette.

My Oscar now has a place of honour at my house. Whenever I appear at special events to talk about my career, I bring Oscar with me and people always ask to have their picture taken with it. I get a kick out of seeing how excited people become when they're given a chance to hold it.

I feel very fortunate to have been honoured with an Academy Award at such a young age. Two of my nephews, Neil and Chris Corbould, have since won their own Oscars for their special-effects work on *Gladiator*, *Inception* and *Gravity*.

Even today, *Superman* is considered the pinnacle of superhero movie adaptations. Some of the special effects may look a bit dated now compared to the state-of-the-art CGI in modern Hollywood blockbusters, but the work we did was cutting edge in the late seventies.

Celebrating our Oscar win. From the personal collection of Colin Chilvers.

Nowadays, audiences are a bit spoiled because they've seen everything imaginable at the movies. Digital technology has expanded the horizon of moviemaking significantly, but back in 1978, everything about *Superman* was new. Nobody had ever seen a man fly convincingly on screen before. Even the opening credits, with the names of the cast and crew swooshing through space, were astonishing for audiences to behold because they were unlike anything seen up to that point.

Sometimes I think it would be fun to see a special edition of *Superman* released by Warner Bros. with all of the special effects redone with the latest digital technology, like George Lucas did when he re-released his original three *Star Wars* movies, but I doubt it would be financially feasible to do.

I think the great success of *Superman* goes far beyond its special effects though. Dick Donner understood that the character of Superman is as American as apple pie, an important part of modern mythology that must be taken seriously. Hence his commitment to verisimilitude, which he always held dear to his heart.

The humour in the film is always within the context of the story's reality and never strays into straight-out parody like Richard Lester ended up doing on *Superman III*. Dick found the right balance between drama and humour to create a movie that isn't just for kids. *Superman* is an adult film that even kids can enjoy. That's why it's still the benchmark for all superhero movies to follow. It proved that superheroes on film didn't have to be goofy sendups like the *Batman* TV show from the sixties.

Everyone can enjoy the special effects and sheer spectacle of such an epic film, but adults can also appreciate the subtleties in the characters' relationships. The underlying sexual tension and wordplay between Lois and Superman during the balcony scene, for example, carries a whole new level of meaning for older viewers.

All philosophizing aside, *Superman* succeeds because it's a hell of a lot of fun. I recently saw Zack Snyder's *Man of Steel*, and with all due respect to him and his talented filmmaking team, it isn't nearly as much fun to watch as the original *Superman*. Dick's vision had a great deal of heart to go along with the spectacle, and I found the newer film to be quite cold and depressing.

Man of Steel is also extremely overproduced, with so much of its budget and running time devoted to shots of buildings being turned to rubble as characters punch each other through walls. After a while, it all starts to feel generic and I'm not sure if I'm watching a Superman story or a Michael Bay movie.

I'm amazed at what an impact *Superman* has had on other filmmakers. Years later, when I was the special-effects supervisor on *X-Men*, I learned that director Bryan Singer absolutely loved *Superman: The Movie*. It was a dream come true for him to direct *Superman Returns*, which was essentially his love letter to Dick Donner's film.

My collaborator on this autobiography, Aaron Lam, was inspired to pursue his career as a filmmaker after seeing *Superman* at the age of five. He's a hardcore fan, having travelled throughout Alberta to visit shooting locations for *Superman* and *Superman III*. He even brought his poor wife along with him! That's commitment for you.

In 2012, I lent Oscar to the Innisfil Public Library in Ontario, where it was displayed for the summer. The head librarian was visiting local schools to get students excited about reading and taking part in the library's special events, so she took Oscar with her. At one school, she met a ten-year-old boy with autism who usually didn't speak to anyone in class. He just kept his head low and tried to get through the day without talking to anybody.

When she showed him Oscar, he immediately came to life and started talking about the films I'd done. The boy knew all about my career and he was so excited to see the Academy Award for *Superman*. She said it was amazing to see him blossom and come out of his shell.

I was truly touched to hear about this. If Oscar can inspire people to be creative and reach for the stars, then it's all been worthwhile.

CHAPTER 6
WHAT GOES UP MUST STAY UP

Superman was flying high at the box office, and so was the sci-fi/fantasy genre in general. With films like *Superman*, *Star Wars*, *Close Encounters of the Third Kind* and *Alien* attracting moviegoers like never before, it seemed like every producer in Hollywood wanted a piece of the action. And for every hit genre film came several unsuccessful attempts to ride their coattails.

One such film was *Saturn 3*, a futuristic thriller about a killer robot on the loose at a hydroponics research station on one of Saturn's moons. Despite the high-profile cast that included Kirk Douglas, Farrah Fawcett and Harvey Keitel, the film was poorly received by critics and it barely made a dent at the box office. Stanley Donen, the legendary director of Hollywood musicals like *Singin' in the Rain*, ended up directing *Saturn 3* after the original director was removed from the project.

John Barry, the production designer of *Star Wars* and *Superman* (not to be confused with film composer John Barry), was signed to direct *Saturn 3* with Stanley serving as producer. It was a great opportunity for him to direct a high-profile feature film based on a story he wrote. John was a great guy and a talented artist, and I was looking forward to seeing how he would bring the world of *Saturn 3* to life on the big screen.

However, that never got to happen. Due to various reasons that have never been clearly explained, John did not continue with the production and Stanley quickly stepped in to direct.

I stayed on to work on *Saturn 3* and John went to work on *The Empire Strikes Back*. A couple of weeks into working on the *Star Wars* sequel, we received the shocking news that John had passed away. He'd collapsed on set and was taken to the hospital, where he died shortly after from meningitis. It was such an unexpected tragedy. John was only in his forties and he had so much more to contribute to the world, both as a human being and a filmmaker. Production on *Saturn 3* continued with the cloud of John's passing hanging over us.

Although it must have been awkward for Stanley to step in as director at the last minute, he was a pleasure to work with and he was always open to input from the special-effects department. I was excited to be working with a man who had directed so many classic films I'd grown up watching.

Stanley's experience with musicals showed in his staging of *Saturn 3*'s opening sequence, in which a bug-like space pod is prepared for takeoff in the landing bay of a space station. Stanley choreographed the sequence like a musical, with crewmembers walking in perfect lines in synchronized rhythm while framed dramatically within the bold geometric patterns of the set. It played like an outer-space version of an Esther Williams swimming-pool number - without the smiling ladies in bikinis of course. What a visually stunning way to begin the film.

As production designer, Stuart Craig did an amazing job coming up with interesting designs for the spacecraft and the sets of the film. He loved using curved lines on everything from vehicles to hallways with nary a straight line to be seen, giving the film a distinctive look that still holds up over thirty years later. Stuart had worked as art director on *Superman* and it was great seeing him move up to the position of production designer. His later work on the Harry Potter films would bring him much-deserved acclaim.

Director of photography Billy Williams also did a great job capturing the moodiness of the story with his menacing use of shadow. Billy later worked on classics like *On Golden Pond* and *Gandhi*.

Kirk Douglas, who was already in his sixties at the time, was paired up with the much younger Farrah Fawcett as his love interest. Even though they were separated by more than a few years in age, Kirk was still in remarkable shape and had no problem keeping up with the physical demands of the action sequences. He wasn't shy about his body and was keen to play a number of scenes without a shirt.

Whenever his character isn't battling the killer robot, he's busy skipping rope, jogging through the halls of the station or making love to his sexy co-worker. He seems to have more stamina than men half his age, which helps to make the romantic relationship believable.

Farrah gives a good performance in *Saturn 3*. She was a talented actress and I think people were surprised at her dramatic range. It's a shame she didn't have more high-profile dramatic roles in her career to show what she could really do.

Another major character in *Saturn 3* is Hector, the killer robot brought to the station by Harvey Keitel's character. Hector has an armoured body with a thin, curved neck that sports a tiny head - he looks kind of like a medieval knight with a desk lamp for a cranium. Before I even came aboard the film, the art department had designed Hector and an outside company was hired to build him.

Hector was brought to life on screen by a performer in a suit with fake robotic arms. The remote-controlled head kept breaking down and needed continual repair. Unfortunately, the company that built Hector had little experience working in the motion picture industry and they built him in such a way that made it difficult to remove parts and access the guts inside.

A friend once told me a similar story about his experience as a crew member on *Star Wars*. An outside company had fabricated R2-D2 using these tiny custom-made screws to hold the panels together. This caused problems when the crew was filming in the middle of the Tunisian desert. Whenever they had to remove a panel to make a repair, the tiny screws would fall to the ground and become lost in the sand because they were so small.

The company that made Artoo didn't have experience working on movies, so the use of these screws hadn't occurred to them as a potential problem. Later, the droid was modified by the film crew with standard screws that were larger and made for easier removal and replacement of panels.

The people who constructed Hector also didn't take into account that the robot's head would take a real beating during the course of filming. *Saturn 3* required the robot to be knocked about during various action sequences, often for numerous takes. Hector's dainty head and thin neck were particularly vulnerable to damage and proved to be a pain in the ass to work with.

Even though my effects department hadn't built Hector, we kept finding ourselves in the uncomfortable position of having the entire cast and crew staring at us impatiently while we made repairs. The only solution was to rebuild the head and neck entirely so it could withstand the wear and tear of filming. Once we did that, Hector performed a lot more reliably and made for a much happier set.

Because Hector was designed to have such skinny arms with hollow areas you could see right through, an actor's real arms could not be used inside. For the scene in which Hector plays chess, we created a cable-controlled arm and hand for manipulating chess pieces. It was really quite simple, like those cheap lobster-claw toys you can buy with pincers that open and close when you squeeze the handle. It took a few takes before the puppeteers could control the chess pieces smoothly without dropping them, but they soon got into a groove and really sold the effect.

During the film's finale, the robot is pushed into a vat of chemicals and blows apart into a million pieces. I suggested to Stanley that he shoot the sequence at a high frame rate so the explosion would take place in extreme slow motion on screen. Because he had done such a great job choreographing the takeoff sequence at the beginning of the film, I thought something equally artistic would be suitable for the ending.

I mentioned an incredible sequence from the film *Zabriskie Point*, in which a house explodes in slow motion. Shooting at such a high frame rate made the explosion beautiful and graceful, like a dance of flame and debris, and I suggested that we try something similar with the ending of *Saturn 3*. Stanley liked my suggestion and we ended up shooting the destruction of Hector at something like 1,500 frames per second instead of the regular 24.

The final effect is visually striking, like a ballet of robotic parts dancing in the air as Hector is blown sky high. Especially when coupled with the creepy robotic sound effects, which are like digital cries, the dramatic death of Hector caps off the story in memorable fashion.

This is an example of bringing more to a special-effects sequence than what was written in the script. The screenplay called for the robot to "blow up," but I thought we could film it in a unique way to heighten the dramatic impact. I've always been grateful to work with directors like Stanley Donen and Dick Donner who were open to considering my ideas.

Despite its talented high-profile cast and accomplished crew, *Saturn 3* was quickly forgotten by the world at large and only the most dedicated of cult fans remember the film today. More than three decades after its theatrical release, I received a phone call from Scream Factory, which was planning to release a special edition Blu-ray of *Saturn 3*. They interviewed me for the special features of the release and it was the first time I'd given the film any thought for many years. I was surprised and flattered that anyone was still interested in the film after so long.

To help prepare me for the interview, Scream Factory sent me a DVD of *Saturn 3* to review because I hadn't seen the film since its original release in 1980. It was fun revisiting that world again and memories started flooding back to me.

Although some of the film's miniature effects look a little shaky nowadays, I'm still proud of the ambitious work we did given the limited budget and schedule. The film's production design still looks great and it offers a truly unique vision of the future. Ultimately though, I didn't find the story particularly engaging and I'm not surprised that moviegoers didn't embrace *Saturn 3*.

Luckily, the next film on my schedule was destined to find much greater levels of success and would top the box-office charts in 1981. *Superman II* was one of the most hotly anticipated movies of the year, largely because audiences wanted to see how the first *Superman* could be topped. For many fans, we succeeded in doing just that.

After *Superman: The Movie* was released to critical acclaim and amazing box office, Dick Donner was scheduled to complete the filming of *Superman II*, which he had already begun during production of the first film. However, a war of words erupted in the press between Dick and the producers about their unpleasant experience working together, and Dick was officially fired from the production.

In his place, the Salkinds hired Richard Lester to take over the director's chair. He had already directed *The Three Musketeers* and *The Four Musketeers* for them, and he had proven his ability to deliver epics on schedule and within budget. Because Richard had his own ideas about how *Superman II* should play out, he had screenwriters David and Leslie Newman rewrite a number of scenes to his liking. Richard kept some of the footage that Dick Donner had already shot for the second movie, but he also discarded a lot of what Dick had done because it no longer fit with his vision.

David and Leslie Newman were talented writers who were married to each another, and they had an office in the art department where the special-effects team was based. The Newmans had huge arguments about the script, nothing ever personal, and their voices could be heard echoing throughout the whole art department.

The pair worked closely with Richard Lester to ensure the screenplay suited his sensibilities as a storyteller. Richard would often meet with myself, the Newmans and storyboard artist Michael Ploog to pin down the specifics of the action sequences. Involving me in these meetings allowed me to advise them on what special effects were and weren't possible to accomplish in terms of our timeframe and resources.

Richard Lester was a talented director and a really nice guy to work with, but his style of filmmaking was quite different from Dick Donner's. For one thing, Richard favoured physical comedy more heavily in his films and ended up using more exaggerated characters in supporting roles. It's true that Dick explored a lot of comedic situations with Clark Kent and the villains in the first *Superman* movie, but Richard tended to take things a step further.

Just look at the bumbling police officers or the gum-chewing bellboy from *Superman II*. Dick Donner would never have gone that far into cartoon territory just for a laugh. I think Richard Lester ultimately moved the *Superman* series away from Dick's philosophy of "verisimilitude" and more into the realm of fantasy.

Richard also liked to shoot with multiple cameras, whereas Dick always shot with only one. Shooting with more than one camera allowed Richard to get more coverage with each take and he could shoot script pages more quickly. While Dick Donner would often shoot a scene many times until he was satisfied, Richard was usually happy with far fewer takes. Since the action was being captured from numerous angles, he knew he'd have lots of footage to choose from in the editing room.

Shooting with multiple cameras posed special challenges for director of photography Bob Paynter. Bob always had to ensure that no lights or lighting stands would be picked up by any of the cameras. He also had to ensure that all of the characters within a scene were lit well simultaneously. This meant that Bob couldn't be as precise with his lighting and would need to blast high levels of light over the entire set so it could be shot from any direction. As such, *Superman II* has a flatter, less polished look.

This differed from cinematographer Geoffrey Unsworth's approach on the first movie. Geoffrey meticulously lit each shot specifically for the angle that was framed up by the single camera. Then when the camera was repositioned to film from another angle, Geoffrey adjusted his lights for the new shot. This allowed him to make every shot a Rembrandt, whereas Bob Paynter never had that option on parts II and III.

I was surprised to learn that Richard rarely attended production meetings and he never watched dailies. Dick was always at production meetings and dailies on the first film, so it was a bit of an adjustment for me when I saw how differently Richard worked. As a joke, we ended up enlarging a photo of Richard into a life-sized cutout that we propped up on a stand. We brought it out whenever we had a production meeting so it would feel like he was involved.

It wasn't that Richard didn't care about the film. He was always quite thorough and well prepared, but he enjoyed the shooting part of filmmaking far more than the planning and editing aspects of it. When asked why he never attended dailies, he responded by saying, "Because I already saw everything yesterday during shooting. If there's a problem, the editor will tell me."

Despite constant pressure from the producers to stay within budget, Richard was always very personable and cool-headed. I never saw him lose his temper during production and he was always collaborative with his department heads. Richard kept an office at Twickenham Studios and you could always stop by and talk to him about anything, much like it was with Dick Donner.

To call Richard Lester an intellectual is an understatement. He would often philosophize about the meaning of life, love and the universe. His reflections on the deeper meanings of human existence would usually go over my head and I wouldn't know what the hell he was talking about, but at least we could relate to each other about our love of movies.

If you look at Richard's filmography, he's made some pretty artsy and experimental films in his time. His more mainstream work, like the Musketeer and Superman films, have been better received by audiences at the box office. Because he could become so philosophical and abstract in his thinking as an artist, I think it led him to create intellectually dense films that tended to alienate filmgoers who weren't on the same wavelength.

In my opinion, Dick Donner had stronger mainstream filmmaking sensibilities, as has been demonstrated by his string of hit films after *Superman*. Richard once explained how he didn't like rock music, despite the fact that he's best known for directing the Beatles in *A Hard Day's Night*. Likewise, he wasn't a big fan of the Superman character when he signed on to direct *Superman II*. Dick Donner *was* a fan of the character before directing the first film, so I think Dick had a better grasp of what the Man of Steel and his mythology were all about.

Many people actually prefer *Superman II* over the original, probably because of the dynamic villains and the increased level of action, but I think it veered too far into the realm of comedy and it didn't capture the essence of Superman as well as the first film. Still, I enjoyed working on *Superman II* and I think we managed to create some astonishing special effects long before the days of CGI.

I was still living in England when *Superman II* was entering production. A significant portion of the story takes place in Niagara Falls, so a bunch of us took a flight to the Falls during pre-production to do some location scouting. We got off the plane, did a single hectic day of scouting, then got on the plane for the tiring flight back home. Luckily, our two major locations, Table Rock at the Horseshoe Falls and the Whirlpool Rapids boardwalk at the Great Gorge, were fairly close to one another and would serve our shooting purposes perfectly.

Shooting on *Superman II* began about six months after the first movie hit theatres. Our Niagara shoot came early in the production schedule, and one of the first scenes we shot was Superman's rescue of a little boy who tumbles over the edge of the falls. The night before filming that scene, Christopher Reeve was flown into Toronto and driven to Niagara Falls, where he joined the special-effects team for dinner at Mama Mia's restaurant in the Clifton Hill tourist district. We hadn't seen Chris since the premiere of *Superman* six months before, so it was like a nice little family reunion.

As you can imagine, Chris turned a lot of heads when he walked into the restaurant. Diners certainly weren't expecting to see Superman strolling in. Quite a few people came around to our table and asked Chris for an autograph, and he was happy to oblige. Chris was always very good with fans and he appreciated their support.

Filming at the Horseshoe Falls. Photo courtesy of the Niagara Falls (Ontario) Public Library.

The next day, we were outside of Table Rock House preparing for our location shoot.   For the scene, Superman was to land with the boy in his arms, return the young man to his mother, then fly off again. We used a giant crane from a local company called Modern Crane to hang Chris and the boy from wires. During my few weeks in Niagara, I became friends with Bob Thiel from Modern Crane, and I gave him one of the production's Superman capes as a souvenir after the shoot.

Word had gotten out that *Superman II* would be filming by the falls, and a crowd of about 300 people gathered to watch the action unfold. Chris had his Superman costume on and was ready to go, but he was staying warm under a big bathrobe. As the flying crew prepared the wire rig, Bob Harman asked Chris if he'd like to do a rehearsal before they rolled cameras because it had been quite a few months since Chris had flown as Superman.

"I don't think I need a rehearsal," Chris replied. "Let's just do it."

Then he removed his robe and revealed the Superman suit in all its glory. The spectators all went nuts with applause upon seeing the iconic costume glowing in the sunlight. Even though I'd spent a year and a half working with Chris on the first movie, seeing him in the suit again made the hairs on the back of my neck stand up.

Chris transforms into Superman. Photo courtesy of the Niagara Falls (Ontario) Public Library.

Chris wasn't just *playing* Superman. In that moment, he *was* Superman in my mind, and when the wires hanging from the crane pulled him into the air, the wires suddenly became invisible and he was really taking flight. It was one of those magical moments in my career that I'll never forget. Chris was so utterly perfect in the role.

The little boy was a good actor who wasn't the least bit shy. The scene required him to play recklessly on the safety railing at the edge of the falls. A safety mat was placed just out of shot below the kid and he was hooked up to safety wires in case he accidentally lost his balance. The boy was having a ball because he was getting to do something that no other kids would ever have a chance to do.

Superman to the rescue. Photo courtesy of The Niagara Parks Commission Archives.

My future wife Colleen watches Superman in action.

The other major sequence we shot in Niagara Falls involved Lois Lane jumping into the Whirlpool Rapids. I'm told that a sign at the Great Gorge boardwalk used to tell visitors that *Superman II* was filmed there, but the sign kept being stolen and they eventually stopped replacing it.

Because the Niagara River at the Whirlpool Rapids is some of the most dangerous white water in the world, we couldn't afford to have Margot Kidder jump in for real. Just past the boardwalk, the raging waters form a deadly whirlpool. For the shot of Margot jumping over the railing, we positioned a crash mat below her so she never actually hit the water.

The sequence of Lois being swept downstream combines different shots taken on location and at the studio. Whenever you see a close-up of Lois struggling in the water and you can clearly recognize Margot's face, the shot was done in a water tank at the studio to simulate the rapids. Those shots were purposely taken from a high angle so you could never see the edge of the water tank.

Shots taken on location in Niagara were done with a stunt performer and a mannequin. The stuntwoman was used in shallower and less dangerous portions of the rapids. The mannequin was used for extremely wide shots of Lois being swept through the fiercest parts of the river that were too dangerous for even the stuntwoman to navigate.

At the end of the sequence, Clark uses his heat vision to blast a branch from a tree, which we accomplished using a small explosive charge and an animated laser beam added in post-production. Lois then grabs onto the branch and floats into a calm and shallow cove, where Clark wades in to help. The concluding shots of Lois and Clark in the water were done by Margot and Chris themselves, completing the illusion that it was really Margot in the sequence all along.

The scenes at the hotel in Niagara Falls were written by the Newmans for Richard Lester, who added a great deal of comedy that wasn't in the original script. Lois and Clark's hotel room is an exercise in bad taste, where pink is the order of the day and any sense of class is thrown out the window. Adding to the garishness are a fake bearskin rug, a fireplace that would make Satan envious and a bellboy who couldn't care less about customer service.

When negotiating with the Niagara Parks Commission for permission to film on location, the production had to submit the script for approval. The Commission wanted to ensure that we weren't portraying the city in a negative light. I wonder if the hotel scenes were omitted in the version of the script they were sent. Luckily, the Commission never expressed any objections. At any rate, those scenes were all in good fun and nobody seemed to be upset when the film was released.

Since we needed to control traffic at Table Rock House, which was one of the busiest locations in the city, the production worked closely with the local police department. The Chief of Police, Bill Derbyshire, was an enormous help in making our shoot go smoothly. I also worked with Wes Hill, the legendary riverman who was responsible for pulling bodies out of the river. Wes knew the Niagara River better than anyone and he was an invaluable advisor for the sequence we shot at the Whirlpool Rapids.

I would often visit the police station for meetings with Bill and Wes, where a young lady named Colleen worked as a dispatcher. As fate would have it, Colleen and I would end up getting married and she would be my second wife.

We first met at a party and then I'd see her every time I dropped by the police station. During one of those visits, I asked her if she'd join me for a date later that week, on the upcoming Thursday evening. She turned me down, saying she didn't make plans that far ahead. And besides, she had to work on Thursday. Luckily, Bill was there and he told her to take Thursday off. Colleen didn't have much of a choice but to go out with me.

We hit it off right away and we saw as much of each other as possible over those three weeks of production in Niagara Falls. On a Sunday when we weren't shooting, Bill suggested we go for a romantic picnic on Navy Island, which is on the Niagara River a couple of miles above the falls. The island was accessible only by water, so Wes lent us his boat for the day. We were getting ready to launch the boat when Wes gave us some words of advice.

"If you have any problems with the engine, throw the anchor overboard. If the anchor doesn't work, tie a rope around the engine and throw that over. And if that doesn't work, I'll pick you up in about ten days because all the bodies that go over the falls end up circling the whirlpool."

It wasn't very reassuring, but I'm happy to report that neither the anchor nor the engine needed to go overboard and the picnic was indeed romantic.

After filming wrapped in Niagara Falls and I was back in England, we had a long-distance courtship for three months from October to December. We talked over the phone a few times a week and we really got to know each other.

I visited Colleen in Canada during a weekend after Christmas. It was an unusual way to start a relationship, but it was obviously meant to be. If I hadn't been asked to go on location for *Superman II*, I wouldn't have met Colleen and I wouldn't be living in Canada right now. All the stars were aligned.

While preparing this book, I realized that I hadn't seen *Superman II* since its original theatrical release in 1981. I sat down to watch it again and was surprised at how ambitious we were with the special effects. In addition to Niagara Falls, the film involves major effects sequences set in Paris, a small town in the southern United States, downtown Metropolis and the Fortress of Solitude in the Arctic. The film is much more international in scope than the first one.

In a new sequence written for Richard Lester when he took over as director, the film opens with a subplot involving terrorists taking hostages at the Eiffel Tower and threatening to detonate a hydrogen bomb if their demands aren't met. It was a rainy, dreary day when we filmed in Paris, probably not the best weather to capture the vibrance of the city, but Richard was a strong believer in realism and he would shoot in any type of weather.

The Paris sequence is a suspenseful and visually exciting way to get *Superman II* underway. Lois Lane, always eager to be in the middle of the action and always the first to find trouble, tricks her way past the police barriers and hides in a nook underneath one of the tower's elevators.

French police complicate matters by detonating explosives they'd planted on the elevator's pulley system, causing the elevator and the trapped Lois to plummet toward the earth. The hydrogen bomb is also accidentally armed in the process, adding an extra level of suspense to the proceedings. Luckily, the Man of Steel arrives just in time to catch the falling elevator, rescue Lois, and launch the elevator into space, where it can explode harmlessly. The firing box used by the French police to detonate their charges is actually my own firing box that I'd used on numerous productions, and I still have it in the garage somewhere.

Considering how many different types of effects techniques were used, the sequence cuts together remarkably well. Shots of Lois hiding beneath the elevator were accomplished with front projection and miniatures were used for wide shots of the elevator moving up and down in the tower. Derek Meddings also did some outstanding model shots of the elevator's pulley system blowing up with belts flying off the wheels.

When we were planning the elevator sequence, we talked to the people who designed the elevators for the Eiffel Tower. They said our script was unrealistic because the elevator wouldn't fall like it did in the movie. If the elevator starting moving even slightly faster than usual, automatic safety brakes would kick in and stop the descent. And besides, if the elevator really did fall that quickly, the floor would probably fall out. At the end of the day though, we were making a fantasy movie and were willing to take some dramatic license for the sake of an exciting scene.

When the elevator is hurled into space by Superman, the explosion of the hydrogen bomb frees the Kryptonian villains Zod, Ursa and Non from their extra-dimensional prison in the Phantom Zone. The effect of the Phantom Zone exploding was achieved with some nifty animated effects overlaid with footage of a shattering plastic sheet. I always found it an odd coincidence that the villains happened to be travelling so close to earth at the time, but I guess it was just another example of artistic license to move the plot along.

The sequence of the three Kryptonians wreaking havoc on the moon was filmed by Dick Donner before Richard Lester came aboard the production. Many of the shots were filmed at a higher frame rate to simulate the lower gravity on the moon's surface. The astronauts hopping along in their spacesuits were actually on wires so they could achieve greater heights with their strides.

Because we were now dealing with more than one person flying at the same time, more harnesses and wire rigs were needed. *Superman II* took a "bigger is better" approach to everything. Although we employed many of the same techniques we used to create the effects for the original film, the sequel's level of complexity seemed to go up exponentially.

For example, one of the astronauts flees from the bloodthirsty Ursa on the moon. As he hobbles away in a clumsy attempt to escape, she gracefully flies right over his head and lands directly in his path. Both Ursa and the astronaut required movement on different axes at the same time. These seemingly simple shots took precise manipulation on the part of the wire handlers to make things run smoothly.

To simulate the lunar lander being crushed by Non when it attempts to lift off, we used hydraulics to compress the breakaway walls and pyrotechnics to augment the destruction of the lander's onboard computers. The panicking voice of the trapped astronaut really helps to sell the effect and create a sense of jeopardy. As always, the safety of the performer was of the utmost importance and he was never really in danger.

Sometimes the simplest of special-effects techniques are the most effective. No blue-screen processing or front-screen projection were used for the moon sequence. The lunar landscape was a simple set that was surrounded by black walls to simulate the darkness of space.

Visible in the background of some shots was the sun peeking out from behind the earth. The sun was nothing more than a small light mounted on a stand, which meant the "sun" would actually cast its own light and create a natural glare in the camera lens. Why spend millions of dollars when ten bucks will do the trick?

Then the film's action shifts back to earth. When the Kryptonian villains first arrive on the planet, General Zod lands in a waist-deep lake. He uses his powers to defy gravity by rising to the lake's surface and walking atop the water as though it's a solid surface. The whole incident is witnessed by a man in a fishing boat who can't believe his eyes.

Eagle-eyed viewers will notice that the actor playing the fisherman is Gordon Rollings, the same guy who gets the pie in the face at the beginning of *Superman III*. The actor who plays the meek deputy in *Superman II*, Peter Whitman, also appears in part three as the man at the cash machine. Richard Lester enjoyed using character actors like them in a number of his films.

To make Zod rise to the surface of the lake, we stood actor Terence Stamp on a small lift under the water. Once the lift reached the surface, he proceeded to walk on a platform that was positioned just under the water. The camera had to be positioned at a certain angle for the glistening of the sun to hide the lift and the platform. It took a long time to get those shots because the effect wouldn't work until the lighting was just right.

While walking through the forest, Ursa uses her heat vision to burn up a snake that's foolish enough to bite her. A prop snake was set aflame for the shot by detonating a charge with wires hidden under the ground. Animated laser beams were added during post-production to complete the illusion.

Even though the villains' landing on earth is supposed to take place in the States, we filmed the whole sequence in Black Park, which is close to Pinewood Studios in England. In fact, the entire American town invaded by the villains was a giant set built in the UK. This gave us full control over traffic and we were free to destroy buildings as needed. Trouble follows the baddies wherever they go, and soon they're smashing locals through bar tables and throwing them through walls. We had fun simulating the Kryptonians' super powers with the breakaway props and sets.

Zod even demonstrates a previously unknown power - the ability to levitate a man with an energy beam that shoots from his fingertip. One of my biggest problems with *Superman II* is the introduction of new powers that were never a part of the Superman mythology. I don't think it's keeping with Dick Donner's philosophy of verisimilitude.

When Zod disengages the levitation beam and lets the man crash to the ground, the stunt performer bounces considerably when he makes impact with the earth. That's because a crash mat was positioned just under the dirt to soften his fall.

The tense situation in the small town escalates when the armed forces arrive to confront the extra-terrestrial invaders. This sequence allowed the special-effects team to utilize almost every technique in the book. Animation was used to show Zod deflecting a flamethrower's fiery blast, which curves back toward the soldiers thanks to his super-breath. Explosions and fire effects added to the onscreen carnage as the villains continued to obliterate the town. A miniature helicopter on wires was crashed into a miniature barn and blown to smithereens by Derek Meddings' team, which added even greater scope to the mayhem.

The script called for Non to use his heat vision against approaching army jeeps. The fronts of the jeeps were required to explode, causing the vehicles to swerve violently and throw stunt performers afar. Because the explosions had to take place so close to the stuntmen, we had the challenge of making the blasts suitably spectacular without endangering anyone. We used naphthalene, an organic compound that smells like mothballs. When it's powdered and liberated with a small explosive charge, it burns with a bright orange flame and black smoke without causing a lot of damage.

In an attempt to stop the bad guys, the army helicopter shoots rockets that explode in huge showers of dirt all around the Kryptonians. Some of the blasts were set off extremely close to the actors, which made for some stunning visuals. Although the explosions look extremely powerful on screen, they were actually quite weak for safety reasons. We used small black-powder mortars buried under the ground that shot pieces of cork high into the air on cue. The flying shreds of cork shrapnel looked spectacular on camera without posing a danger to anyone.

One reason why many moviegoers prefer *Superman II* over the original is the greater emphasis on action in the sequel, especially with the Man of Steel squaring off against the three baddies in a no-holds-barred battle royale on the streets of Metropolis. Even though more than 30 years have passed since we shot this battle, it still packs a dramatic punch when you watch it today. Superman and the Kryptonians duke it out using their full array of powers, leaving much of Metropolis in ruins along the way. Buses are tossed about like toys, cars are detonated with heat vision, and villains are punched with enough force to send them crashing through buildings.

Because so much destruction was required for this sequence, shutting down Times Square and filming in Manhattan was out of the question. Entire city blocks were built on the backlot to simulate downtown Metropolis, right down to the finest detail. The streets were made realistically grimy, dozens of vehicles were brought in to create urban congestion, and the storefronts were fully dressed with products and signage. The amount of product placement on display was just ridiculous, but it did help to make set believable. Painted backdrops were used to hide the ends of the set, and they made it appear as though the city continued beyond the confines of the backlot.

Derek Meddings and his team did a remarkable job recreating the city set as a miniature for various shots. The full-sized set was used whenever possible for maximum realism, but some shots, like those involving a miniature Superman flying on wires through the labyrinth of skyscrapers, or the top of the Empire State Building blowing up, were best achieved by taking advantage of Derek Meddings' expertise.

The Metropolis battle was designed to be the centrepiece of the film, so we spared no expense in creating a big fireworks display for the audience. At one point, General Zod uses his heat vision to destroy a number of cars, and it was fun for us to really let loose and blow the shit out of them. It was yet another opportunity for the effects guys to play around in a really cool (and expensive) sandbox and fulfill our most primitive desires to see stuff get trashed.

Zod then focuses his laser vision on a tanker truck, hoping to create an even bigger fireball . Luckily, Superman swoops to the rescue at the last minute and uses his super-breath to put the truck on ice. The old trick of spraying wax came in handy once again.

The slugfest is hardly a fair fight, with three baddies teaming up against our poor hero and attacking him from all sides. Superman doesn't even know what hits him when Non pounces from above, driving both of them through the pavement and into the sewers beneath the city streets. The pavement was just lightweight material painted to look real and the stunt performers broke through easily.

The fisticuffs continue between Superman and Non, with the ground shaking to the sounds of punches exchanged below the earth. Then manhole covers start blowing high into the air with gusts of steam, presumably the exhalations of the titans in combat. The manhole covers were also made of lightweight material so they could be blown high with bursts of compressed air. Dramatic sound effects sell the illusion of real metal as the manhole covers crash to the ground with echoing clangs.

Non finds himself on the receiving end of a particularly persuasive knuckle sandwich, which sends him airborne through the pavement, into one side of an office building and right out the other. A stuntman was pulled up through the fake pavement on wires to achieve the effect of Non being launched into the air by Superman's punch.

The shot of Non smashing through the office was done with an upside-down set that was tilted on an angle. All of the office workers, as well as the furniture and set dressing, were fastened upside down from the roof of the set, and the stuntman was simply dropped through the flimsy set walls. The camera was mounted upside down, so when the shot was played back normally, it appeared as though Non was flying up and through the office at a 45 degree angle.

At one point in the battle, Zod tosses Superman right through the side of a delivery truck. It was built of light-gauge aluminum by a contractor named Stan Giles, who I first met on *Battle of Britain* and consequently hired on various projects. Stan was a car-body specialist who made a name for himself in the English film industry for specializing in sheet metal.

For *Superman II*, the truck had to be safe enough for the stuntman to crash through without risk of being cut. Stan even built the ribs of the truck in lightweight metal to reduce the chances of injury. I think the truck wall looks a bit too flimsy on film to be convincing, but hopefully audiences are so caught up in the action that they don't notice. The great sound effects once again go a long way in selling the illusion.

Zod is the next to receive some punishment when Superman scoops him up, twirls him in circles like a carnival ride, then pitches him straight into a giant Coca-Cola sign. The spinning shots were done with a dummy on wires to create the illusion of Superman's great strength, and the effect of Zod crashing into the billboard was achieved by optically inserting him into a shot of an exploding miniature sign. Coke must have paid a hefty sum to be featured so prominently in the sequence, which finishes with the letters on the sign burning off in a dazzling array of sparks.

Non and Ursa soon gain the upper hand by grabbing onto the ends of a bus and hurling it toward Superman. The bus was suspended on wires and lifted by a crane as actors Jack O'Halloran and Sarah Douglas pretended to do the heavy lifting.

For shots of the bus in flight, an aluminum miniature was used that was ten feet long and weighed two hundred pounds. Instead of resorting to costly optical effects, the effect of the bus flying through the air was achieved completely in-camera using forced perspective.

Like the full-sized bus, the miniature was also manipulated on wires that were suspended from a crane. The model bus was lined up with the camera in such a way that it appeared full-sized when viewed through the lens. In reality, the model was only a few feet in front of Christopher Reeve, but the two-dimensional nature of film and the relative size of the miniature gave the illusion that it was actually much farther from the actor.

With Superman pinned by the crashed bus, the three villains proceed to use their super-breath to fend off the angry citizens of Metropolis, who are hell-bent on avenging their hero. The people of the city find themselves literally blown away by the breath of the Kryptonians. We used wind machines made from aircraft engines with eight-foot blades like you'd find in a Spitfire. They were so powerful that they had to be anchored into the ground or they'd go shooting off like rockets.

This sequence allowed Richard Lester to indulge in his love of slapstick comedy. A wig is blown right off a man's head. Ice cream flies off a cone and into a guy's face. A man tries to continue his call even after his phone booth is blown onto its side. Such side trips into the absurd were the calling card of the director and would become even more pronounced with the next Superman sequel.

During this sequence of comedic carnage, a group of firefighters is seen struggling with their hose in the mighty winds as they attempt to extinguish the flaming car wrecks. I had my own memorable struggle with that hose. In between takes, I was walking down the set where the hose was laid out on the ground. It suddenly split open and sent a high-pressured shower of icy water my way. I was completely drenched and I did not find it funny at the time. Everybody else did.

Some of Derek Meddings' miniature shots are featured in this sequence. Cars are shown blowing down the street in a veritable smash-up derby. To achieve these shots, a section of miniature street was turned on its side and model cars were dropped down its length. The camera captured the action while also turned on its side, creating the illusion that cars were flying horizontally across the screen because of the gale-force winds. A high-speed camera was used to slow the action and give everything a greater sense of mass.

The cars themselves looks great in the miniature shots, but the model people blowing around in the background are far less convincing. They are clearly miniatures and they sway with the wind in awkwardly inhuman fashion. I think the shots would have been more convincing if the people were left out entirely.

Richard Lester's disregard for the established rules of the Superman legend is especially apparent during the film's climax. Superman and the villains demonstrate powers that were never established in the original comic-book source material. The Kryptonians can now shoot lasers from their fingertips. They can teleport themselves in the blink of an eye. Superman can even turn his chest insignia into an energy weapon that he tosses like a frisbee!

Despite any weaknesses in the storytelling, the cast members were all wonderful in their roles. When Superman reveals his true identity to Lois in the Niagara Falls hotel room, it's amazing to see how quickly and effortlessly Chris Reeve transforms from Clark Kent to the Man of Steel. As soon as he removes his glasses, he seems to gain two inches in height by straightening his back and relaxing his shoulders, and his eyes and voice suddenly gain the confidence more befitting a superhero.

Margot Kidder has wonderful onscreen chemistry with Chris, adding a true sense of heart to the story. Gene Hackman is great as Luthor, who is simultaneously evil, charming and funny. Terence Stamp, Sarah Douglas and Jack O'Halloran are truly frightening as the escaped convicts from Krypton. None of our special effects would have been convincing without good performances to back them up.

When *Superman II* premiered in Niagara Falls, a fancy dinner for the cast and crew was held in the revolving dining room of the Skylon Tower, which afforded a spectacular view of the falls. That evening, I was asked by the Warner Bros. marketing department to project the Superman "S" logo onto the falls themselves after the sun had gone down.

The special menu prepared for the *Superman II* party. Photo courtesy of the Skylon Tower.

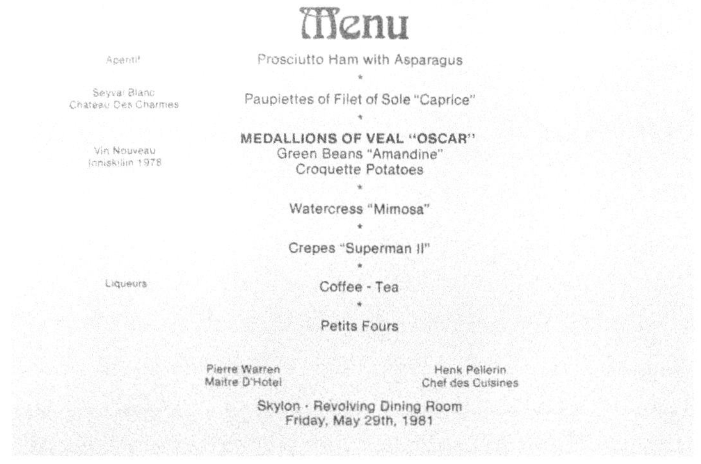

Menu

Aperitif	Prosciutto Ham with Asparagus
	*
Seyval Blanc Chateau Des Charmes	Paupiettes of Filet of Sole "Caprice"
	*
Vin Nouveau Inniskillin 1978	MEDALLIONS OF VEAL "OSCAR" Green Beans "Amandine" Croquette Potatoes
	*
	Watercress "Mimosa"
	*
	Crepes "Superman II"
	*
Liqueurs	Coffee - Tea
	*
	Petits Fours

Pierre Warren
Maitre D'Hotel

Henk Pellerin
Chef des Cuisines

Skylon · Revolving Dining Room
Friday, May 29th, 1981

The inside of the menu. Photo courtesy of the Skylon Tower.

Christopher Reeve and Gene Hackman left their mark at the party.
Photo courtesy of the Skylon Tower.

Every night, the falls are illuminated by brilliantly coloured spotlights so tourists can enjoy the spectacle even after dark. I was given special permission that night to set up my own powerful light atop the abandoned power station at the base of the Horseshoe Falls, which would project the Superman emblem onto the cascades.

It was no surprise when *Superman II* was another blockbuster at the box office. Despite negative press about the replacement of Dick Donner as director, audiences flocked to cinemas and made it one of the year's biggest hits. Moviegoers and critics alike were charmed by the balance of action, humour and romance.

With the villains defeated and Superman's secret identity safe once again (thanks to a rather convenient magical kiss), the slate was clean for future adventures. It was a foregone conclusion that a *Superman III* would follow, but I'd be involved with a number of other productions before reteaming with Richard Lester for the third instalment.

Right after *Superman II*, I traveled to France to work on the live-action Disney film *Condorman*. Starring Michael Crawford, Barbara Carrera and Oliver Reed, *Condorman* was Disney's attempt to enter the world of big-screen superheroes, and I had the perfect pedigree to head up their special-effects department. The film was a goofy adventure about a comic book creator who assumes the identity of his fictional character and finds himself caught in a web of espionage.

Much of *Condorman* was filmed in the south of France, a beautiful place to shoot with its warm weather and picturesque coast on the Mediterranean. As with my early experience on *Superman* when pre-production was still based out of Italy, the craft services were far beyond anything I'd ever experienced working in England. The food-services people set up a tent wherever we were shooting, then the gourmet dishes would start to flow over the next two hours. Somehow, we never felt rushed during those meals, but we still managed to get our shooting done within schedule.

The chef prepared the most amazing French dishes that would have cost a fortune in a North American restaurant. Two or three bottles of French wine awaited us on each table, and we'd enjoy eating, drinking and socializing with nary a mention of work. It was amazing how strong the coffee was (you could almost chew it) and there was never a shortage of chocolate croissants to get you through the day. The French crew was wonderful and they really knew how to enjoy life. It was a very civilized way to do things on a film shoot.

Condorman was a movie with a lot of spectacular action sequences in the tradition of the James Bond films. We crashed six Porches for *Condorman*, destroying them in the most spectacular ways possible for the camera. My favourite way to kill a car was to fly it off the side of a cliff and have it explode midair. I remember asking director Charles Jarrott how soon he wanted the car to blow up after it flew off the edge. Did he want it to happen 20, 30 or 40 feet out? He decided that he wanted to see it explode at about 40 feet.

Discussing details like this with Charles ahead of time allowed him to plan his shots with the camera operators. In reality, it didn't make sense for a vehicle to spontaneously combust while flying through the air, but it sure made for some great shots in the final film.

My effects team had an impact switch that controlled when the blast was detonated. The switch was positioned inside of the car and attached to 40 feet of cable plus a bit of extra slack that was tied off on land, with the extra cable looped so the cable wasn't too taught. Parts of the vehicle were precut to ensure it would break apart easily once the explosives were detonated.

Three gallons of gasoline wrapped in primer cord were placed inside the car. For extra safety, we used what we called a leaf switch, which was like a handle with two connectors on the sides shaped like leaves. When you pushed the switch down, it would lock down onto the leaves and break the circuit to the explosives until the cable pulled it during filming and triggered the detonation.

The car was towed down the road and flung off the cliff. When the car was forty feet out and the cable pulled tight, it activated the leaf switch and obliterated the car midair. Fun stuff.

When you shoot in the water, like we did for the boat chase in *Condorman*, it's considerably more difficult to control the elements than it is when filming on dry land. The script required Condorman's boat to pass through a gauntlet of explosions in the Mediterranean and barely escape destruction. Easier said than done.

We're talking about water that's anywhere from 100 to 300 feet deep, and we had to anchor the explosives in specific locations, then set them off in meticulously timed fashion. As always, safety was a concern with the explosives. We couldn't have the detonations go off too close to the boats, but they had to be close enough to create a sense of danger.

I had some personality conflicts with a second-unit director on the film, who didn't always have much patience for the special-effects department. One day, when the water was particularly rough, I was out in a boat trying to rig the explosives for the big chase. Everything needed to be set precisely and properly, but high winds were making our work difficult.

The second-unit director and his team were on land, waiting eagerly for us to finish so they could begin filming the sequence. Every 15 minutes or so, my radio would crackle to life and a voice from land would express a growing sense of impatience.

"How much longer do you need? We want to get going."

"We're working as fast as we can. We'll let you know."

Fifteen minutes would pass.

"What's taking so long? How much longer?"

"We're working on it. The water's really rough out here, so we're doing our best."

I could tell from the tone of the person on the other end that he didn't believe me. What did he think we were doing, having a party?

Another fifteen minutes went by.

"The director's tired of waiting. He's coming out to see what's taking you guys so long."

"Fine. Come out."

We watched as the second-unit director and his camera crew piled into a 50-foot boat and left shore. Only about 300 metres out, they realized how rough the water was and they immediately made a u-turn back for shore. The radio crackled to life again soon afterwards.

"The water's too rough," said the voice from land. "We're not shooting today."

Sometimes, people have to learn the hard way. Overall though, *Condorman* was a wonderful experience, both for the lovely shooting locations and the great crew. It was on that film that I became good friends with Marc Wolff, a talented helicopter pilot and aerial coordinator. Any big movie that requires helicopter work is sure to seek out Marc's services. From *Star Wars* to the Harry Potter films, he's done it all. I had the pleasure of working with him again on various projects in the future.

In addition to being such an accomplished helicopter pilot, Marc also flew fixed-wing aircraft and was an avid hot-air balloonist. He was extremely passionate about flying and absolutely loved what he did for a living. One time, he took me up in a helicopter and let me take the controls for a while. After years of flying radio-controlled helicopters, it was exciting to fly a real one at last.

Marc was a great guy with a wicked sense of humour. One shooting day, he was hanging out with the special-effects department after we'd finished rigging the explosives for the big boat chase. Just for fun, I offered to take him out in a boat. The water was a bit choppy, and I purposely hit all the waves I could so he'd get totally drenched. Marc was pretty soggy by the time we made it back to land.

A couple of days later, we were back in the harbor filming the bad guys firing rockets at Condorman from their speedboats. Marc was flying overhead for aerial shots of the chase. Everything went well and we got all the shots we needed.

The weather was beautiful, so I started sunbathing on the deck of the boat. Marc flew overhead, so I playfully gave him the finger. Circling back around, he came in really low and used the blades of the helicopter to whip up quite a storm. It was like a tsunami hitting me and he totally drowned me on that deck.

I also spent a few weeks in Paris for the sequence of Condorman flying from the Eiffel Tower. We flew the stuntman from the first level of the tower by wires suspended from a crane. It was quite a showstopper to film this sequence in Paris. Especially with the Eiffel Tower sequence having just appeared in *Superman II*, there was a lot of interest from onlookers to watch another superhero taking flight from this famous landmark. Condorman looked particularly spectacular with his twenty-foot wingspan fully outstretched.

When we filmed another flying sequence, this time in Monte Carlo, the large wingspan presented challenges in making the flight look suitably elegant. The stuntman was flown around Monte Carlo Harbor while suspended from a helicopter by wires. When taking off, the poor stunt guy was getting buffeted in every direction by the winds that were catching his outstretched wings like a sail. Once they picked up enough speed and climbed high enough, things eventually balanced out and Condorman's flight looked fantastic.

We also did some filming in the mountains of Zermatt in Switzerland, which was breathtaking to say the least. The scenes made use of the famous cable car, which seemed to dangle over a bottomless abyss. As someone who isn't very fond of heights, it wasn't the most comfortable experience for me. To further compound my discomfort, I got food poisoning during my first day there and had to deal with it during our entire shoot in Switzerland. I was still feeling ill during our trip back to the south of France, which made for an extremely unpleasant journey.

My nephews Ian, Chris and Paul Corbould worked with me on the special effects of *Condorman*. Ian had just started in the business, and he was determined to save his money so he could buy the car of his dreams, a Triumph Spitfire. In addition to staying in a nice hotel in the south of France and having unbelievable French cuisine served on set, we were each given a living allowance. Ian figured if he saved up his living allowance and didn't spend it eating out all the time, he'd have enough money to put a deposit on a Spitfire when he got back to England.

Instead of going to restaurants, Ian would buy a can of spaghetti and eat it in his hotel room. About halfway through our shooting in the south of France, I received a phone call from the hotel manager, who asked if I'd join him to see something. He took me into the bathroom in Ian's suite, and I was surprised to find that the fancy mirror next to the tub was completely covered in spaghetti-can labels.

I later learned that Ian would take a hot bath after each day of shooting to unwind. He'd bring that evening's can of spaghetti into the bath with him to heat it up. The label would always come loose from the can, and he made a habit of sticking the labels onto the nearby mirror. This unusual explanation did little to satisfy the hotel manager, who insisted that we pay a cleaning fee to rid the mirror of all the sticky label residue. Ian could be a bit eccentric, but most creative geniuses tend to have a unique way of viewing the world.

Condorman was a fun but intense experience because it relied so heavily on practical effects to tell its story. It was made all the more intense by drama in my personal life that was playing out at the same time. Colleen was still living in Canada, and we had been keeping up our long-distance relationship. While I was in France, a "friend" had let my wife Josie know that I'd met someone special when I was shooting *Superman II* in Niagara Falls. Our rocky marriage was already hitting rock bottom, so I flew back to England to face the music with Josie and prepare for our impending divorce.

After *Condorman* was finished production, I flew to Canada for a little while to recuperate, then I returned to England to finalize details of the separation. It was decided that my daughter would stay in England and be raised by Josie, who was an exceptional mother to Lucy.

With my clapper board from *Superman III*, which I recently discovered in my garage after all these years.

The following year, I moved to Canada so I could be with Colleen. I received a phone call from Bob Simmonds, who would be serving as associate producer on *Superman III*, asking if I'd be interested in working on the film. Richard Lester was once again taking the director's chair, and he wanted as much continuity as possible with crew members from part two, so I was asked to return. Derek Meddings, however, would not be returning for the film, so I was asked to supervise the miniature effects as well as the practical effects.

Working on the production took me to Pinewood Studios in England and to Alberta, Canada, where exterior locations for Metropolis and Smallville were filmed. I was happy that Colleen could accompany me to England so we wouldn't have to spend months apart like we had previously.

With my daughter Lucy.

At this time, Lucy was five years old, and my time on *Superman III* included my first Christmas way from Lucy and Josie. I was used to seeing my daughter during Christmas, so it was a tough time for me emotionally. During production of *Superman III*, I kept in touch with Lucy as much as possible and let her know I was thinking of her. Luckily, Lucy never held it against me for leaving. I think she was too young at the time to fully understand the situation. Lucy has since become acquainted with Colleen and the two of them get along very well.

Right from the start of production, I could sense that *Superman III* was in danger of losing its way. So many elements that had made the first two films successful were missing from the new screenplay by David and Leslie Newman. For one thing, Lex Luthor was replaced by a watered-down villain named Ross Webster, who was played by Robert Vaughn. I think he was really miscast for the part because he didn't exude any of Gene Hackman's underlying menace. Audiences had come to know Robert for his suave character in *The Man from U.N.C.L.E.* and I feared that people would have trouble accepting him as the bad guy.

Although Margot Kidder returned for *Superman III*, her part amounted to a scant few minutes. The romance between Superman and Lois Lane that was so magical in the first two movies was nowhere to be found here. A new love interest played by Annette O'Toole was introduced to take the story in a new direction.

Even Christopher Reeve himself was given far less screen time for this adventure. Much of the focus was shifted to Richard Pryor, who was brought in to share the spotlight as a bumbling computer specialist involved in a plot to control the world. Pryor was a talented comedic actor, but he just didn't belong in a Superman movie.

Right from the beginning of the movie, it's obvious that *Superman III* is straying far from the verisimilitude that Dick Donner had worked so hard to achieve. The opening sequence is a silly hodge-podge of pratfalls that have nothing to do with the central plot. For example, an out-of-control rollerskater causes a series of phone booths to topple like dominoes. A toy penguin walks down the street with its head on fire. A man even gets a pie in the face. If you think none of this makes any sense, then you'd be right. It's director Richard Lester indulging in his love of goofy comedy. Verisimilitude be damned.

Storyboard for the insane opening sequence of *Superman III*.
From the personal collection of Aaron Lam.

The sequence is well-executed, but it doesn't belong in this particular movie series. By the time a man gets a metal bucket stuck on his head and a mime starts tripping over gumballs, you might expect Buster Keaton or Charlie Chaplin to appear and join the mayhem.

Instead, you get Superman saving a man from drowning in his own car. The Man of Steel makes his first appearance when a stray bullet from a shootout hits the tire of a passing car, causing the driver to swerve into a fire hydrant. The vehicle quickly fills with water and the man inside is unable to escape. It's Superman to the rescue!

With Christopher Reeve in downtown Calgary. My nephew Chris Corbould is standing behind me. Photo courtesy of Jim Bowers at CapedWonder.com.

We filmed this sequence in downtown Calgary, where hundreds of curious onlookers wanted to catch a glimpse of Christopher Reeve in costume. The stunt driver knocked over a fake fire hydrant, then the car was pumped full of water as the man struggled within. Chris was flown in on wires suspended from a crane, much to the delight of the cheering crowd behind the barricades. Then he landed on the car, tore off the sunroof and hauled the man to safety. Not a very dramatic rescue for the beginning of the movie, but thankfully the next action sequence was more befitting a Superman epic.

During a bus ride to Smallville, Clark encounters a raging fire at a chemical factory. Housed within the factory are containers of a volatile acid that, if overheated, will form a giant cloud that can eat through anything. Superman must stop the inferno and save the Eastern Seaboard from total disaster.

This sequence is one of the film's highlights, but it played out far differently in the first drafts of the script. As originally written, Superman was supposed to put out a forest fire instead. I was sent to scout a remote area north of Edmonton, where we considered using controlled fires for the sequence.

Upon my return, I told Bob Simmonds my thoughts on using that location. For one thing, it would take us hours to drive the cast and crew up there for shooting. Then there was the problem of getting all our equipment up there by helicopter, which would cost a fortune. Also, I wasn't convinced that we could control the flames and I didn't think we should risk burning down the whole forest for the sake of our movie.

The script was changed so it featured a fire at a factory instead. Bob suggested using an oil refinery just outside of Calgary that looked perfect for the scene, but he doubted they'd let us use the location because fire and oil aren't good bedfellows. Surprisingly, they were agreeable to letting us film there and they were confident in our ability to keep the shoot safe.

In order to create the thick black smoke we wanted, we set two truckloads of tires ablaze at the refinery. Unfortunately, the wind blew the smoke directly over the runways of Calgary International Airport, which had to be closed because planes couldn't take off or land. We got into trouble with the aviation authority over that, but the smoke looked fantastic on screen.

The shoot was carefully orchestrated with a number of controlled mini-fires to give the impression of utter chaos. Some of the wider shots of the factory on fire, such as those showing oil tankers exploding, were accomplished with miniatures. Other shots that involved stunt performers, like a cutaway of a factory worker running out of the building with his clothing on fire, were done later at the studio.

To save people trapped on the roof, Superman pulls a metal silo from its foundation and leans it against the building so they can use it as a slide. It's a really creative use of his powers and it allows us to see something we'd never seen before in the series. The silo was actually manipulated by wires hanging from a crane, and it's a testament to Chris Reeve's acting ability that he was able to sell the illusion of great strength so convincingly.

Photographer Jimmy Olsen, always out to get the perfect picture for the *Daily Planet*, climbs up a fire truck ladder to get a good view of the inferno. Unfortunately, the ladder is knocked over by debris from an explosion and Jimmy crashes to the ground, breaking his leg in the process. More miniature effects were used in this sequence, with the suspenseful editing and dramatic sound effects adding greatly to the visceral impact.

After being carried from the danger zone by Superman, the audience is treated to a peek at Jimmy's fractured leg bone thanks to the Man of Steel's x-ray vision. It's a simple but effective shot achieved by superimposing the image of the broken bone over the live-action footage of Jimmy's leg.

When the firefighters suddenly run out of water for their hoses, Superman combats the fire with a truly outlandish display of his superpowers. He flies to a lake five miles away, freezes the top layer using his super-breath, flies off into the sky with the giant sheet of ice in his hands, then drops it while hovering over the factory. Luckily, the heat of the fire melts the ice during its fall. Lo and behold, it starts raining and the fire is quickly extinguished.

The effect of the lake's surface icing up was done with an animated freezing effect, and the shot of him prying the lid off the frozen lake was accomplished by having Chris lift a lightweight plastic sheet that was painted to look like ice. The overhead view of the ice breaking up as it falls from the sky was accomplished by optically matting a small sheet of ice into the shot. It was broken up bit by bit using stop-motion animation. Roy Field and his optical-effects department did a wonderful job with this sequence.

One of the biggest laughs in *Superman III* comes when Clark sneezes at a bowling alley, which sends a bowling ball flying down the lane at incredible speed and the pins shatter in spectacular fashion. We rigged the pins with explosives and detonated them with the camera running at a high frame rate so they would blow apart in slow motion. The speeding ball was an animated effect added during post-production to complete the illusion.

Some of the film's potentially exciting effects sequences were totally undermined by Richard Lester's decision to focus on slapstick comedy. One such example is the scene in which Richard Pryor wears a pink tablecloth like a superhero cape and describes Superman's incredible feats. Instead of showing the Man of Steel's heroics firsthand, information is revealed to the audience through Pryor's jokey storytelling as he pantomimes Superman's actions.

The sequence occasionally cuts to shots of Superman saving the day, but they are used only in brief cuts with Pryor's over-the-top narration taking centre stage. As such, the effects end up as little more than the punch line to his jokes.

One effect we created for the scene shows Superman flying up through the base of a tornado and turning it inside out. The tornado was created in a cloud tank, which is essentially a giant aquarium filled with saltwater and freshwater, which naturally separate into distinct layers. Dyes were injected into the tank, which formed cloud-like structures in the zone where the water of differing densities refused to mix.

The water in the tank was churned to create the twister, and a blue screen was placed behind the tank so the tornado could be matted into a separate background plate of a landscape. Roy Field completed the effect by adding a wipe with the optical printer to show the tornado being turned inside out by the Man of Steel.

It was a nice effect that was undermined by the lack of a dramatic set up within the context of the story. As such, it lacked the visceral impact of something like the helicopter sequence from the first movie, which took its time establishing a real sense of jeopardy and built to an exciting climax.

The script of *Superman III* enters darker territory in its final third, giving Chris a chance to show his acting range and allowing us to create some effects with greater emotional resonance. After exposure to artificial Kryptonite, Superman transforms into an evil version of himself. While drinking excessively at a bar, he uses his super-strength to flick peanuts at bottles behind the counter, shattering them one by one. A pellet gun was actually used to destroy the bottles.

Superman then ponders his own reflection in a mirror behind the counter. With an expression of pure loathing, he uses his heat-vision to melt the mirror into a warped mess. This effect could be done easily using CGI today, as seen in films like *Terminator 2: Judgment Day*, but we needed to rely on more practical means back then. The mirror was actually a thin piece of plexiglass that was blasted with a wave of intense heat from behind, causing it to warp out of shape. An animated glow was added to create the impression that the mirror was red hot.

Wanting to rid himself of the darkness that has gripped him, Superman flies to a junkyard and splits into two separate selves - the evil Superman and the good Clark Kent. They proceed to battle one another to the death in one of the film's major set pieces. The junkyard was actually a set built on the backlot of Pinewood Studios, and if you look carefully, you can see a little bit of Pinewood's famous 007 Stage in the background of one shot.

Clark takes quite a beating at the hands of the evil Superman. The mild-mannered reporter is thrown into a pile of cars, beaten with a metal fender, and (seemingly) flattened inside of a car crusher after being engulfed in an avalanche of vehicle parts. Much of the junkyard was actually constructed of lightweight plastics that were painted to look like metal on screen. That way, the stuntman could be tossed about and beaten up on screen without any real injury.

The car masher is particularly effective in the sequence. Chris really sells the illusion that Clark is being crushed to death in the machine, even though he really has a comfortable safety zone inside. To the evil Superman's surprise, Clark escapes from the car crusher unscathed and manages to defeat his foe once and for all.

Superman then flies to the Grand Canyon, where the baddies have set up their base inside of a cave that is guarded by a giant supercomputer. I remember giving Colleen a tour of the impressive cave set at Pinewood, which resembled something out of a James Bond movie. The set was a few stories high, allowing the actors to move around on different levels of the supercomputer. Whenever the ceiling of the cave is shown, with the top of the computer complex reaching up several additional stories, a miniature was used instead of a full-sized set.

As Superman approaches the base, the villains launch rockets and try to blast him out of the sky. The missile launchers that rise up from the rocks were radio-controlled miniatures, and the shots of the rockets in flight were achieved using miniatures shot in front of a blue screen. We filmed explosions against the sky for some shots, then had Roy Field matte in the image of Superman dodging the blasts later on.

Once Superman enters the cave, the bad guys unleash an arsenal of futuristic weapons that allowed the animation department to go crazy. The various energy weapons, like the laser beams and the Kryptonite ray, were animated effects added during post-production.

At one point, Superman becomes trapped in a giant bubble that is impervious to his super-strength and he must use his heat vision to break free. Animation was used to create the illusion of the bubble being launched by the supercomputer and engulfing him. The shots of Superman struggling inside the bubble were done with Chris suspended on wires inside of a plastic bubble.

It was decided that the bubble should have a web of vine-like tendrils covering its surface to make it look a little organic. I locked an air gun together with a silicone gun to create irregular patterns that stuck to the outside of the bubble, which gave it a lot of personality and made it feel almost alive.

The supercomputer eventually gains consciousness and transforms the unfortunate Vera into a vicious cyborg. A tractor beam pulls her into the heart of the computer, where the transformation takes place in a matter of seconds. To create the effect of the various cybernetic enhancements being grafted to her face in rapid succession, the sequence was filmed in reverse. We started with the actress covered with all the prosthetic implants, then we yanked them off one at a time with wires. When played backward, the shot was quite effective and unsettling to watch.

Superman saves the day by destroying the computer with a canister of acid taken from the chemical factory that was seen earlier in the film. Polycell wallpaper paste was used for the bubbling acid, which I had also used in *Saturn 3* for the pit of chemicals that ultimately destroys the robot Hector.

The canister of acid eats right through the floor and falls into the abyss below. The floor was constructed of a soft foam material that melted when covered in a solvent, and it was lit dramatically from below to give the impression of great heat.

For the grand finale, we blew up both the full-sized cave set and the miniature version, and I think they intercut quite seamlessly. Since it can be difficult to make miniature pyrotechnics convincing on screen, we shot at a high frame rate to slow everything down and add a greater sense of scale. The climactic action sequence lacked the epic quality that Dick Donner captured with the first film, but at least we got to end *Superman III* with a bang.

With the world now safe and Superman back to his normal "good" self, he still has some business to take care of before the movie ends. Earlier in the story, when he was under the influence of the manmade Kryptonite, he mischievously straightened the Leaning Tower of Pisa just for the hell of it. At the conclusion of the film, Superman makes things right by restoring the tower to its natural tilt.

The wide shot of Superman pushing the tower back to its original position was accomplished with a miniature, and the two Italian men in the foreground were added to the shot after being filmed in front of a blue screen. It was a nice effect, but a rather silly way to conclude the story. Compared to the emotionally satisfying finales of the first two films, this was a rather limp way to wrap things up.

Although *Superman III* ended up doing decent business at the box office, it wasn't nearly as successful as parts one and two. Critics and audiences had a field day with the film, lamenting the loss of gravitas that had made the previous films so engaging. The ill-advised attempts at slapstick comedy fell flat for the most part, and none of the new villains were nearly as interesting as Gene Hackman or Ned Beatty.

Ultimately, *Superman III* just didn't feel like a Superman film. The spotlight on Richard Pryor was so strong that Christopher Reeve seemed to play second fiddle. I'm proud of the effects work we did on *Superman III*, but the film never came together as a cohesive whole.

Had Dick Donner been allowed to continue as director of the series, it's possible that we would have seen several more successful Superman films, but that was not to be. *Superman III* was the last film in the series I worked on, and I wish that my involvement with the *Superman* films could have ended on a higher note. Instead of flying high, *Superman III* spun out of control at the very beginning and never quite found its flight path.

CHAPTER 7
A NEW DIRECTION

I got to know Richard Lester quite well during the production of *Superman II* and *III*, and we often spoke about the art of directing. I was developing an interest in becoming a director myself, and I was grateful that Richard allowed me to direct the miniature-effects shots for the third film.

In reality, my ambitions to direct had started a few years earlier. After I'd received the Academy Award for the first *Superman*, I felt it was time to take the next step in the industry and try my hand at directing. My interest in directing didn't stem from any need to boost my ego. To me, it was a matter of creative control. I came from a fine-arts background, where my photographs and illustrations were the product of my own creative vision, and I liked the idea of gaining greater creative control as a filmmaker.

As a director, I find it satisfying to set up each shot and tell the story through my own creative lens. It's also creatively gratifying to see a project through all stages of development and production, from concept to delivery of the final product. Directing also allows me to work with the different production departments instead of being limited to special effects. Getting to play in a bigger sandbox can be fun once in a while.

I never even considered film directing as a possible career until one memorable occasion during my student days. I went for a job interview with British Rail, which had its own film unit for shooting commercials and promotional films. The interview was for the position of trainee cameraman, which I thought would be a great deal of fun. Imagine being paid to learn about cinematography while riding the rails through the beautiful countryside! Not the worst way to break into the business.

I brought along some storyboards I'd created for a school project. The interviewer complimented me on my visual storytelling and he suggested that I consider directing as a possible career instead of cinematography. I didn't end up getting the job with British rail, but his advice stuck with me over the years.

Even after I'd moved to Canada in the early eighties, I had an agent in London named Maureen Moore who worked for London Management, one of the biggest agencies in England. Another one of Maureen's clients was a talented and well-known Iraqi cinematographer living in Canada named Ousama "Ossi" Rawi, who ran a production company called Rawi Films that specialized in television commercials.

At the time, he was married to the popular British actress Rita Tushingham of *Doctor Zhivago* fame. Maureen introduced me to Ossi and we hit it off right away. He hired me because he wanted someone who could direct commercials that involved a lot of special effects.

Maureen also introduced me to her friend Peter Cooper, who had a production company in Los Angeles, and I began to direct commercials for him as well. He felt more comfortable working with actors than he did with special effects, so I took on the effects-driven ads for his company while he concentrated on the "people" commercials.

Since I was now living in North America, I worked with a rep out of

New York named Jeff Devlin, who would receive storyboards for potential television commercial jobs from various advertising agencies. Jeff would then send out my demo reel for projects he thought might be a good fit for me.

Directing baseball legend Gary Carter on the set of a commercial for *New York Newsday*.

If the ad agencies were interested in speaking with me further about a commercial, they'd ask for either a conference call or a meeting in person. Sometimes I'd fly out to L.A., Chicago or Washington to do a presentation for an agency, where we'd discuss their storyboards and my approach to directing the commercial. If our visions were in sync and our personalities clicked, then I'd move on to the next level of consideration. Agencies tended to have three different people bid for each job, and if they chose me, we'd agree on a budget and then start pre-production.

I soon became busy directing commercials and I found myself becoming known for specializing in toy advertisements. There's an old saying in the business: never work with children or animals. Personally, I never agreed with that saying because I always loved working with young actors on set and going through the casting process with them.

We usually looked for kids who were natural on screen - kids who would act like kids instead of trying to emulate adult actors. For a single commercial, we often saw 150 candidates brought in by the casting director. Sometimes we'd get kids who came in and had the perfect look for the commercial, but they didn't have the acting ability. Other times they would hit the nail on the head right away and our casting was over quick and easy. We also tried to cast kids who could take direction well and stay focused - time is money in this business and we usually had a lot of ground to cover in a single day.

The producers, ad-agency representative, copywriter and art director would also sit in on casting sessions to weigh in with their opinions. My producer usually attended to ensure that the actors and their representatives weren't asking for additional payment or perks that weren't a part of our offer.

Sometimes, I'd have disagreements with others at the casting session who wanted me to choose a particular candidate based solely on appearance.

"He's got the perfect look," they'd tell me. "You should go with him."

"But he can't act," I'd point out.

"Don't worry about it," they'd say. "You're a good director. You can get a good performance out of him."

I'd always hold my ground: "You can't get a good performance out of a kid who isn't a natural actor."

Children can't perform well in front of the camera unless they're having fun. It's not something you can coax out of them like you can with an adult. If you try coaching kids too much, they end up feeling stagey. They have to be naturals to begin with. In order to get the best possible performances, we tried to keep a relaxed environment for the kids, and when it was fun for them, it was fun for me too. Knowing that they'd be getting free toys at the end of the shoot was probably extra motivation to do a good job.

One time, we were shooting a doll commercial that was set in a girl's bedroom. Our actress was the cutest little girl, no older than six or seven years old, and she was doing a great job. Numerous takes are usually required, sometimes a seemingly ridiculous number of takes, in order to get the performances right and cover all the necessary angles. The girl patiently did take after take. When we were setting up for the sixth take, she motioned for me to come over.

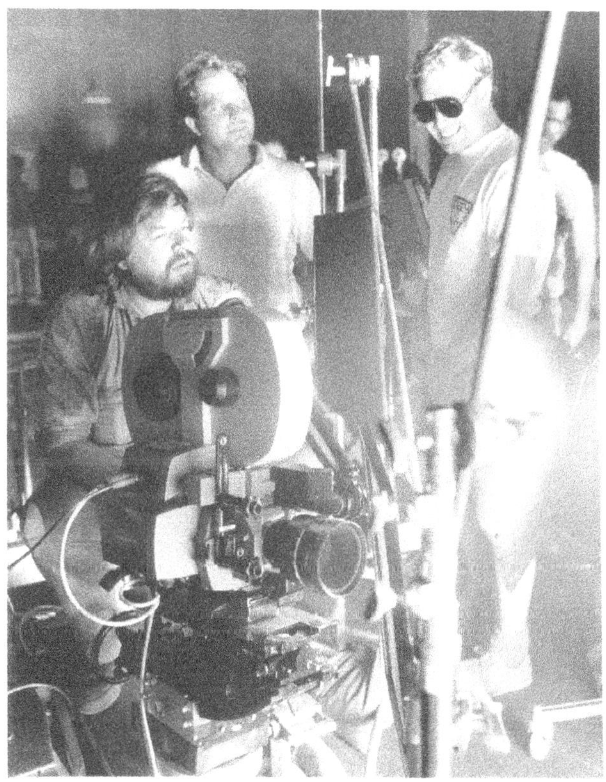

"One more take and I'm outta here," she said without a touch of irony. I couldn't help but laugh. She'd probably heard an adult say that at some point.

I've worked with so many wonderful child actors over the years and sometimes I wonder what they're up to nowadays. Many of them would be in their thirties by now and hopefully I played a small role in helping them on their path to a successful adulthood. At the very least, I hope their experience helped to teach them discipline, responsibility and respect.

Although I enjoyed directing commercials, the experience was much more restrictive creatively than directing music videos, episodic television and feature-length films - all of which would come later in my career. The scripts for commercials were completely vetted by the client, who wanted to keep tight control over how their product or service was being represented to the public.

Directing a commercial for 7-Eleven.

As a director, I could present my own ideas for their consideration, but I couldn't make any changes to the script without going through the agency, the client and the writer. I wouldn't usually recommend any changes unless I felt strongly that a certain piece of dialogue didn't work and could be improved. And whenever changes were made, we had to ensure they adhered to all broadcasting standards.

All commercials, especially ones that are selling products aimed at children, must be approved by various regulatory bodies before they can go to air. This is to ensure that commercials aren't making false claims or presenting material that viewers would deem offensive or unsuitable for television.

When I first started shooting toy commercials, some of the advertising guidelines were much looser in terms of how the toys could be presented on screen. Some of my earliest commercials were for Micro Machines, a line of small toy vehicles from Galoob. Back then, we used a lot of stop-motion animation to show the small cars zooming around and we'd set off tiny explosions to add excitement.

Then a whole new set of regulations came in - we were no longer allowed to showcase the toys like that because it didn't accurately represent the experience of playing with them. Using stop-motion animation to bring inanimate toys to life was limited to a certain amount of screen time, and animation in general could be used only if it was clearly presented as being for dramatic purposes only.

This applied to Barbie as well. We weren't allowed to use photorealistic CGI to animate her, only stylized animation that clearly wasn't the actual the doll. We also weren't allowed to show Barbie moving by herself, as this would imply that she'd take on a life of her own when removed from the box.

Whenever she moved on screen, we were required to show a person's hands manipulating the doll. Barbie had to come alive on screen without bringing too much attention to the hands. The emphasis had to be on Barbie as an actual character, so sometimes only the slightest hint of the puppeteers' fingertips would appear within the frame.

We had a couple of regular hand models who did an amazing job bringing Barbie to life with the most subtle of nuances. Sometimes, it was just a slight turn of the head or a barely perceptible move of an arm, but they were able to communicate a remarkable amount of personality. Sometimes we'd put a little bit of glue on their fingertips so they could maneuver the doll more easily.

I always treated Barbie like a real person who needed direction like any other actor, only I was directing through the puppeteer's hands. I ended up shooting a number of Barbie commercials because the agency thought I was the only director who could really bring Barbie to life.

One of the trade magazines for the television-commercial industry picked my ad for Olympic Gymnast Barbie as the top commercial of the month. The puppeteer did an amazing job transforming the inanimate Barbie doll into a fully performing gymnast. I don't know how she managed to do it without tying her fingers into knots.

I directed TV spots for various companies over the next several years, including ads for toys based on characters from Marvel Comics. In 2000, I shot commercials for the X-Men and Spider-Man toys when their respective movies were hitting theatres. Avi Arad was in charge of the toys at the time, and he has since gone on to be a major producer in Hollywood.

Avi was a brilliant man who started off as a toy entrepreneur. He deserves every bit of his success because he was able to raise the marketing of Marvel's characters to a whole new level. Now that the X-Men, Spider-Man and Avengers films are regularly smashing box-office records around the world, you can't even walk down the street without seeing a T-shirt or a toy featuring the likeness of a Marvel Comics character.

Around this time, I directed a commercial for jeans that I'm particularly proud of. The ad starts on a breathtaking shot of mountains taken from a helicopter, and without cutting away, the camera begins to zoom in on a mountain peak. As we get closer, a man becomes visible standing atop the precipice. Without cutting away, the shot keeps moving in tighter until the screen is filled with a close-up of the logo on the guy's jeans.

People have often asked me how we accomplished that sequence without crashing into him. In reality, we filmed the shot starting with the close-up on the jeans and then pulled the helicopter back. When the film was played in reverse, it appeared as though the helicopter was zooming in toward the actor.

This commercial reunited me with helicopter pilot Marc Wolff, who once again demonstrated his amazing level of control over a helicopter. In order to film the close-up of the jeans and keep the shot nicely framed, the copter had to hover steadily in just the right position. Because of the naturally high winds and the draft created by the helicopter blades, we anchored the actor safely into place.

Marc and I shot a couple of commercials together, and he always traveled with the same engineer who did serious safety checks on the helicopters no matter how short or simple the shoot was. I always admired his dedication to safety and we shared the same philosophy - a film is just a film and isn't worth getting people hurt.

One time we rented a helicopter to shoot a commercial in Calgary, and Marc received a radio call from the police while he was in the air. Some people needed rescuing in the Albertan wilderness, so Marc went off to pick them up. He was the best possible candidate for the job, as he had performed similar duties in Vietnam. On top of that, he had also captured 007 in action by working on aerial shots for several James Bond pictures. The people he rescued in Alberta never knew they had the best in the world at their disposal.

Lining up a shot.

Directing commercials was fun and a good source of steady income, but I knew I'd never be satisfied working exclusively on ads and I always had greater ambitions. While I was shooting commercials in the eighties, I was still working as a special-effects supervisor on various projects while keeping my eyes open for opportunities to become a director of episodic television and feature films.

I was spending much of my time in L.A. because that's where the majority of commercial work was at the time, but I came back to Canada in 1983 to supervise the physical effects on a little-seen movie called *The Wars*, which was written by the celebrated playwright and novelist Timothy Findley. The film was shot around the Toronto area and it was nice to be back in Canada again after spending so long south of the border.

In *The Wars*, the main character joins the Canadian army during the Great War to escape his dysfunctional family, and he soon finds himself on the front lines in Europe. Originally, the producers wanted to film the trench warfare sequences outdoors, in the backlot of the studios in Kleinburg, Ontario. Filming these scenes outside would put us at the mercy of the weather, so I asked the art director if he'd be able to duplicate the trenches inside of the studio instead of on the backlot. He was confident that he could, so I spoke to the producer and convinced him to move those scenes indoors.

The art department did an amazing job recreating the trenches inside, which gave us full control of the "weather" for the scenes. If we wanted rain, we turned on the sprinklers. If we wanted dry weather, we didn't need to worry about the fickle skies overhead. It also gave us a greater level of control using our smoke machines without Mother Nature intruding with unwanted gusts of wind. Shooting the battles inside also gave the director and the cinematographer a greater variety of angles to shoot from, as they were now able to hang cameras from the studio grid for more creative and dramatic shots.

It had been years since I'd worked on war films like *Battle of Britain* and *Murphy's War*, so it was fun returning to the battlefield. I got to rig lots of explosions and bullet hits for the trench scenes, which I always enjoyed doing. Working on *The Wars* was a very positive experience and I wish it had reached a wider audience.

About a year later, I worked on another film shot in Ontario - one that was worlds apart in terms of subject matter and tone. *Sesame Street Presents: Follow That Bird* was a musical children's adventure that involved such classic characters as Big Bird, Kermit the Frog and Cookie Monster.

I was originally hired as special-effects director, with my main work on the film involving the creation of a hanging-foreground miniature for

Big Bird's house. However, my duties were extended during production to second-unit directing.

It was surreal working on a film with so many iconic TV characters from *Sesame Street*. Caroll Spinney was a wonderful man and it was amazing to see how he was able to instill so much character into Big Bird once he donned the famous yellow suit. Because his facial expressions couldn't be seen behind the mask, he used his entire body to convey subtleties of mood and emotion.

I didn't have much involvement working on Caroll's scenes, but I was lucky enough to direct a scene with the legendary Bert and Ernie. It was a fascinating experience because I was required to communicate directly with the characters, not the puppeteers hidden underneath. I'd give them direction, the puppets would look at each other and discuss things between themselves, then they would turn back to me and respond. After a while, it was easy to forget the puppeteers even existed and I spoke directly to Bert and Ernie as though it was the most natural thing in the world. My years of directing Barbie served as a good foundation for this unusual experience.

As I continued directing commercials, I also had meetings with producers about possible work as a feature-film director. After working on *Follow That Bird*, I had a meeting in New York with Martha Schumacher, who was married to the legendary Italian producer Dino De Laurentiis. They were gearing up to produce a horror movie called *Maximum Overdrive*, with bestselling novelist Stephen King scheduled to make his directorial debut with the film.

Martha came up with the idea that I co-direct the film with Stephen, who didn't have any experience as a director, and I could help him with my background in special effects. *Maximum Overdrive* was a violent but humorous tale of machines coming to life and trying to exterminate humanity. With scenes involving killer trucks and lawn mowers chasing people, the film would provide many opportunities for fun physical effects.

At Martha's suggestion, I flew to Maine and visited Stephen at his home. I met his family and had a pleasant afternoon visit. He was extremely excited about *Maximum Overdrive* and was eager to discuss the project with me. Unfortunately, it appeared as though Stephen thought I was visiting to be interviewed for the job of special-effects supervisor. We had a nice lunch and talked about the movie, but I purposely didn't mention my discussion with Martha about co-directing.

I flew back to Toronto and never heard from anyone about the movie again. I think he probably found out about the plan for me to co-direct the film and was none too happy about it. Maybe it was for the best that I wasn't involved. It certainly wasn't my intention to steal any of his thunder or to force my way onto a project when I wasn't needed or wanted. At the end of the day, *Maximum Overdrive* was a box-office and critical disaster anyway.

That same year, I was lucky to have said "no" to another project that came my way. Menahem Golan of the Cannon Group called and asked if I'd like to direct second unit on an epic jungle adventure called *King Solomon's Mines*, which was to be their version of Indiana Jones. They sent me the script and I didn't care for it. Everything was so over the top and cartoony.

The film would be shot in Africa and I was hesitant to go there after my challenging experience in the Venezuelan jungle working on *Murphy's War*. On top of that, they weren't prepared to offer much money for my services. The Cannon Group was known for its low-budget exploitation movies and the less-than-great quality of their productions. I'd also heard through the grapevine that it could be hard to get your paycheck from them, so I decided to pass on the project.

It was a good thing too, as *King Solomon's Mines* ended up being a dreadful clone of *Raiders of the Lost Ark* that was crucified by critics. The film was even nominated for two Razzie Awards - Herbert Lom as Worst Supporting Actor and Worst Musical Score by Jerry Goldsmith.

In 1985, I was given the opportunity to direct my first feature-length film, a made-for-TV version of *Pippi Longstocking* for the anthology series *ABC Weekend Specials*. It was one of those wonderful experiences when everyone bonded and had a blast together. The talented cast included Carrie Kei Heim as Pippi, Eric Hebert as Tommy and Alyson Court as Annika. Ossi Rawi's wife Rita Tushingham did me a favour and played the antagonist Mrs. Prysselius, and she was brilliant in the role.

Filming took place around Lake Simcoe in Ontario, which was a beautiful area that served as a perfect backdrop for the story. We didn't have a very big budget and we had to complete shooting in only ten days, but it was a remarkably stress-free experience for me.

Carrie was an extremely capable young performer and she really brought Pippi to life on screen. In one scene, she had to cry because Pippi's father was going to leave. In order to get a heartfelt performance, I asked her to internalize how she'd feel if her pet had just died. On an emotional level, she couldn't relate to the actor pretending to leave, but the thought of losing a beloved pet hit the mark and Carrie gave the scene a wonderful sense of sincerity.

She was also good at improvisation, which was necessary since she was required to act with a monkey. Animals usually add a level of unpredictability to a shoot, and monkeys are even looser cannons than most. Carrie had a wonderful chemistry with the monkey and she made you believe he was her friend.

Concept art for *Pippi Longstocking*. © ABC. From the personal collection of Colin Chilvers.

Joanne A. Curley was a great producer on *Pippi Longstocking* who set a collaborative tone and gave me a lot of creative freedom. Sometimes producers can be aggressive personalities who tend to overpower the director, but Joanne decided to work *with* me and do everything she could to support me.

My art directors Susan Longmire and Marlene Graham did an extraordinary job dressing all the locations with so little money. My cinematographer David Herrington also played a major role in making the film look like it had a much bigger budget than it actually did.

The script required us to locate an old ship for use in the film. Luckily, we found an English gentleman living in Ontario who owned a ship that would suit our purposes perfectly. Joanne warned me that he was a difficult person who might not be open to letting us use it.

I had recently returned from a visit to England, where I'd bought a big rum jug. When we went to meet the gentleman, I took the jug with me and presented it to him as a gift. That softened him up immediately, as did the fact that we were both English. We soon discovered we'd both attended the same art college. Before I knew it, we were like old friends and he was happy to let us do anything we wanted with his ship.

With our short production schedule, we had only one day to shoot at a local fair. On a regular movie shoot, a director can be expected to get through 14 to 20 camera setups a day. We did an insane 47 setups that day.

In order to capture the kinetic atmosphere of the fair, we shot everything handheld instead of locking the camera down on a tripod. Although many directors use handheld camerawork nowadays, it was far less common back in the day. We basically just followed the kids around and tried to capture their sense of excitement. When you watch the film, you can see the wonderful level of raw energy that was captured by the camera, making you feel like you're right there with the kids.

As a director, I've been able to stay within tight schedules because I carefully plan what coverage I'll need and I don't waste a lot of time shooting material I'll never use. Whether it's a commercial or a feature-length film like

Pippi, once I have all of the necessary angles covered and the producers are happy, I don't do more takes just for the sake of it. I keep moving forward so I don't lose momentum.

The cast and crew went out for a nice dinner every night and we enjoyed our time together as friends. There were no egos, power struggles or conflicting visions. It was one of the happiest experiences of my career and I wish I had more like it over the years.

Our hair stylist Sherry Baker won an Emmy for *Pippi* and we were all proud when she was recognized for her outstanding work. Every department was totally dedicated to making *Pipi* the best it could be, for which I am extremely grateful.

Directing brings its own share of headaches, including the potential for politics when working with producers, but I enjoy the challenge of bringing a diverse group of people together to create something from the ground up. Everybody's coming up to you and asking questions because they want to know the director's vision. You'd better have an answer for them, because if you don't tell your people what you want, you ain't gonna get it. Directors must be fairly decisive and opinionated if they want to stay on schedule and within budget.

One of the most important relationships on set for a director is with the cinematographer, or director of photography (DOP). The DOP is responsible for how the film will ultimate look from a photographic perspective, so the director and the DOP must be on the same page at all times. A director can't express his vision fully if the DOP has completely different ideas.

After we worked together so well on *Pippi Longstocking*, I was lucky to work with cameraman David Herrington on a number of projects. We became good friends and we always had a great rapport on set. My arts background helped me to develop my director's eye and I could clearly articulate what I wanted when speaking with David.

After a while, it was almost like he could read my mind. He knew exactly what I'd ask for because he got to know me as a director. At the same time, David wasn't afraid to offer suggestions on how to make a scene work better, which I always appreciated. Even though the director has the final say creatively, it's important for a director to realize that he isn't an expert at everything and he should be open to collaboration with the specialists on his team.

As I continued to work steadily on television commercials, Superman returned to the silver screen in a most regrettable way. In 1987, the film series continued without me when Cannon Films released *Superman IV: The Quest For Peace*. After *Superman III*, the Salkinds licensed the movie rights to Menahem Golan and his partner Yoram Globus. They wanted to elevate Cannon's level of respectability in the industry by producing bigger-budgeted films, and they thought another Superman sequel would be their ticket to the big time.

Unfortunately, their idea of a bigger-budgeted film was still low-budget compared to the three previous Superman adventures and they didn't allocate enough money to produce adequate special effects. Most of the crew from *Superman III* was replaced, myself included. Even though the main cast members of the other Superman films returned for part four, including Christopher Reeve, Gene Hackman and Margot Kidder, audiences stayed away in record numbers and the film flopped upon release.

Over the years, I never had any interest in seeing *Superman IV*. It has a reputation for being one of the worst sequels of all time. Only recently has my writing partner Aaron Lam convinced me to watch some of *Superman IV*. With all due respect to the cast and crew who worked hard on the production, I'm glad I wasn't involved. You can't make a good movie if you don't have the proper resources at your disposal.

Just as *Superman IV* was dooming the film franchise, a unique career opportunity came my way that I never anticipated. I was becoming well known in the industry for directing commercials that involved special effects and children, and this new opportunity would allow me to combine my experience with both. It would take the next two years of my life and give me an opportunity to work with a true legend of pop culture. Some would even call him "the King."

CHAPTER 8
WALKING ON THE MOON WITH THE KING

I've had the opportunity to work with a lot of big names from the world of entertainment, including Peter O'Toole, Alan Arkin, Roger Daltrey, Ringo Starr, Marlon Brando, Gene Hackman, Harrison Ford and Liam Neeson. First and foremost, I see them as artists who are doing a job. I've never been one to become starstruck, probably because I've always been too busy with my own responsibilities to think much about the superstars in front of the camera.

However, there are exceptions to every rule. In my case, the big exception was Michael Jackson. I was in awe of him the first time I met him in 1986 and I'm still in awe of him now that he's passed on. A major highlight of my career was working for two years on the "Smooth Criminal" music video alongside the King of Pop himself. The offer to work with Michael seemed to come out of left field, but that's the story of my life.

I was in Los Angeles directing a television commercial for antifreeze, which required a car to stand on its end and blasts off like a rocket. The special-effects supervisor on the commercial was Kevin Pike, who had been the effects supervisor on *Back to the Future*. Michael wanted to do a music video for "Smooth Criminal" that involved himself transforming into a car, a robot and a spaceship. He didn't have the full story worked out yet, but he knew that his transformations would play a key role in the concept.

Back to the Future had been released the year before and Michael absolutely loved the movie, especially the modified DeLorean that had served as the story's time machine, so he contacted Kevin to discuss working on the music video. After they'd had a few meetings, Kevin asked who was going to direct "Smooth Criminal." It turned out that no director was hired yet. Michael had approached some feature-film directors he admired, but everyone he'd spoken with was already busy with other projects and couldn't start "Smooth Criminal" right away. A lot of the top Hollywood directors can be booked solid for two years in advance.

Kevin then recommended me for the job and he told Michael about the fun we had on the antifreeze commercial. He also told Michael I'd be an ideal candidate because I had lots of experience working with children, which would be valuable because the music video would feature a number of young actors. And it certainly didn't hurt that I'd won an Academy Award for the special effects of *Superman*.

Michael was interested in speaking with me, so a meeting was arranged at his parents' Hayvenhurst mansion. Arriving at the Jackson estate was a memorable but intimidating experience. After being led through the giant gate surrounding the property, the guard walked me to the impressive trophy room, where I was asked to wait for Michael's arrival.

The room was a comfortable lounge with a big fireplace and an elegant settee. Three of the walls were covered with Gold records, plaques and trophy cases. Every conceivable kind of honor and award was on display. Looking back, I think Michael purposely made me wait for him in the trophy room

- it gave me time to peruse his awards and it allowed the magnitude of his accomplishments to sink in before meeting him.

The room was connected to a huge reception area with a grand staircase that led to Michael's quarters. He looked every bit the celebrity when he gracefully descended the stairs, dramatically lit from behind. The man knew how to make a memorable entrance.

Michael was extremely pleasant and quite shy. *I* was the one who was in awe, so I was surprised to discover that he was shy about meeting me. I learned that Michael was tentative around anybody he didn't know well, so he always surrounded himself with people he felt comfortable with and trusted completely.

We talked extensively about our ideas for "Smooth Criminal," and I was delighted that we got along right away. He wanted the music video to resemble a classic gangster movie, so we screened *The Third Man* for reference in his private movie theater. Our overall visions for the video were in sync and we began to jot down the basics of the story.

Michael and me.

Michael and I decided to involve a screenwriter to finesse our ideas into a cohesive whole, so we invited David Newman to fly from New York to discuss the project. I'd already worked with David on the Superman films and I thought he'd be perfect for "Smooth Criminal." Over the next several months, Michael and I worked with David as he drafted a script for the video.

David did his usual great job and we continued to build upon his screenplay, which evolved organically as Michael contributed his impromptu ideas during production.

Originally, "Smooth Criminal" was going to be a music video of regular length, only a few minutes long, but it soon evolved into a longer dramatic film that was designed to feature a performance of the song as its centerpiece. Early in pre-production, we talked to various music-video production companies about the possibility of taking on the project. When the scope of "Smooth Criminal" kept expanding, we changed our approach and decided to put together our own film company.

Producer Dennis Jones came on board, then we hired John Romeyn as production manager. John was a mutual friend of ours who had produced commercials that I'd directed. Michael and I picked a cinematographer that we both admired, John Hora, who had shot many of Joe Dante's films, and I suggested that we hire my friend Mike Ploog as production designer. He was a talented storyboard and comic artist, which Michael loved because he wanted "Smooth Criminal" to look like a comic-book adventure come to life.

Mike was living in England at the time, so we flew him over to Los Angeles and he began designing the monster-sized sets. Betty Madden was hired to design the costumes, many of which were based on clothes worn by Fred Astaire and Cyd Charisse in *The Band Wagon*, which had been a major inspiration for Michael.

It was becoming apparent that making "Smooth Criminal" was going to be epic in scope and would require months to complete, so Colleen and I moved to Los Angeles for production. Michael put us up in a beautiful four-bedroom house in Woodland Hills, complete with orange trees blossoming in the backyard, a swimming pool and lots of room to host fancy parties. I was living the Hollywood dream! We ended up staying there for almost two years until "Smooth Criminal" was completed.

When we moved to L.A., Colleen wasn't going to spend her time moping around the house all day. She knew I'd be spending long hours working and she was determined to make the most of her time too. With a keen interest in antique jewelry, Colleen signed up for courses at the Gemological Institute of America, where she graduated as a gemologist. This helped to keep our marriage healthy because we were both busy pursuing our own interests.

We got a cat and Colleen bought a little car so she could get around while I was working. Some of our friends were already living in L.A., so she could keep an active social life while I was busy. Although Colleen hadn't done a lot of traveling before we became a couple, she was very adaptable and didn't have any problem picking up and moving for months at a time. If she ever felt the need to spend time with family, she could always fly back to Canada for a while. Colleen had a much different temperament than Josie and I didn't have to worry about coming home from a day of shooting to find Colleen stewing about being left alone all day.

One of my key responsibilities during pre-production on "Smooth Criminal" was casting the child actors. Michael suggested using some of his friends' children if possible. I visited Michael Douglas, whose son was the right age to play one of the young leads. After carefully consideration, he decided against having his son involved in the film business at such a young age. He wanted the boy to have a regular childhood away from the pressures of acting.

Michael also suggested talking to Yoko Ono to see if her son Sean Lennon might be a good candidate. I visited them at their Dakota Building apartment in New York and spent a couple of hours discussing the project. Sean was a great kid who was a very natural actor, so we cast him as the suitably named "Sean."

For the role of Zeke, Michael suggested a boy who hung out by the gate of the Jackson mansion on a regular basis. Every time Michael left or arrived at the house, the boy demonstrated his amazing ability to mimic Michael's dancing. We met with the boy, Brandon Adams, who was another natural actor, and we quickly cast him as Zeke. Brandon was so good at mimicking Michael's dance moves that we included a bit of his dancing in "Smooth Criminal."

That left the role of Katie, who was played by the talented Kellie Parker. We arranged a meeting between Michael and Katie, who hit it off right away and had a natural chemistry on screen. Michael found it easier relating to children than adults, probably because he was a big kid at heart.

With Michael during production of "Smooth Criminal." Standing in front of me are the talented Kellie Parker and Brandon Adams.

The child actors all gave strong performances and brought their characters to life. At the beginning of the shoot, however, I did have a little trouble keeping Brandon focused. He didn't have any experience on a film set and he had a tendency to goof around when we needed him to perform. I reminded Brandon that he was there to work, not to play games. We were fine after that and it was great working with him for the duration of production. Years later, I ended up using Brandon again in television commercials I directed.

In casting the bad guy, Mr. Big, we were looking for a performer who could appear devious with black shades, slicked-back hair and a gangster's ensemble. Someone suggested casting our production designer, Mike Ploog, so we held a casting session and dressed him up as Mr. Big. It just didn't work because Mike wasn't an actor, but Michael got a real kick out of seeing our production designer dressed as a supervillain.

Production designer Mike Ploog trying out for the role of Mr. Big. © Warner Bros. From the personal collection of Colin Chilvers.

Frank DiLeo suggested that we cast Joe Pesci, who was a friend of his. Joe was perfect in the role and he was a lot of fun to work with. With his energetic performance, he brought a real sense of danger to the character that was a wonderful contrast to Michael's innocence.

As an in-joke, we added a line in the script to reveal that Mr. Big's real name was "Frankie *LiDeo*," a reference to Michael's manager. Actually, the real Frank could have played the part because he had the right look. Frank looked scarier than Joe Pesci! He was a larger-than-life character who smoked a big cigar like a tycoon from the Golden Age of Hollywood.

Frank and Michael seemed like an odd duo at first glance, but once you saw how well they communicated and worked together, you realized what an amazing team they made. Frank was rightfully protective of Michael, and Michael could trust Frank with anything He was Michael's go-to person if he had any problems.

The sets for "Smooth Criminal" were built at Culver Studios, where *Gone with the Wind* was filmed. Mike designed a spectacular nightclub for the song-and-dance portion of the film that was stunning in its scope and level of detail. It was exciting to see his detailed illustrations become a reality in three dimensions. After production wrapped, I kept a couple of chairs from the nightclub set and they now reside in my dining room.

A maquette of the nightclub set. © Warner Bros.
From the personal collection of Colin Chilvers.

The nightclub sequence required 48 dancers of the highest calibre, as they would be dancing alongside Michael Jackson himself. We held a casting session with choreographer Vince Paterson and more than 3,000 dancers were auditioned. Michael himself worked as choreographer alongside Paterson and assistant choreographer Chester A. Whitmore. Paterson and Whitmore didn't always see eye to eye, which caused occasional tension on set, but Michael always had the final word on everything.

As Michael continued to contribute his ideas during the script's development, the project became increasingly ambitious. Before long, "Smooth Criminal" had evolved into a 40-minute movie with a music video in the middle of it. It was a creatively-charged environment where Michael's imagination was allowed to run wild. At the end of the day, we were all there to bring Michael's vision to fruition because he was the one bankrolling the entire production.

Once the script was fine-tuned to everyone's satisfaction, we began our four weeks of scheduled rehearsal before the start of shooting. I was surprised when Frank called for an emergency meeting only a couple of weeks through the rehearsal period. He told us the start of shooting was being postponed for three months because Michael had to concentrate on finishing his album.

It was a shame to lose all of our momentum, but at least it was Christmas time and we'd all be able to relax for the holidays before returning to the project in the New Year. We held our big Christmas party on the sets that had been constructed so far, then Colleen and I went back to Canada so we could spend time with family.

After Michael finished his album, he turned his attention back to "Smooth Criminal." Michael was fascinated by the idea of having his character transform into a car for the film and he began to look at various models. After considerable research, he became obsessed with a prototype sports car called the Bertone Stratos, which was a sleek and futuristic vehicle like one you'd see in a sci-fi movie. Michael made up his mind - he wanted the Stratos for "Smooth Criminal." Unfortunately, only two of them had ever been constructed and it would be remarkably expensive to acquire one for filming.

I remember having conversations with Frank, who was very much against the idea of wasting so much money to get this specific vehicle. "It's just a car," he'd say, then he'd give me a bunch of books with photos of other sports cars. "Tell Michael he can have any other car. Anything *except* the Stratos."

Each time I'd show pictures of other cars to Michael, he refused to back down and he insisted that we use a Stratos. We did some digging and discovered that the Fiat Museum in Milan had one. The museum allowed us to bring the Stratos to L.A., where the art department used it as a guide to build five prop cars for use in "Smooth Criminal."

At Michael's request, all five of them were outfitted with genuine Porsche engines, which probably cost the production an additional million dollars or so. Once he set his mind on something, he wouldn't stop until he got it, no matter how expensive it was.

A miniature Bertone Stratos is prepared for visual-effects photography. © Warner Bros. From the personal collection of Colin Chilvers.

Michael would often change his mind and ask for things that weren't in the original plans. After reviewing footage we'd shot, he'd think of ways to make things even more spectacular. One of his cinematic heroes was Charlie Chaplin, who would often change his mind at the drop of a hat and ask for numerous reshoots. Chaplin's way of making a movie was to shoot a scene, watch the footage, make notes, shoot it again with modifications, watch it again, make more notes, then shoot it again until he was happy with it. Michael shared Chaplin's philosophy of filmmaking, which was against the Hollywood grain because it was nearly impossible to stay on any sort of schedule or budget.

I had an ongoing disagreement with producer Dennis Jones about this approach to filming. Jones became increasingly frustrated with Michael's endless retakes and his constant stream of expensive new ideas. For example, we had just finished building the full-sized robot for "Smooth Criminal" when Michael saw *RoboCop* at the theatre. Loving what he saw, he asked us to modify our robot so it had giant arm cannons like the character ED-209 from the movie. We had already spent our budget building the robot prop, so altering its appearance at this point would be an unplanned expense.

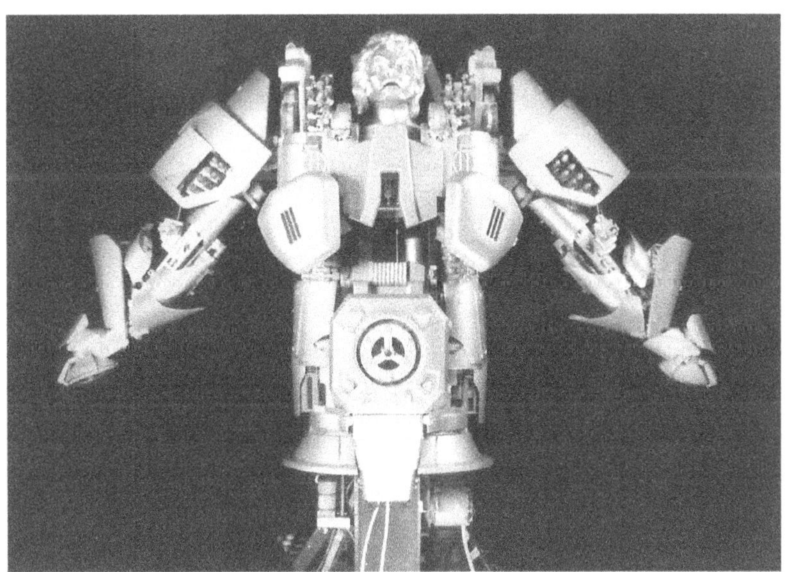

The full-sized robot prop. © Warner Bros. From the personal collection of Colin Chilvers.

After speaking with Michael about updating the robot, I conveyed Michael's notes to Dennis. "Absolutely not," he said. "There's no way we're going to do that." Every time Michael had a flash of inspiration like that, Dennis would put his foot down. He was failing to recognize that "Smooth Criminal" was Michael's baby and the money was ultimately coming from Michael anyway.

Instead of arguing with Dennis, I found a way of working around the problem so Michael could get his way. A week or two later, Michael would ask me how the new cannons on the robot were coming along. I'd tell Michael that he'd need to talk to Dennis about it directly. I knew that Michael avoided conflict whenever possible and he would always go to Frank with his problems.

Then I'd sit back and watch - Michael would talk to Frank, Frank would talk to Dennis, then Dennis would talk to me and say, "You know those cannons Michael wanted? We should get started on those." This ended up happening three or four times with things that Michael wanted but Dennis had kyboshed.

Dennis usually sat right next to me on the set. I'd get up from my chair to speak with the actors or members of the crew before the cameras rolled for each setup. Each time I'd return to my chair, Dennis would make a show of checking his watch. He didn't really need to check the time - it was his passive-aggressive way of letting me know that the clock was ticking and he wanted me to work faster.

Producer Jerry Kramer, who was directing the "making-of" documentary, noticed what Dennis was doing. Jerry walked over to him and said, "When you're working with Michael, you don't need a watch. You need a calendar."

I couldn't understand why Dennis was always on my case. The footage we were getting looked spectacular and Michael was happy with the way things were going. In my opinion, that was all that mattered. I wonder if Frank was putting pressure on Dennis to move things along because he thought Michael was spending too much time, energy and money on the project. Whatever the reason, Dennis clearly wanted to let me know he was in charge. A producer's job is to help the director do his or her job, not vice versa. I think Dennis had it backward in his head. As a director, my job was to help Michael achieve his vision, and I was determined to see it to the end no matter how long it took.

The original song and dance section of "Smooth Criminal" was scheduled for five days, but we ended up shooting for 16 because Michael kept requesting reshoots. We shot with five cameras capturing the action, along with a documentary unit of five cameras shooting behind-the-scenes footage. It took 18 weeks in total to complete principal photography.

In addition to filming at Culver Studios, we also shot scenes on the backlot of 20th Century Studios. The sequence with the dogs chasing Michael was done there, as was the scene involving the car. It felt like a real city because the streets and buildings were so detailed, which helped us get into the mindset of the story.

Directing "Smooth Criminal" at 20th Century Studios. © Warner Bros.
From the personal collection of Colin Chilvers.

Our first evening there, we were just about to start rolling cameras when an anonymous person phoned and claimed to have planted a bomb on the backlot. We had to cancel shooting for the evening while the set was searched. No bomb was ever found, but it was still an unsettling experience. It's unfortunate that some sick people get a kick out of pulling stunts like that.

We filmed for a couple of weeks at night, which can be an adjustment for a cast and crew not accustomed to sleeping during the day and working after dark, but Michael seemed to enjoy the night shoots.

John Hora did a wonderful job lighting the street scenes in dramatic film-noir fashion, with silhouettes and long shadows creating an air of mystery. Michael loved all that stuff. He'd always wanted to be a movie star and "Smooth Criminal" brought him a step closer to his idols from the old days of Hollywood.

Storyboard by Mike Ploog. © Warner Bros. From the personal collection of Colin Chilvers.

Michael has a wonderful entrance at the very beginning of "Smooth Criminal" when we first see the kids on the rooftop looking down at the street. The soft lighting and Bruce Broughton's lovely score bring to mind the magic of classic films like *Peter Pan* and *Mary Poppins*. Michael steps out of his front door, all dressed for an evening on the town. Looking sharp in his fedora and suit, he conveys the aura of a timeless movie star. We purposely made the film ambiguous in terms of its time period because we wanted the story to exist in a fictional universe of its own.

Then all hell breaks loose. Machine guns open up and spray bullets as Michael dives out of harm's way. Kevin Pike supervised the physical effects and he enjoyed blowing away the front of the music store and all of the instruments on display. I didn't want to see Michael getting injured on screen, not only because it would have been upsetting to children watching the film, but also because Michael was supposed to be a magical figure who couldn't be killed with something simple like bullets.

Filming action sequences like this was a dream come true for Michael, who was like a kid in a candy store. He was fascinated by the filmmaking process and he loved to see how bullet hits and pyrotechnics were achieved by the special-effects crew.

Seeing the musical instruments being blasted to pieces by machine-gun fire made a powerful statement in itself. It was meant to represent the death of music, creativity and childhood innocence, all of which Michael came to represent to his legions of fans around the world.

Storyboard for an unused opening that would have shown Michael in action with a machine gun. © Warner Bros. From the personal collection of Colin Chilvers.

We wanted Mr. Big's troopers to be completely devoid of personality, like brainless drones at the command of a single evil mind. It was Michael's suggestion that we focus on the technology used by the soldiers to further dehumanize them. The close-ups of the gun muzzles flashing and the bullet casings falling to the ground emphasized the troopers' unquestioning and mechanical adherence to duty.

In casting Mr. Big's troopers, I chose guys from the L.A. Reserve Officers' Training Corps who were training to be in the military. The producers thought I could use untrained extras because we wouldn't see any of their faces behind the masks, but I wanted people with a military background. I think my decision paid off - the ROTC guys had a crispness to their movements from learning how to march and they felt comfortable with their prop weapons.

The flashback scene of Michael and the kids running across the field was shot at Disney Ranch. We had to clear out some rattlesnakes before the cameras rolled, but filming went without a hitch. John did a great job of creating a joyous, dream-like quality to the scene that was drastically different from the film-noir look he achieved on the street sets.

Michael posing with the "Smooth Criminal" title created with bullet holes. © Warner Bros. From the personal collection of Colin Chilvers.

Scenes were also filmed at Rocketdyne, which was a facility where they used to test rockets and engines for NASA. The building wasn't being used at the time, so it served as a shooting location for Mr. Big's bunker. The cold, industrial look of Rocketdyne worked perfectly for the sequence and it ended up saving money because we didn't need to construct a set.

The centerpiece of "Smooth Criminal" is the song-and-dance number in the nightclub that serves as the music video for Michael's song. During shooting, we played the song through these enormous speakers that shook the whole soundstage. During a break one day, Michael asked me if we could get even bigger speakers for the following day's shoot. He liked the music playback to be extremely loud, with bass so heavy that it would shake his internal organs. Michael wanted to *feel* the music reverberating through his entire body.

Michael "feeling" the music. © Warner Bros. From the personal collection of Colin Chilvers.

Part of the dance sequence required Michael to defy gravity by leaning forward at an unnaturally steep angle. For that effect, we came up with the idea of specially designed shoes that had a slot in each heel. Pins were built into the floor that fit into the slots, which allowed Michael to lean forward without fear of falling over. After returning to his normal standing position, he slid his feet backward, which unlocked the shoes from the pins and allowed him to dance freely. Wires were also used, but only for extra safety. Michael went on to patent this design and use it for his stage shows.

At one point during the shoot, Paul Simon was in town performing with Ladysmith Black Mambazo, an amazing male choral group from South Africa. Michael and I went to see them perform with a bunch of the crew from "Smooth Criminal." After the show, Michael suggested using Ladysmith Black Mambazo in the video, which was a great idea.

I told Michael about something we used to call a "happening" in England, which was a completely unrehearsed setup with the cameras rolling, during which anything could happen. I thought it would be fun to have the guys from Ladysmith Black Mambazo make a surprise appearance on the set of "Smooth Criminal" as we rolled. Michael agreed and he talked to Ladysmith Black Mambazo, who immediately agreed to be a part of it. In fact, they had written a song for Michael called "The Moon is Walking," which they wanted to perform on set.

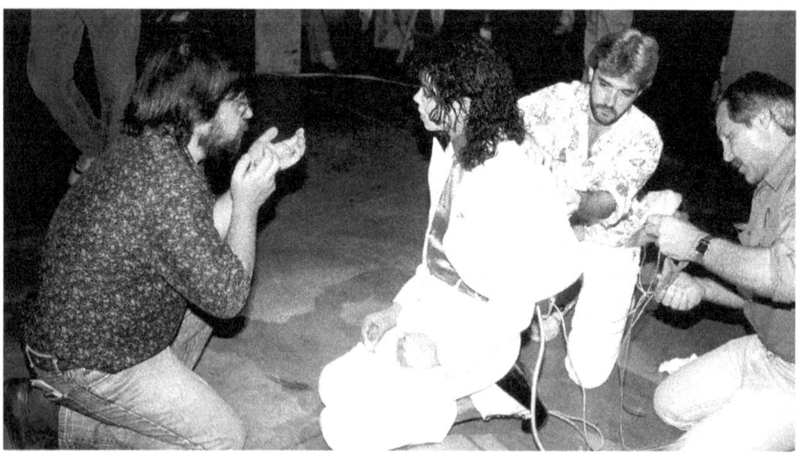

Directing Michael on the nightclub set. © Warner Bros.
From the personal collection of Colin Chilvers.

It was decided to let only a few select people on set know what was going to happen. Other than myself and Michael, only the camera operator, the assistant director and the wardrobe department were in on the secret.

We outfit Ladysmith Black Mambazo in 1940s gangster clothes and had them wait just outside the set as we prepared to start shooting. On cue, they entered through the doors and started singing. Before long, tears were flowing freely because it was so beautiful. The guys from Ladysmith Black Mambazo were so nice, and I have to thank them for one of the most memorable moments from my experience on "Smooth Criminal." Because their performance was totally out of context with the rest of the film, we ended up using their song under the end credits.

One day, Michael came up with an idea for the song-and-dance sequence that wasn't in the script. Partway through the song, he wanted the windows of the nightclub to implode, showering glass all over the dancers. Everyone would enter a trance-like state and the music would end abruptly. The performers would softly chant, "Annie, are you okay?" over and over again, slowly building in speed and volume. Eventually, the music would resume and the sequence would continue at its regular pace.

Michael asked to do this sequence as improv without any rehearsal, wanting to see what would happen if the performers were allowed to follow their instincts with the cameras rolling. We talked about the general concept before filming, but we had no idea how long the sequence would go or exactly what Michael was going to do. I asked John to stagger all five cameras slightly just to be safe. This way, if one of them ran out of film, it could be reloaded as the other four continued rolling. The performers were rigged with wireless microphones so even the softest of their chanting would be recorded. We wanted to capture the moment in only one take.

We shot thousands of feet of film, but I think it was worth it. With John's haunting cinematography and the almost animalistic performances of the dancers, the sequence is like a surrealist's bad dream. To this day, I still don't know what the sequence actually means, but it sure is cool.

When we were shooting the song-and-dance sequence at Culver Studios, the entire cast and crew would take lunch in the theatre and watch dailies from the previous day's shooting. It was like a big party with lots of whooping and hollering, and it got everybody jazzed about shooting again after lunch. The energy was wonderful and the enthusiasm generated at the dailies was contagious.

Then one day, the producers decided to put an end to it. They thought the crew was taking too long to calm down and concentrate on work after the dailies. Only myself, Michael and John were allowed to attend after that. I thought it was a shame because sharing the dailies generated so much positive energy and goodwill. We would get 200 percent out of everyone after a lunchtime screening. Preventing the rest of the cast and crew from participating only served to deflate people's spirits.

As the villain, Joe Pesci took his role extremely seriously. Toward the end of the film, Mr. Big had to push Katie around as Michael was held back by some of the villain's henchmen. While we filmed Michael's close-ups, Joe stood behind the camera and started to shout some really rude things, swearing and insulting Michael to get him all wound up. You can see in the final film that Michael was getting genuinely upset and the goons were struggling to keep him from getting his hands on Joe. Michael appreciated it at the end of the day because Joe had gotten the best possible performance out of him.

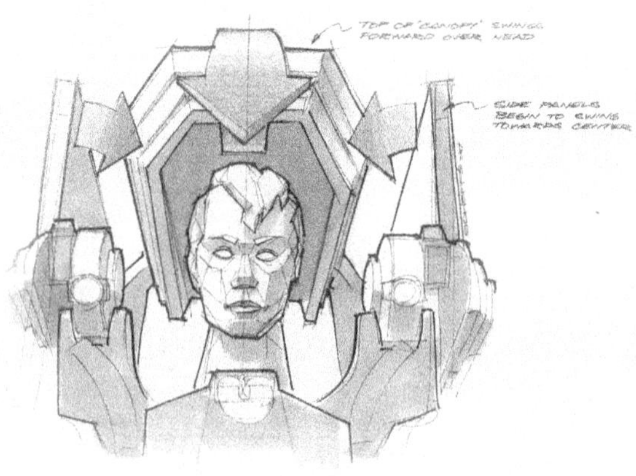

Concept art showing how Michael transforms into a robot. © Warner Bros.
From the personal collection of Colin Chilvers.

We had a top-notch team of effects artists working on "Smooth Criminal." The climax of the film called for Michael to transform into a robot and a spaceship. Dream Quest Images used impressive miniatures and state-of-the-art computer animation to achieve these effects, the likes of which had never been seen before in a music video. Shortly afterward, the wizards at Dream Quest Images went on to win an Academy Award for their work on James Cameron's underwater epic *The Abyss*.

At the finale of "Smooth Criminal," Mr. Big temporarily gains the upper hand when he shoots down Michael's spaceship using an enormous laser cannon. His victory is short-lived, however, as the ship strikes back with a laser weapon of its own. Pyrotechnics expert Joe Viskocil was brought on board to destroy a detailed model of the cannon. Joe was absolutely brilliant at blowing up miniatures and he did a great job giving "Smooth Criminal" an explosive climax. He went on to destroy miniatures of the Empire State Building and the White House for *Independence Day*.

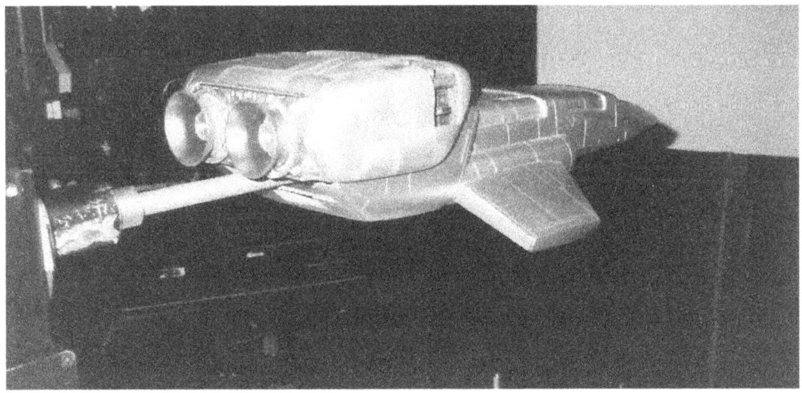

Preparing the miniature spaceship for photography. © Warner Bros.
From the personal collection of Colin Chilvers.

Michael was closely involved with all aspects of the production to ensure that everything met with his satisfaction. We assembled rough edits of the footage as we went along, which helped us decide what needed reshooting and what new material could elevate the film to the next level.

Ready for liftoff. © Warner Bros. From the personal collection of Colin Chilvers.

We worked very well together and never found ourselves fighting over creative control of the project. He had chosen me to direct "Smooth Criminal" because of my past experience and technical expertise, but I was ultimately hired to help Michael bring *his* vision to life. It was a fruitful and enjoyable collaboration, and I felt privileged to work so closely with such a legend. He was always bursting with creative energy, which proved contagious and gave everyone the passion needed to see this two-year odyssey to its end.

If Michael wasn't so consumed with his career as a musical entertainer, I think he would have pursued a career as a filmmaker. He'd spent a fortune on top-of-the-line Panavision film cameras, lenses and equipment so he could dabble in his filmmaking passion. Unfortunately, he never had an opportunity to develop as a filmmaker and share that talent with the world.

I spent a lot of time with Michael outside of the set and eventually broke past his shy exterior. If you put him in an amphitheater with thousands of people and cranked up the music, he was completely fearless. However, he was remarkably introverted when it came to one-on-one interactions, especially with people he didn't know.

"People tend to stare at me and they don't know what to say," he told me. "That makes me really uncomfortable."

I explained how I could relate to his shyness. When starting out in the film business, I was extremely self-conscious about my young appearance. I didn't think anyone would take me seriously, so I grew a beard when I was 24 and I've kept it ever since. He laughed and told me that George Lucas had related a similar story to him.

Michael often appeared in public with a surgical mask covering his mouth. Many people thought he used the mask because he was a germophobe, but he actually used it for a sense of security. It gave him something to hide behind when facing the world.

On one occasion, I was scheduled to meet with Michael and some of the special-effects guys at his house to discuss the production. I arrived about twenty minutes early to talk about various things and we met in the trophy room as usual. Since he'd become quite comfortable working with me, he was casual and we joked around while we chatted. Then the front gate called to let him know that the effects guys had arrived and would be escorted to the house. Michael's demeanour changed immediately. He became the shy Michael Jackson.

The trophy room was lit dramatically with splashes of light punctuating trophy cases and awards. On both sides of the fireplace were these fairly dark recesses where he could stand and feel more secure. When the effects guys arrived, Michael was wearing his mask and he had retreated into one of those dark alcoves to greet them from a position of safety. It wasn't that Michael was trying to be rude; he was just being tentative because he didn't know them.

I came to think of Michael as Peter Pan because he was an eternal child. He got along well with children because he could identify with them so well. Years later, when allegations of child molestation came up in the press, I found them difficult to believe. Michael just wasn't that kind of person.

He'd led an extremely sheltered existence since he was young and nobody ever said "no" to him, so he didn't grow into "normal" adulthood like everyone else. Even as an adult, he was like a child who lived in a fantasy land, only the toys had gotten more expensive. Now he could afford the most expensive mansions, sports cars and fine art. Anything he wanted was just a phone call away.

We would go to an expensive bookstore in Santa Monica that specialized in art books. They closed to the public at 6:00 but would stay open afterward specifically for us. We'd wander around the store for an hour and Michael would buy an enormous pile of books worth thousands of dollars. Then the store would pack them all up and ship them later.

Fine art was a particular passion for Michael. Priceless paintings filled his house, including an original Maxfield Parrish work that hung on his wall. I love art myself, so it was amazing to see his personal collection. It was like visiting an art gallery. Spectacular sculptures of children were everywhere, which reflected his desire to stay childlike even into adulthood.

Colleen joined us at the mansion a few times, and it was surreal having dinner with Michael at a 15-foot-long table in a giant dining room with opulent chandeliers hanging overhead. His pet monkey Bubbles also joined us for dinner and provided an extra level of surrealism. Just another day in the life of Michael Jackson.

I found Michael to be a charming, funny guy who liked to joke around. With all of his eccentricities, he was really just a normal guy underneath. It was interesting to see a side of him usually seen only by his inner circle. Michael tried to teach me to dance one time, which was a complete flop. When he saw how uncoordinated I was, he gave up pretty quickly. Although Michael made it look so easy, his level of skill came from countless hours of hard work perfecting his craft since childhood.

He had a private space above one of the garages where he could practice dancing and work on choreography. It was like a little museum with a lot of his iconic clothing on display, including several different suits he'd worn over the years and his famed white glove. In the middle of the room was a dance floor and a mirror so he could watch himself practice.

While Michael was genuinely young at heart, he was also an extremely smart guy, especially when it came to marketing himself. He knew exactly how to run his business. In fact, Michael *was* his business and he was in complete control of how he presented himself to the public.

When I first started working on "Smooth Criminal," the *Bad* album hadn't been released yet. The press was on fire because someone had reportedly stolen tapes from Michael that included songs from *Bad*. These were sold to some disc jockeys, who proceeded to play them on the radio before the album's official release date. It was reported that Michael was furious about the leaked songs and he was threatening to sue. In reality, it was a publicity stunt dreamed up by Michael himself to generate interest in the upcoming release of *Bad*, and it worked like a charm.

Editing "Smooth Criminal" took a lot longer to complete than the actual shooting. Michael was heavily involved in post-production and he requested change after change until he felt we'd done the best possible job in the editing room. Our final edit was over 40 minutes long, which captured the epic quality we were aiming for without bogging down the story.

The music of Michael Jackson was at the heart of the film, but composer Bruce Broughton also played a crucial role in the success of "Smooth Criminal" by writing a large-scale symphonic score for the scenes outside of the nightclub. It was exciting to attend the scoring sessions and watch him conduct a huge orchestra as the film was projected onto a large screen. Bruce is a classically trained film composer like John Williams who can punctuate every subtle moment on screen and create sheer magic with his music. We were lucky to have such a talented artist to add that finishing touch.

"Smooth Criminal" was the grand finale of a compilation film called *Moonwalker*, which featured other short films that explored different aspects of the Michael Jackson mythos. *Moonwalker* was born out of the realization that "Smooth Criminal" was too short to be released as a feature film. It was only about 40 minutes long, but we would have a full theatrical feature if we added another 45 minutes of content.

Originally, Michael wanted the film to be much shorter so he could submit it to the Academy of Motion Picture Arts and Sciences for consideration as Best Short Film. He eventually abandoned that plan when the scope of the film kept growing. Besides, "Smooth Criminal" wasn't the sort of film that generally wins an Oscar. First and foremost, it was an extended music video to showcase Michael's talents.

Moonwalker featured a number of charming segments from other directors, including a parody of Michael's music video for "Bad" with all of the roles played by children. It was only natural that the younger version of Michael should be portrayed by Brandon Adams, since he could do such a good impersonation of Michael's dancing. Other sequences featured humorous Claymation by Will Vinton, experimental collages of Michael's stage performances and 2D cut-out animation. The film ends with Michael performing the Beatles song "Come Together" on stage as the kids from "Smooth Criminal" cheer from offstage.

Michael was traveling the world on his *Bad* tour in October of 1988, so it was the perfect time for the release of *Moonwalker* in theaters. The film was released theatrically in Europe and South America, where it did exceptionally well at the box office. I was looking forward to the planned release of *Moonwalker* in North-American theaters that Christmas. Having directed the biggest segment of such a high-profile project, it could only help my career as a director. My hope was to start directing feature films, so Christmas 1988 would be extremely important to me professionally.

Then it fell apart. Warner Bros. suddenly canceled the theatrical release of *Moonwalker* in North America, where it was released straight to video instead. I was disappointed to say the least. After two years on the project, it wouldn't be shown in a single North-American theater.

Especially during the eighties, projects with the "straight-to-video" label lacked the prestige and credibility of films that were released theatrically. Quite often straight-to-video fare wasn't of sufficient quality to be shown on the big screen, but that certainly wasn't the case with *Moonwalker* or "Smooth Criminal."

To this day, I don't know exactly why the theatrical release was canceled, but I've heard a few different theories. One rumour was that Michael and Frank were putting together a deal with CAA (Creative Artists Agency),

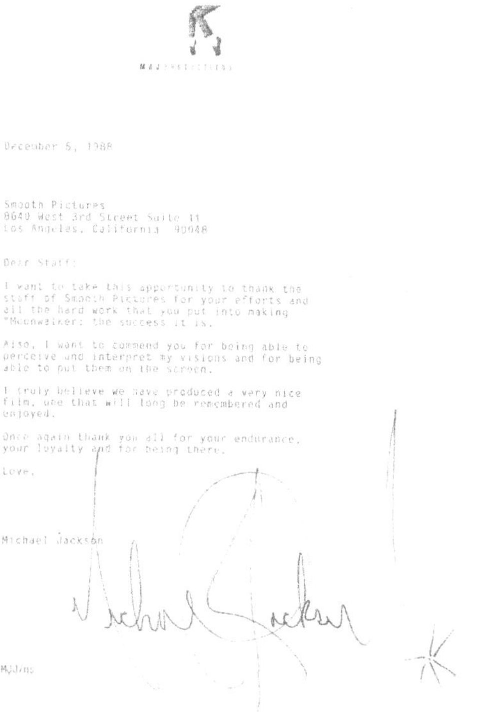

A thank-you letter from Michael Jackson.

which wanted to be the driving force behind Michael's first foray into motion pictures as a leading man. Recognizing Michael's ability to market himself, CAA thought the King of Pop had a good chance of making it big as an actor, and they were keen on introducing "movie-star Michael" to the public at large.

The rumour goes on to say that *Moonwalker* was released straight-to-video in Canada and the States to avoid upsetting such an influential agency. I have no idea if there's any truth to the story, but that's what I've heard. Ultimately though, Michael never did break through as a movie star.

I'd also heard the story that Warner Bros. simply couldn't find a suitable time to release *Moonwalker* in their schedule, which I have a hard time believing. They obviously had a lot at stake with the film, and I don't understand why they couldn't have found a time to release it theatrically in North America after being so successful in other parts of the world.

At least the video release did very well and stayed at the top of the sales charts. Even to this day, *Moonwalker* has quite a cult following because it was so ambitious. "Smooth Criminal" remains one of Michael's most memorable performances, which says a lot when you consider how many memorable performances that man had in his career. It was also satisfying to see "Smooth Criminal" win a Brit Award for Best Music Video.

Because *Moonwalker* never hit theaters in North America, my directing career didn't receive the boost I was hoping for. However, I did get my name out there by doing a lot of press interviews on both sides of the Atlantic, which helped my name become known in the industry. All during production, I had to be fairly hush-hush about what I was doing, and it was great to finally talk openly about my two-year journey with Michael Jackson.

Theatrical release or not, just being associated with a superstar like Michael was a great boost to my career. Thanks to this experience, I went on to direct movies for television and episodes of various TV series.

I remember visiting Dick Donner in L.A. while shooting "Smooth Criminal." We started talking about *The Goonies*, a film he'd directed a couple of years earlier. A sequel was being considered, and I was flattered when he said I'd be a good candidate to direct part two. Unfortunately, nothing came of it and the world has yet to see a second adventure of the Goonies.

Michael and I never kept in touch after our experience on "Smooth Criminal." He wasn't the kind of person to keep in contact unless you were working together. I think you could have counted his intimate friends on one hand because he valued his privacy so much. He'd even change his personal assistant every several months because he didn't want people to know too much about him or his business. I don't know if that was his personal decision or if it was advice he was given, but he was a very cautious person that way. His phone numbers would change every once in a while too. He even parted ways with Frank DiLeo for a while and went with a new manager.

It would have been interesting to see Neverland Ranch after he moved there in 1988, but that was after we lost contact. Years later, I contacted his office to get a print of *Moonwalker*, but I never communicated with Michael directly. We never spoke again after we finished working together. Such was the reality of working with the King of Pop.

Michael's death was shocking and tragic. He was such a talented person on so many levels - as a singer, dancer and businessman. After facing so much negative press for his eccentricities and allegations of inappropriate behavior with children, he was set to make his big comeback and was just about the embark on his new tour. Buzz was in the air, and whether you were a fan of Michael's eccentricities or not, the collective anticipation was undeniable.

Then he passed away. Such a sudden end to one of the great artists of our time. Even though I hadn't been in contact with Michael for several years, his passing was still very upsetting to me. The world would never have the opportunity to enjoy a new Michael Jackson song, and I would never have the opportunity to share another laugh with him. I ended up naming one of my beloved cats "MJ" in his honour.

In 2012, I received a phone call from filmmaker Spike Lee, who had directed the Michael Jackson video for "This is It." He was directing a documentary called *Bad 25* to celebrate the 25th anniversary of the album's release, and he wanted to interview me on camera for the film. I flew down to New York and visited his studio in Brooklyn. We sat down for a nice lunch before we began the interview. Spike was very pleasant and articulate, and it was obvious he was in complete awe of Michael. Making *Bad 25* was clearly something Spike was doing out of passion.

For about an hour and a half, we talked about how I first met Michael, our creative process working together and our two-year experience on "Smooth Criminal." It stirred up a lot of memories and it brought back the sadness of Michael's passing, but it also brought back my sense of pride about the work we did together.

The legend of Michael Jackson will live on forever, and I feel extremely fortunate to have joined him for a small part of his extraordinary journey.

CHAPTER 9
HEROES OF A NEW AGE

Although I was disappointed about *Moonwalker's* lack of a theatrical release, I was grateful that my involvement with the film still raised awareness of my name within Hollywood circles. A producer from New York named John Williams (not to be confused with the Oscar-winning film composer) called and told me how much he'd enjoyed "Smooth Criminal."

He was putting together a musical feature film called *Stagger Lee* that took place in New Orleans during Mardi Gras, and it had a film-noir tone similar to "Smooth Criminal." I thought it sounded great and I could see how it would make a compelling motion picture, so we teamed up and began to shop the project around.

I had a meeting with New Line Cinema, the studio we were hoping would back *Stagger Lee*. Unfortunately, the producers at New Line decided not to proceed with production of the film, but because I had such a background in both directing and special effects, they asked if I would read the script for *A Nightmare on Elm Street 4* and give my comments. They were considering me as a potential director for the latest Freddy Krueger movie.

I went away, read the script, then had another meeting at New Line. Unfortunately, I didn't like the script at all and I didn't hesitate to tell them. The producers said they wanted my notes on the script, so that's what I gave them. For example, one of the gorgeous teenage girls was supposed to be playing pool when Freddy appeared out of nowhere and turned her into minced meat. The scene didn't have much drama and I didn't think the pool hall made a very scary place for the murder.

As an alternative, I suggested that the scene take place in the girl's apartment basement when she goes down to do laundry. I thought it would work better because more people could relate to the experience of going into a dark and sinister basement. Unfortunately, the producers at New Line didn't agree with me. They also didn't appreciate my honesty - especially one of the producers at the meeting. He had also written the script and didn't like my criticism. The job went to another director.

I did however get hired by Paramount Television to direct the two-hour premiere of the *War of the Worlds* TV series in 1988. To keep the budget down and to take advantage of tax incentives, the show was shot in Toronto with a Canadian crew. The series was conceived by producer Greg Strangis, whose father Sam Strangis was executive producer.

The premiere episode, called "The Resurrection," continues the story of the Martian invasion as told in the 1953 *War of the Worlds* movie produced by George Pal. The alien invaders are awakened from their decades-long hibernation and attempt to conquer the world again, this time by taking over human bodies.

It was fun bringing back the manta-like Martian war machines from George Pal's film to create a sense of continuity. I was very pleased with how the finale of the premiere turned out, with the war machines blasting their way free from a government warehouse. We filmed the sequence at a garbage dump in Pickering, Ontario, where the spaceships pursue our heroes and use their heat rays to incinerate everything in sight. Having such a large-scale action sequence in the premiere started the series on a great note.

Martin Malivoire did a nice job on the practical effects. With our combined experience working on feature films, we were able to create this spectacular finale with our limited budget and resources. We wanted to make the sequence feel more like something from a big-budget feature film than a made-for-TV pilot, and I think we succeeded for the most part.

I directed another two episodes of the show during its first season. Although I was always under the gun to shoot as quickly as possible, which is a common story when it comes to episodic television, I tried not to compromise in terms of quality because my name would ultimately end up on screen as the director.

The producers weren't looking for artistic flourish - they were looking for a director who could deliver within the allotted schedule and budget. I like to take the time necessary to set up each shot as effectively as possible, adding camera movement whenever possible and setting my dialogue scenes against visually interesting backgrounds. This didn't always go over well with the producers, who were always watching the clock.

"Why are you spending so much time setting up your shots?" Sam would ask me. "It's just a dialogue scene. Just put the actors up against a brick wall and get it over with."

I didn't agree with that approach to filming, which is a major reason why I didn't find it particularly satisfying to direct episodic television. For me, just sticking the camera on a tripod and filming actors against a brick wall is the most boring and creatively stifling thing you can do as a director. It felt like my hands were always tied and very little of my artistic vision was allowed to find itself onto the screen.

As a result of our conflicting views, Sam and I tended to bump heads. I certainly respected where he was coming from as producer. Staying within budget and keeping on schedule were always priorities. However, I felt that some level of artistic directorial vision needed to guide filming if the series was to sustain itself in the long run. In episodic television, the director doesn't have as much control as a director of feature films. Producers hold a lot more power on a series and episodic directors are more like glorified assistant directors.

Early during the production of the premiere, Sam and I had a major disagreement over how I'd directed a scene. I was lucky enough to have a talented cast at my disposal and I wanted to take advantage of their acting abilities. The scene involved an argument between the characters played by Richard Chaves and Jared Martin at a toxic-waste facility. When the actors performed the scene, they really got into it and I loved what they were doing. They had a lot of passion and I thought the scene played out realistically. After all, when the future of humankind is at stake, people are going to take an argument very seriously.

The next day, Sam called me into his office after having seen the dailies. Before I knew it, Sam was tearing a strip out of me because he didn't like the way the scene had turned out. He thought it should have been played with more restraint and I was being held responsible for "ruining" the scene.

In the middle of our meeting, Sam's son Greg called. Sam picked up the phone, spoke to Greg, then handed the phone over to me.

"It's Greg and he wants to speak with you."

I was expecting to be the recipient of more yelling over the phone.

"I just saw the scene you directed," Greg said. "Wow! That was great! It was perfect."

I handed the phone back to Sam. "Talk to Greg," I said. "You guys need to work this out between yourselves."

Although we'd started off on the wrong foot, Sam ended up being happy with my overall work on the series. Television production is stressful enough as it is, so I was always happy to avoid confrontation whenever possible.

By the time I directed my second episode of *War of the Worlds*, it was apparent that the series was quickly running out of ideas. How many ways can you have Martians kill people and take over their bodies? The scripts were already feeling uninspired. With audience interest in the series waning by the end of the first season, the second season was completely revamped so it took place in a post-apocalyptic future, by which time the Martians had succeeded in destroying much of earth.

I wasn't involved with the second season, but I wasn't surprised when it didn't catch on with audiences and it brought the series to an end. *War of the Worlds* never became popular in North America, but it fared much better in Europe, especially Germany for some reason.

More than two decades later, a gentleman would approach me at Niagara Falls Comic Con and tell me how much he loved the series. I was happy to sign his rare *War of the Worlds* press kit and it was gratifying for me to know that my work on the series had been appreciated. He told me about how the series has since gone on to become a "cult favourite."

I was briefly involved with another TV series shot in Toronto that has become a cult classic, mainly for its ambitious special effects and the popular toy line that inspired it. *Captain Power and the Soldiers of the Future* was unique in how it involved viewers as active participants. Kids could buy a battery-operated spaceship and aim it like a gun at the TV set. Whenever they hit one of the bad guys, the toy registered a point and kept a running score.

Douglas Netter was a producer on *Captain Power* who was concerned about how long it was taking to create the special effects for each episode. He had to find a way to save money if the series was to continue production. Knowing about my background in special effects, he asked if I would come in for a couple of weeks to study how they were creating their effects and then provide feedback on how to improve efficiency and lower costs.

My time on *Captain Power* wasn't very long, but it was exhaustive. I studied their methods of working and I prepared a detailed report on how they could streamline their processes. The production team of *Captain Power* wasn't receptive to my presence at all, probably because of my association with Douglas, who they saw as the hatchet man. The truth of the matter was that Douglas was trying to save the show, but our efforts resulted in defensive pushback.

Ultimately, none of my recommendations were implemented and the show discontinued production soon after. I honestly wasn't trying to step on anyone's toes or take over the production for myself, but nobody other than Douglas really wanted to hear what I had to say. Implementing my recommendations might not have saved the show, but it's impossible to know for sure either way.

Shortly afterward, another opportunity to direct episodic television came my way from an old friend. I received a phone call from Bob Simmonds, who was the production manager on *Superman*. Ilya Salkind was gearing up to produce a new half-hour Superboy television series and I was being considered to direct some of the episodes.

Bob dropped by the house to discuss *Superboy*, and it was nice to get caught up after so many years. He explained how the Salkinds had kept the film rights to the character Superboy, who was legally considered a different character than Superman. The film rights to the Man of Steel still resided with the Cannon Group, the production company behind *Superman IV: The Quest For Peace*.

Ilya thought he could update the legend of Kal-El for the small screen and introduce the character to a whole new audience. Bob thought I might be a good choice to direct episodes of the new series because I was comfortable working with both actors and special effects. Wanting to gain further directing experience with the hope of graduating to feature films, I agreed to come aboard for *Superboy*.

Although it wasn't technically a "Superman" series, working on *Superboy* still felt like a family reunion after having left the Man of Steel behind me when *Superman III* wrapped. In addition to working with Bob Simmonds again, I was reunited with Bob Harman, the harness and wire-flying specialist who had made Christopher Reeve take flight for the feature films.

I was one of a few different directors who helmed episodes of *Superboy* in rotation. In total, I directed five episodes of the series with actor John Haymes Newton in the lead role and actress Stacey Haiduk as Lana Lang.

On the set of *Superboy* with actress Stacey Haiduk.

Superboy suffered from extreme budget limitations, which meant we had to rush through the production of each episode and the special effects never managed to be that "special" at all. One of the episodes I directed required the construction of a spaceship's interior, but because we had no money at all, we were forced to go with a "minimalist" approach and just slap up pieces of black polythene sheeting. We always made the best of it and trudged onward. This was a far cry from the mega-budget days of Dick Donner's *Superman*.

Despite limitations of time and budget, directing *Superboy* was still an enjoyable experience. It was nice filming in Florida and we had a good cast and crew, even if they weren't given much to work with in terms of scripts. John Haymes Newton was a good kid, but he was replaced by actor Gerard Christopher for the remaining seasons.

I never returned to direct more episodes after the first year, which I don't regret. However, it's unfortunate that the five episodes I directed with John in the leading role were never rerun after the part was recast.

Apparently, *Superboy* has gone on to become another cult favorite. Maybe I should start marketing myself as the guy who works on projects that are destined to become cult favorites!

The late eighties were an eclectic time for me as a director. In addition to my TV work, I also had the opportunity to direct a couple of big-budget music videos. One was for the song "Too Much" by Bros, a popular band formed by twin brothers Matt and Luke Goss. It was nice being given a little more artistic freedom than I had with episodic television. The record label was open to my ideas as long as 60 percent of the music video consisted of performance, with the remaining 40 percent being story or concept.

The brothers were great to work with and I appreciated their collaborative nature. Matt was the lead vocalist and Luke was the drummer, and they were somewhat competitive in nature. Because they wanted equal billing, I had to be sure that both of them received equal screen time in the final edit.

Matt and Luke loved "Smooth Criminal" and they were keen to work with me because of my history with Michael Jackson. I came up with a concept for "Too Much" that involved the brothers romancing a beautiful young lady atop spectacular oceanside cliffs. They liked the idea and we began to search for shooting locations.

When I suggested filming in England, they asked if I would mind filming in the south of France instead because they were recording their latest album in Provence. I had such a wonderful time in the south of France while filming *Condorman*, so I quickly agreed.

A French location manager joined me for scouting along the Mediterranean coast and we spotted a beautiful lookout with dramatic cliffs near Nice. It was perfect for the video.

"You'll never get permission to shoot there," said the location manager.

"Why not?" I asked.

"A rich couple owns the land and they're very private. They'll never give you permission."

We couldn't find a better location after a week of scouting, so the location manager reluctantly arranged a meeting with the couple at their villa. I brought my Academy Award along to help establish my credibility. It never hurts to bring Oscar with me at times like this.

A gentleman answered the door, and he walked us down to his private beach where his wife was working on her tan. She was about 30 years old, gorgeous, and completely nude. Trying to have a conversation with her as she faced us in the buff was awkward and distracting, but they ended up being extremely pleasant and they agreed to let us film there. It was the easiest "negotiation" I'd ever been a part of. We shot in their villa, flew a helicopter all around their property and scaled their seaside cliffs. I couldn't have asked for a better shooting location. It never hurts to ask.

Working once again with helicopter pilot Marc Wolff, we captured some spectacular aerial shots of the brothers walking along the cliffs and driving along winding roads in a Porsche. The aerial footage really captured the beauty of the French countryside and added an epic quality to the video that we couldn't have achieved without Marc's expertise.

The final shots of the video show one of the brothers kissing the young lady on a cliff top as the sun sets behind them. We ended up shooting at dawn instead of dusk because we were able to get a better shot in the direction of the rising sun.

For the actual musical performance in the video, my location manager recommended an abandoned casino along the waterfront in Nice. Reportedly, the people who ran the casino didn't keep up their payments to the mafia, so enforcers were sent in to close down and trash the place. The casino never reopened and it had been sitting empty for years.

The building was enormous and it would have been beautiful in its day, with its ornately decorated lobby and classy furniture, but that was in the past now. All the tables were overturned and refuse was scattered about. Nobody had bothered to clean up. It looked like the owners just locked the doors and walked away after the place was trashed.

A huge staircase was the centerpiece of the lobby, which we put to good use in a couple of shots. I posed the brothers in silhouette at the top of the stairs for their big introduction at the beginning of the video, and we also had hordes of teen fans rush down the stairs toward the camera.

After getting to know the brothers on a social level, I learned that Luke sometimes felt left out because his brother Matt tended to get more attention as the lead singer. I told Luke my idea for making his drumming more dramatic on screen, which in turn would make his appearance more memorable. The idea was to cover the tops of his drums with water, which would spray when he pounded away with his sticks. Luke was all for that because it would help put him in the spotlight. The splashing looked fantastic when backlit and it added a great deal of kinetic energy to the performance.

Colleen joined me for the shoot in France and it was nice that she could join us for dinners in the evening. Being the south of France, we always had wonderful wines and the best cuisine the area could offer. Back then, it seemed like *everyone* smoked and the thought of having a no-smoking policy at a restaurant was ludicrous. Neither Colleen nor I smoked, so we were definitely in the minority. Trying not to look conspicuous, we tried our best not to inhale the smoke of the 13 other people at our table who were lighting up one cigarette after another. It's a nasty habit and a terrible way to go if you get lung cancer, but it was the reality of the film business in the eighties.

I'm still proud of the work we all did on "Too Much" and I think we really lucked out in terms of shooting locations. It's a shame that Bros' popularity didn't extend into the 90s and beyond, as they certainly had the talent for long-lived success. Pop culture can be fickle and you can never tell who's going to have staying power.

While I was working with Bros, I was being considered to direct two other music videos. One of them was the last video that Freddie Mercury did with Queen, which would have been a blast. Unfortunately, the video ended up going to another director who was pitching for the job.

The second music video was for the song "Atomic City" by Holly Johnson, best known as the lead singer of Frankie Goes to Hollywood. I got the gig and started conceptualizing with Holly, but we immediately had a difference of opinion about how the video should look. Because the lyrics described how "there's a party going on in Atomic City," I wanted to film a dark journey into a post-apocalyptic underworld. Holly wanted to go with a stylized vision of 1950s innocence. In the end, we ended up incorporating both of our visions into the video, which was a lot of fun and allowed us to contrast the squeaky clean 50s with a futuristic punk sensibility.

Richard O'Brien, the writer of *The Rocky Horror Show*, was friends with Holly and was invited to appear as an extra in "Atomic City." Holly was a big fan of Richard's work and he was over the moon that Richard would be a part of the music video. It was fun to see Richard again and we talked about our surprise that *The Rocky Horror Picture Show* had garnered such a cult following. We never dreamed it would continue to play at midnight screenings so many years later.

In "Atomic City," Holly plays a sort of pied piper that leads a clean-cut young couple into a grungy underworld populated by a group of punk-inspired denizens. Many of them wore riské S&M outfits that clashed wonderfully with the couple's conservative dress.

One dancer was wearing an outfit that was too revealing for a record executive on set, who thought the costume was unsuitable for television. I approached the dancer and asked if he could report to wardrobe and trade his outfit for another one that was less revealing. I was surprised to learn that he'd brought that outfit from home!

Richard had also brought his own wardrobe for the shoot. He wore short skin-tight black jeans, a fishnet T-shirt and a black feather boa. If you watch the video, you can see him having a ball and hamming it up like you wouldn't believe.

Music videos like this were fun to shoot because they didn't require the same long shooting schedule as a feature. We shot "Atomic City" in only two days, getting loads of coverage so we had lots of takes and angles to choose from during post-production. Editing took a lot longer than actually shooting it, as so much of a music video's success is determined in the editing suite.

We had fun letting our imaginations run wild and seeing what strange imagery we could create for the video. I was grateful that Holly was willing to take some of my ideas and combine them with his own instead of shutting me out of the creative process. I think the resulting music video still holds up well today.

Shortly after shooting "Atomic City," I was shooting a commercial for BMW in Milan when I received a call from producer James G. Robinson at Morgan Creek Productions in L.A. He was beginning production on *The Exorcist III*, which was to be directed by William Peter Blatty. Best known as the novelist who had written *The Exorcist*, William was also a filmmaker who had directed *The Ninth Configuration* in 1980.

James said he was calling me on the recommendation of Dennis Jones, the producer of "Smooth Criminal." I was surprised that Dennis would recommend me for any work, especially given our differences of opinion in the past, but he must have been satisfied with the results of our collaboration.

Apparently James was concerned about William's take on *The Exorcist III*, which the director saw as more of a psychological thriller than an effects-driven thrill ride. Morgan Creek wanted a more typical horror movie that would fall in line with the previous two *Exorcist* movies and they feared that William's subdued approach would not deliver the gross-out chills that audiences expected.

They wanted me to work with William and co-direct a rescripted sequence for the climax that featured more action and special effects. When I returned to L.A., I visited William and we had a nice conversation about collaborating on the new ending, but he was hell-bent on sticking to his guns and making the movie that he wanted to make.

I had to think hard about whether I wanted to get in the middle of this disagreement. On one hand, it would give me a co-directing credit on a major Hollywood feature. On the other hand, it meant becoming involved in a potentially sticky political situation.

My friend Skip Short warned me about the potential consequences of diving in. In his opinion, if I worked on the film and it was a success, William would receive all the credit - and if it wasn't a success, I would receive all the blame. A no-win situation. Skip suggested that I offer to help them with *The Exorcist III* only if they agreed to give me my own modestly budgeted feature film to direct afterwards. I took Skip's advice and asked Morgan Creek for my own movie in exchange for my help. They said no. Ultimately though, I'm glad I wasn't involved with *The Exorcist III* because it was considered a disappointment that didn't live up to the classic original.

Would the film have turned out better had I worked with William on a different finale full of special effects and gore? Is it possible that working on *The Exorcist III* could have kickstarted a lucrative career as a big-time motion-picture director? Who knows? It's easy to second guess yourself with the benefit of 20/20 hindsight, so I don't like to dwell on decisions I've made in the past.

By the early 90s, having won an Academy Award and working steadily as a director of commercials, television shows and music videos, I was feeling pretty invincible. Then January 22, 1991 arrived.

I was in L.A. editing a toy commercial when I suddenly felt ill, as though I was coming down with the flu. A cold shiver took hold of my entire body, then I started to feel nauscous. I told the guys in the editing suite that I needed to throw up and I rushed to the washroom. I wasn't able to vomit, so I returned to the editing room despite the lingering nausea.

We tried resuming work on the commercial, but I just couldn't concentrate and I started to feel even worse. Then the world started going black on me. My editor called an ambulance, which arrived promptly and took me to Cedars-Sinai Hospital.

The cardiologist did an angiogram, which revealed that I'd had a heart attack. A catheter was inserted into my leg, which administered drugs to thin my blood and hopefully clear the blockage that had formed in my artery. In case the medication wasn't enough, the doctor decided to leave the stint in, which could be used if I required an angioplasty to stretch the artery open.

Colleen was back in Canada, so I called to explain the situation and let her know I was okay for the time being. I never thought I'd ever find myself making a phone call like that. She flew down to be at my bedside, and it was a huge comfort having her there during such a scary time.

I was kept in the intensive care unit for a couple of days for observation before being moved to a private room. Luckily, I had insurance coverage through the Director's Guild of America, so I didn't have to worry about the expense of it all. During such a stressful time, money is the last thing you want to be thinking about.

Unfortunately, the tranquilizer they were administering didn't agree with me at all. For a day and a half, I had that terrible sensation of falling that people sometimes get when they start to nod off and suddenly jerk awake. I was glad when they finally took me off that particular drug.

A few days later, the cardiologist said the blockage was cleared and they decided to remove the stint. Unfortunately, it had been left in my leg for so long that it had damaged my artery. I found out later that an artery consists of an outer and an inner layer, and it had ruptured the inner layer. Blood had leaked in between the two layers and had created a new clot.

Within a week of me leaving the hospital, the new clot in my leg was the size of a fist and it was far more painful than the heart attack was. Surgery was required, which involved an eight-inch incision that allowed them to repair the artery. I couldn't be given any general anaesthetic because I'd had a heart attack only a couple of weeks before, so I had an epidural and was awake for the entire operation.

Then I went through three months of rehab in L.A. so I could regain my strength. I was glad that Colleen was with me for the entire time, but it was still hard because most of our family and friends were still up in Canada and the cardiologist didn't want me to fly for three months after the surgery. It was a relief when I could finally return to Canada and sleep in my own bed.

My heart attack was the result of unwise lifestyle choices and stress. Working in the industry often requires long hours and eating out all the time, and it's easy to fall into unhealthy eating habits when you're always on the go. Especially when traveling to other countries, I found myself eating a lot of rich foods that can be high in fat and cholesterol.

Upon reflection, I don't think I was experiencing a high level of stress when I had the heart attack, but that could just be denial on my part. In truth, the film industry is always stressful to at least some degree because it's a deadline business with lots of money at stake, and inflated egos and office politics often rear their ugly heads.

When I was married to my first wife Josie, we rented an apartment in an old Victorian house in London. We became good friends with our neighbour upstairs, who was a psychologist. He was always observing other people to see how they would behave in various circumstances and how they would react to different stimuli. During a conversation one day, he commented on my "interesting" body language, describing it as "feline" in nature. Whenever I sat down to relax, he could see that my entire body was genuinely relaxed. He was amazed at how calm I always appeared, especially given the industry I'd chosen for my career. Signs of stress never seemed to show in my body language.

Special effects in particular can be stressful on a film set, especially when people's safety is a major concern, but I've always managed to stay quite calm and collected at work even when under enormous pressure. Whether creating special effects or directing actors, I've never been one to start yelling to get my point across. I always thought that sort of behavior was anti-productive.

But the stress was still present, building up inside of me over the years and starting to wear away at my health. I've come to realize that I tend to internalize my stress without a proper outlet for releasing it, and I think this build-up was largely responsible for my heart attack.

I eventually came to terms with the whole experience, realizing I needed to lead a healthier lifestyle and reduce stress. My heart attack and slow road to recovery helped me recognize my own mortality and made me grateful for how lucky I was in life. When you're busy just trying to get through each day, it's easy to forget about the important things in life and how fortunate you are to have loved ones around you.

Once I was back on my feet, it was back to directing commercials in

L.A. I did a lot of work for a company called GMS, which stood for Giddens, Marshall and Short. The line producer on "Smooth Criminal," John Romeyn, had introduced me to Skip Short, who was a producer and one of the owners of GMS. Skip and I became good friends and I directed many commercials for his company while also pursuing opportunities to direct television shows and feature films.

The 90s saw me directing hundreds of commercials for a wide range of companies, including IBM, Budweiser, Labatt, BMW, Hertz, Jordache, Konica, Toshiba and Burger King. I wasn't directing Hollywood blockbusters yet, but at least I was working steadily as a director and having fun.

One commercial I directed for RCA never went to air despite turning out well (in my opinion, anyway). The commercial featured a man sitting down to enjoy music playing on his RCA CD player. He was transported by the music into a dreamlike haze as he relaxed in his lounge chair. The final shot featured the trademark RCA puppy and the company logo.

After I delivered my cut of the commercial, everybody seemed happy with the result - until the head of RCA decided that the spot should not be aired. He agreed that it was well shot and edited, but he didn't like the fact that the RCA dog was not featured throughout the commercial. I argued that the dog was shown at the very end, but he said it wasn't good enough, so the ad never made it to television. Oh well. The client is always right.

I also continued directing toy commercials and I found myself becoming known for specializing in toys related to movies. Whether it was *Star Wars*, *Men in Black* or *Starship Troopers*, I was your man. Each commercial took only a day or two of shooting, so they all kind of blur together in my head now. I liked being able to work for short periods on different shoots because no two commercials were alike and things never became boring.

It was fun returning to the world of music videos in 1994, when I directed a video in Toronto for the song "A Future to this Life," performed by Joe Walsh (of the Eagles) and Lita Ford. The song was featured on the soundtrack of *RoboCop: The Series*, which was shooting in Toronto at the time, and they even used portions of the music video under the closing credits of some episodes.

The video intercut footage from the series with shots of Joe and Lita performing on a futuristic set. We used a lot of smoke and fire effects to create a post-apocalyptic atmosphere, which set the stage for RoboCop himself to appear in the video with Joe and Lita. The producers of the series lent us the suit and we had a stuntman play the part. That thing was remarkably heavy and clunky, making it nearly impossible for the performer inside to move. It was no wonder they made the character move so slowly and mechanically in the show.

It's a shame that *RoboCop: The Series* never caught on with the public or fans of the movies. It was an ambitious Canadian-shot program like *War of the Worlds* that didn't lend itself easily to the format of an ongoing series. I'm not sure if it has garnered a cult following yet, but I wouldn't be surprised if it does eventually.

By the late 90s, my opportunities to direct commercials in the States were drying up. It certainly wasn't because I lacked the ability or the experience to do so, but I found myself competing with a wave of newer, younger directors who were taking the industry by storm.

Quite frankly, clients were starting to think I was too old to direct commercials. They're always looking for the youngest, hippest visionaries to shoot their ads, and I wasn't fitting that description. In my opinion, the only reason I managed to survive so long in the field was because I'd found a niche directing commercials that involved special effects and children.

Skip eventually closed down his company, so I briefly went to work directing commercials for another organization. Unfortunately, it wasn't a happy working situation, so I didn't stay for long.

I moved back to Canada in 1998 and settled in Toronto with the hope of finding work north of the border. I directed commercials for a company called Partners and I returned to supervising special effects for movies. Toronto was being hailed as "Hollywood North" because numerous Hollywood productions were shooting there to take advantage of tax incentives. Many opportunities came my way to work on effects because there weren't many people in the country with the necessary skills and experience.

I shared a workshop with Martin Malivoire for a few years and worked on pictures like *Bride of Chucky*, the fourth instalment in the popular *Child's Play* series. My main memory on *Chucky* was blowing up a Winnebago that goes rolling down an embankment. When I instructed the effects guys to rig five wiring harnesses for the explosion, they asked me why we needed five instead of just one. I explained that we needed five so we could stagger the explosion and make it look more dramatic on screen, as Glen Robinson had taught me all those years ago on *Battle of Britain*.

The murderous Chucky. Copyright Kerem Gogus | Dreamstime.com.

I was surprised that these effects technicians hadn't heard of staggering explosions before. They just wanted to load the Winnebago with enough dynamite to disintegrate the whole thing in an instant, which isn't very exciting to watch on screen. I showed them how to precut sections of the vehicle so it would blow apart more easily, and how to use gasoline with a fire charge for some pretty big fireworks. Some of the guys didn't appreciate that I was telling them how to do their jobs, but it was my duty and I was ultimately responsible for the final results.

Next, I worked on a film that went on to spawn one of the biggest motion picture franchises ever - *X-Men*. At the time, nobody knew it would be such a huge success at the box office and lead to so many sequels and spinoffs. In fact, it was a modestly budgeted affair that was produced at a time when superhero films were far from popular. Many of the recent comic-book movies had bombed at the box office, but *X-Men* reversed the trend and demonstrated how big-screen superheroes were still viable.

I didn't know until I signed on that Dick Donner was an executive producer on *X-Men* and his wife Lauren Shuler Donner was the producer. Dick wasn't involved with the on-set production of the film, so I didn't get to work with him directly, but it was nice to know we were being supervised by someone who believed in the verisimilitude of superheroes on the silver screen.

Another executive producer on the film was Avi Arad, who was now developing movies based on characters from Marvel Comics. It was fun being reunited with him on this film after working together on so many toy commercials.

X-Men was filmed in Toronto and Hamilton, so I didn't have very far to drive from my home in the Niagara Region. The producers interviewed a few candidates for the position of special-effects supervisor, but I ultimately got the job because I had more credits to my name than anybody else they were considering. It also didn't hurt that I had experience with other superhero-themed projects, such as *Superman, Condorman* and *Superboy*.

I was told that the director was a young and talented filmmaker known for his strong storytelling ability, but he had no experience working with special effects. The producers wanted someone with a strong effects background to help guide him through this new territory.

Bryan Singer was indeed a good storyteller and he was far more interested in directing the actors than dealing with the technical aspects of the special effects. He knew what kinds of effects he wanted for the film, but he didn't have much interest in how they were achieved as long as they were delivered on time and to his satisfaction. Especially with the film's unusually short production period, Bryan often had his assistant director handle effects sequences so he could concentrate on more character-centric scenes with the cast.

To ensure that everyone was on the same page, all of the effects shots were storyboarded in detail by Michael Ploog. Having worked with Michael on *Superman II*, *Superman III* and "Smooth Criminal," I suggested flying him in from England to work on *X-Men*.

Michael was an extraordinary storyboard artist whose ability to bring a story to life on paper probably came from his background in comic books. Storyboard artists in general tend to be good illustrators, but Michael had a special ability that put him in a league of his own. If I asked him to draw a shot as though it was filmed with a specific lens, he would nail it perfectly.

During our initial conversations, Bryan seemed to have difficulty articulating exactly how he wanted an effects sequence to look. Michael did his usual outstanding job with the storyboards, but it was still difficult to capture a sense of pacing and movement in his drawings. That's when I suggested that we try using previsualization, or "previs" for short.

This is the process of creating 3D-animated storyboards to see how a sequence will play out. All important elements in the scene, including characters and settings, are rendered in low-resolution computer animation. The fine details, like the characters' faces and costumes, aren't the focus here. What's important is the movement within the frame, the movement of the camera and the timing of the shots within the sequence.

The advantage of previs over traditional 2D storyboarding is the ability to get a sense of rhythm that's more difficult to communicate through stationary drawings. Temporary music and sound effects can also be added to help determine how the different elements will mesh together in the final film.

When we were in pre-production for *X-Men*, it was still during the early days of previs. My nephew Neil Corbould had recently used it on the Sean Connery film *Entrapment* and I'd used it on a project I was hoping to get off

the ground. Friends of mine at Keyframe Digital Productions did the previs for me, even though the company specialized in video-game production.

Bryan immediately recognized the potential of using previs on *X-Men*, but it took a while to convince the producers. Previs could save a fortune because all of the planning for effects sequences was done before any shooting was done. The director could experiment with different camera angles in the digital realm and change his mind on the fly without hundreds of people standing around and waiting on set.

The set builders in particular loved previs. Before any hammers were even picked up, it helped them determine how much of a set should be constructed physically and how much would be created afterward using a green screen and visual effects. Previs also allowed the cinematographer to see how the look of a shot would change if the lights were repositioned.

The producers didn't want the expense of flying computer animators up from L.A. to do previs, so we used my friends at Keyframe instead. They did a wonderful job helping us plan some of the most spectacular action sequences in the film. Some of Keyframe's work is included in the special features of the film on DVD and Blu-ray, and it's interesting to see how closely the final shots ended up looking like the previs.

I also used previs for a Swiffer commercial I shot in Montreal that involved an elaborate dance number. When I presented my concept to the client, I was able to show them the entire commercial in rough animation with a temporary soundtrack. Because so much of the planning was done ahead of time and I knew exactly where the camera would be placed for each shot, what should have taken three days to shoot took only two.

One of the most memorable sequences in *X-Men* takes place at a train station, where a number of mutant powers are unleashed upon the public. We filmed at Liuna Station in Hamilton, a beautiful historic building that once served as a train station and has since been converted into a convention hall. Luckily, the front foyer still resembled a train station and required minimal dressing.

The script called for the character Cyclops to blast through the ceiling of the train station with energy beams from his eyes. Usually, we would have filmed a scene like this on a studio set, but it was decided to take advantage of the real location and its beautiful foyer. We constructed a fake section of the ceiling out of breakaway materials that blew apart on cue, showering the people below with lightweight chunks of debris. This way we didn't do any damage to the historic building and the people below weren't in danger of being hurt.

Outside of the train station, Magneto uses his telekinesis power to levitate a number of police cars. We built lightweight versions of the cars that could be pulled up into the air quickly on counterweighted wires suspended from cranes, creating the illusion that they were weightless under Magneto's power. Real cars would have been too heavy to pull up so quickly because you can't move a heavy load with as much speed, especially when you're working against gravity.

For shots of Magneto releasing the vehicles from his telekinetic control, real cars were used. One cue, they were released and dropped onto other cars parked below. I'm glad we used old-fashioned physical effects instead of CGI, as it would have been more difficult to get the proper sense of weight and gravity with computer graphics. If you want to capture the sheer physicality of cars falling from the sky, nothing beats the real thing.

X-Men made effective use of CGI when needed, but it still relied on traditional physical effects whenever possible. Whether it was blowing up vehicles or making characters defy gravity with wires, we used tried-and-true techniques to bring the story to life. For the sequence in which Storm unleashes her weather-controlling powers to fight Toad, we constructed loads of lightweight props and let them all loose in front of giant wind machines, much like we did twenty years earlier on *Superman II*.

Of all the cast members, I worked the most closely with Halle Berry, who was perfect as Storm. She was a wonderful person - always positive, patient and supportive of everyone around her. For New Year's Eve, when the new millennium was about to begin, she bought every crew member a bottle of really nice champagne to show her appreciation for their hard work. What a lovely gesture.

The   om.

The finale of *X-Men* required some high-flying martial-arts action in the vein of *Crouching Tiger, Hidden Dragon*, the film that took kung fu to a new level for international audiences. A number of stunt people for *X-Men* were brought in from China who had experience with that kind of screen fighting, which required the performers to be flipped around on wires like marionettes. This was before computer-assisted wire-removal was perfected, so they used extremely thin wires that were easier to hide on camera. The Chinese methodology of flying people on such thin wires was considered unsafe here in North America, but it was common practice for Asian action films. Luckily, nobody was seriously hurt on *X-Men* and the fights looked spectacular on screen.

X-Men was released to critical acclaim and box-office success in 2000, and it marked the beginning of the superhero-movie explosion. Avi Arad was now the superhero king of Hollywood, producing films based on characters from Marvel Comics, as well as their related toy lines. I found myself busy directing commercials for toys based on *X-Men* and *Spider-Man*, which introduced these classic characters to a whole new generation.

I was proud of the work I'd done on *X-Men*, but it was a stressful experience because of the extremely short production period and tight budget. I found myself working 14-hour days trying to keep up with the workload.

All that stress started to take its toll. After *X-Men* was released, I suffered another heart attack. Luckily, it was a relatively minor blockage that could be treated with medication. Since then, I've been taking blood thinners and medication to help prevent future cardiac issues.

At least now I'm aware of my problem with high cholesterol and I can take preventive measures. Far too many people are walking around in imminent danger of a heart attack who don't even know it. The heart attack gave me incentive to exercise more regularly and cut out foods that are high in cholesterol. I can't leap around like I could when I was a teenager, but I still try to walk on the treadmill four or five times a week. Golf is another passion of mine, so I try to hit the golf course regularly and walk all 18 holes.

I feel lucky to have survived two heart attacks and it helped put things into perspective. The little things in life that used to worry me aren't as important any more. What's important is staying healthy so I can spend more time with family and friends. I continued doing effects work for movies after my second heart attack, but I did slow down a little bit. I wasn't as willing to work 14-hour days on a film set, and I think there's something fundamentally wrong with the film industry if you have to sacrifice your health and your personal life to be considered "successful."

Stress can kill, and I needed outlets to keep that stress from building up inside of me. Colleen and I have a cabin up north where we can escape from urban life and find peace of mind. Seeking refuge in the wilderness allows me to indulge in my love of woodworking, whether it's building a new addition to the cabin or making new shelves for our overflowing collection of books. I've come to realize that work can be an important part of your life, but it shouldn't *be* your life. You've got to have something outside of work that you love doing if you're to stay healthy and sane.

After *X-Men*, Martin Malivoire and I went our separate ways and I started a new company called The Effects Group with a few other guys in the industry. Our first project was the movie *Driven*, starring Sylvester Stallone and Burt Reynolds. I served as special-effects coordinator and had a lot of fun working with director Renny Harlin.

Driven was a movie about auto racing that allowed for lots of spectacular crashes. I admired Renny's commitment to using practical effects instead of CGI whenever possible. We built 12 cars that were "crashable" for the action sequences. We'd wreck them for a take, weld them back together, put some new decals on them, and they'd be good for another go.

One spectacular shot involved a car stalling in the middle of the track while another one plowed into it from behind. Once again, I was able to rely on the towing techniques that Glen Robinson had taught me on *Battle of Britain*. By towing the car on a cable, we were able to execute the crash without endangering any stunt drivers. When you see the final shot, it's pretty clear that a stunt performer would have been killed in that crash.

Sometimes we managed to get spectacular shots by sheer luck, like the time a car accidently crashed into an unmanned camera. Some people think it was achieved with computer animation because it was so perfect, but it was achieved practically.

The visual-effects supervisor on *Driven* was surprised that we were able to achieve so much with practical effects on set. He thought we'd need to rely more heavily on computer animation for a lot of the crashes, so he was grateful that we'd made life easy for him.

Working on the special effects of a film like *Driven* is like unleashing an inner five-year-old who likes to smash up dinky cars and roll them down the stairs. We got to flip cars, bounce them off walls and even crash them into water. What a great way to let all that stress out!

Unfortunately, *Driven* wasn't a hit at the box office, nor was my next movie, *K-19: The Widowmaker*. The submarine thriller was directed by Kathryn Bigelow, who went on to direct such acclaimed films as *The Hurt Locker* and *Zero Dark Thirty*. I remember first meeting *K-19*'s lead actor in the hallway of the production office in Montreal. He warmly extended his hand and introduced himself: "Hi. I'm Harrison Ford." That was the understatement of the year.

Harrison was a wonderful person to work with. Although he was one of the biggest movie stars on the planet, he never showed any sense of an inflated ego. He came across as a down-to-earth guy who seemed more comfortable hanging out with the crew than he did with the glamorous Hollywood crowd.

At the end of one particularly long shoot day, the crew had just finished striking the set and they decided to break open some brewskies. One of the production people, who was extremely uptight and by-the-book, gave the guys shit and told them they weren't allowed to drink on set.

Afterward, Harrison came by to congratulate the crew for doing such a great job that day. When they told him about what happened, Harrison responded with his usual wry wit. He jokingly suggested something that would get them out of trouble if they were ever caught drinking again - they should say that the beers were given to them by Mr. Harrison Ford himself!

When I first went to Montreal for the film, the art department had put together a 6-foot scale model of the submarine set to help Kathryn plan her shots. Every time she came in to look at the model, she'd tear out a section of the model and tell them to rebuild it differently because she'd want more space in a particular section of the sub to fit her camera. The next time she'd look at the model, she'd tear out another piece and ask them to redesign it. This went on and on and she kept changing her mind. The model was constantly being rebuilt. Kathryn would be trying to plan her camera angles

by looking at the model through a viewfinder, which she found to be a slow and frustrating experience.

I suggested using previsualization, which she wasn't familiar with. By building the submarine in the digital realm, she could move through the set in cyberspace and "walk" through the sub in a way that couldn't be achieved with her viewfinder and model. For one particular shot, Kathryn wanted a close-up of the radio operator. Looking at the sets in the digital realm, it became clear that the bulkhead in front of the radio station should be removable so she could get the shot she wanted. It's a lot more cost-effective to do all that planning with previs rather than having 150 crew members standing around while you decide how to rip out a part of your set.

Even though Kathryn accepted the value of previs, she tended to change her mind frequently and come up with new ideas on the fly. Even when things had been planned meticulously with previs and she had given her sign-off, we often found ourselves working through the night after receiving a call at 11:00 p.m. and being told that she'd changed her mind again. Such is life. All directors work differently, and Kathryn liked to remain flexible until the very end.

While working on *K-19*, I received a call from Avi Arad asking if I'd like to be the second-unit director on Sam Raimi's new *Spider-Man* movie. Unfortunately I had to turn down the offer because I was too busy with *K-19*. In hindsight, it probably would have been a better career move to work on *Spider-Man* because it was such a smash hit. I might have gotten to work on the sequels as well.

Alas, nobody can tell the future. Here I was working on a big-budget submarine movie starring Harrison Ford and Liam Neeson. It was destined to be a blockbuster, right? Wrong. There are no guarantees in this crazy industry.

I returned to the director's chair in 2004 with a feature film called *Home Beyond the Sun*, which was aimed at the Christian home-video market. The story chronicled the experiences of a Bible-college student from the West visiting China and befriending a Chinese orphan.

Before directing *Home Beyond the Sun*, I hadn't realized how big and potentially profitable the Christian market was. Just a few years before, a company in Canada called Cloud Ten Pictures had made the Christian-themed movie *Left Behind*, starring Kirk Cameron. The film found crossover success beyond the religious market and became quite popular with a more mainstream audience. It was our hope to duplicate that type of success with *Home Beyond the Sun*.

We shot the film in 14 days using a talented cast from Toronto. Our budget was only about $600,000, so we decided to shoot on video instead of film to keep costs down. I wanted to use David Herrington as my director of photography again, but he was already busy working on another project.

Perci Young took on the cinematography for the film. He was a talented cameraman who had done lots of great work, but I think he was more of a film guy than a video guy. We actually shot the film in 13 days, a full day ahead of schedule, but we had to reshoot an entire day's footage because it ended up out of focus. This was during the early days of digital video cameras and Perci didn't realize that the camera lens needed to be back-focused as well as front-focused to ensure that all the footage stayed sharp. In the end though, the film ended up with a nice look thanks to Perci's skill as a cinematographer.

To simulate China, we shot at a beautiful Buddhist temple in Niagara Falls, which was filled with hundreds of Buddha statues. The 20-foot statue in the main hall was so massive that the temple was actually built around it. I thought it was a shame that we weren't allowed to film inside the temple because it would have looked so spectacular on camera. Still, we managed to get some beautiful exterior shots featuring the fearsome stone lions in the garden and the giant bell in front of the temple, which added an sense of scope to the film that was beyond our meager budget.

The monks generously invited us to share a vegetarian lunch with them every day. It was an interesting place to visit, with the monks regularly walking the grounds while chanting. If it weren't for the sound of passing cars on the Niagara Parkway just beyond the gates, it would have felt like we were in a totally different world. It's ironic that such a meditative oasis can be found just a stone's throw away from the cheesy wax museums and souvenir shops of Niagara.

Unfortunately, *Home Beyond the Sun* wasn't marketed effectively and it hasn't gained a very wide audience. The producer had an interesting idea for distributing the movie that ultimately didn't pan out. He planned to send copies of the film to churches throughout North America and have them hold screenings for their congregations. The churches would then sell copies of the film on behalf of the production company, keeping a certain percentage of sales for themselves. As it turned out, churches weren't as eager to jump on that bandwagon as had been hoped.

Ultimately, I was never paid the full amount of money I was contracted for, but that's all water under the bridge now. I just wish that *Home Beyond the Sun* had better distribution so it could have reached its intended audience more effectively.

The last movie I worked on as special-effects supervisor was *Shoot 'Em Up* in 2007, which was written and directed by the talented Michael Davis. This balls-to-the-walls action movie starred Clive Owen, who was one of the nicest actors I had the pleasure of working with. Clive was a very physical actor who wasn't afraid to get down and dirty for an action sequence (and acquire a few bruises in the process).

"You can hit me with anything," Clive told me early in production. "Just nothing in the face."

He realized that his face was his greatest asset as an actor, so he didn't want any sparks or explosives to go off near it. We did end up grazing his face a bit with some debris from a bullet hit, but he was cool with it and he realized that a certain level of unpredictability is always at play in the middle of a shootout.

Clive was also a die-hard football fan who *had* to watch whenever Liverpool FC was playing. If he hadn't become such a successful actor, he probably would have followed his passion and become a footballer himself. Whenever there was a game going on, it was damn near impossible to tear him away from the television set!

Working on the film was also fun because of director Michael Davis, who had a strong storytelling ability that was probably developed during his years as a storyboard artist. I later realized that I'd considered him for storyboarding "Smooth Criminal."

Michael was the type of person who had a crystal-clear idea of what he wanted to see. For *Shoot 'Em Up*, he prepared the most extraordinary animated storyboards I'd ever seen, complete with music and sound effects. The entire film, from the first shot to the last, was completely planned out. Because of his strength of vision and depth of planning, every department was very clear on what they needed to accomplish for each scene.

That didn't mean Michael was close-minded or wouldn't consider suggestions from people on his crew. Much like Dick Donner, Michael would listen to your suggestions and carefully consider them, but if your suggestion wasn't what he was looking for, he'd move forward with his original plan.

Michael was also remarkably cool-headed on set, which is important on a film like *Shoot 'Em Up*, with all kinds of pyrotechnics unleashing hell everywhere. If a director is yelling all the time, actors and special-effects people are more likely to lose their focus and make a mistake, which can be a matter of life and death.

Many of the directors I've worked with over the years don't have much interest in how special effects are accomplished - they only care about the final product. It was refreshing to discover that Michael was very interested in the technical side of special effects. He was completely immersed in every aspect of the film, which was his baby.

It was fun blowing the shit out of everything on *Shoot 'Em Up*, which required more bullet hits than any other movie in my career. For the big warehouse shootout, we built these fake wall sections that we could just wheel into position and quickly rig up to a sequencer for the bullet hits. We'd do a take, set off the bullet charges, wheel out the wall section, then wheel in a fresh new wall for each subsequent take.

It's a shame that *Shoot 'Em Up* didn't make a bigger impression at the box office. I think it's a great action movie that somehow slid under the radar for many moviegoers. I also think that Michael was deserving of more opportunities to direct big action movies after *Shoot 'Em Up*. He told me about the difficult time he had convincing the studio that he should be hired to direct the movie. Hollywood is always on the lookout for the hottest young filmmaker and the studio felt that Michael was too old to make such a hip movie. And Michael was only in his forties!

Maybe the movie biz really is the for the young. After *Shoot 'Em Up*, I just didn't have the motivation to work those insanely long hours any more. I decided to spend more time with Colleen and do the things that meant the most to me personally. After all, real life isn't a movie.

CHAPTER 10
LEGACIES

I left the world of big-studio feature films behind, but it wasn't an "ending" at all, and definitely not a retirement of any sort. A new phase of my life had begun that would allow me to focus on creative projects that genuinely engaged me. The projects might not be as high-profile as the features I'd worked on, but they would be guided by personal interest and a desire to be a more active member of my community.

My decision to stop working on Hollywood features was not a decision that was forced upon me in any way. The work was still available if I wanted it. In fact, more work was available than ever before. Canada and the Greater Toronto Area in particular continued to attract productions from south of the border that sought to take advantage of tax incentives, skilled crews and a filmmaking infrastructure that continues to grow every year.

Ever since I moved back to Canada from the States, I'd purposely chosen to work on films that were shooting in the Greater Toronto Area so I wouldn't need to travel far from home. I had the pleasure of working with talented performers like Kirsten Dunst, Chow Yun-Fat, Vin Diesel and Tim Allen on films like *Get Over It, Bulletproof Monk, The Pacifier* and *Zoom* while coordinating special effects in Toronto. I had an upper hand over other special-effects guys in the area because I had so many years of experience and an Academy Award to boot.

Despite the availability of work, I found that I wasn't having as much fun on movie sets as I used to. The insanely long hours were certainly a contributing factor, and I didn't think it was sustainable to be working 14-hour days all the time with scarcely a weekend to remind yourself that you had a life beyond the movie. Things didn't used to be like that, especially when I was working in England, and I thought it was ridiculous to expect your crew to be 100-percent effective when they were walking around like exhausted zombies.

Hollywood productions shot in Canada tend to push their crews harder than they would if the films were shot in the States. The big studios usually decide to shoot in Canada as a cost-saving measure, realizing they can take advantage of tax breaks, more affordable crews, less expensive studio facilities, and shooting locations that can easily double for New York or Detroit.

As a result, many of these productions have such a budget-conscious mindset that they try to squeeze every last bit of productivity out of their Canadian crews. Hence, the 14-hour days. The producers kept wanting more for less, and the situation kept getting worse. It was a snowballing situation with producers' expectations growing as their budgets kept shrinking.

I enjoyed working on some of the more recent feature films in my career, but overall, it just wasn't as fulfilling any more. I used to feel like a kid in a candy store when I was working on films like *Battle of Britain* and *Superman*. It was all about creative problem-solving and movie magic. By the mid-2000s, it started to feel like I was working on an assembly line that was struggling to keep pace with the shortened schedules and lack of resources.

Geography was another reason I decided to turn down work on feature films. Even though many high-profile productions were being mounted in Vancouver and Montreal that could have benefitted from my expertise in special effects, I no longer felt a strong desire to spend months away from home.

Shoot 'Em Up in 2007 ended up being my last Hollywood picture, and it was a good note to leave on. Since then, I've enjoyed devoting more time to projects around the Niagara Region. Whether it's helping charitable causes or helping to promote local businesses, being an active member of the community has taken on an increasingly important role in my life. I work out of my home office now, which allows me to spend more time enjoying the beautiful view of Lake Erie behind my house.

Helping out the next generation of filmmakers and special-effects artists is also important to me. I serve on the advisory board of Niagara College and I regularly lecture to film students throughout Southern Ontario, sharing my experiences and hopefully inspiring those with the dream of pursuing filmmaking as an art and a career.

I believe that special effects should be a standard subject of study in any college or university film program because effects are so pervasive in today's media. With CGI allowing filmmakers to alter cinematic reality with increasingly greater ease, film students need to be on the leading edge of the technology that shapes how movies are made and how stories are told.

Digital effects are a powerful tool when used wisely in the service of a good script, and I hope CGI doesn't continue to overwhelm cinema like I've been seeing in recent years. I enjoy watching a blockbuster as much as the next moviegoer, but many of the big summer movies are so overproduced with nonstop CGI fireworks that I stumble out of the theatre in a state of numbness.

You can sit through only so many exploding robots and toppling buildings before the action loses all emotional impact and every movie starts to feel the same. I hope the next generation of filmmakers will remember that the flashiest of CGI rings empty without a meaningful story at the heart of it all.

In May of 2012, I was invited to be a keynote speaker for the graduating class at Brock University in St. Catharines, just outside of Niagara Falls. I enjoyed sharing some of my life experiences from the podium and bringing out Oscar at the very end, which always gets a great reaction. The ceremony was made even more memorable when the university awarded me with an honorary Doctors of Law degree, which was very touching indeed. My honorary degree has found a place of honor at my house, and I had fun referring to myself as "Dr." Chilvers for quite some time afterward.

2013 marked my first appearance at a fan convention, which was held at the Scotiabank Convention Centre in Niagara. We shot a video for the convention's website in front of the falls, where I welcomed visitors to Niagara Falls Comic Con and invited them to visit me at my booth. It was hard to believe that three decades had passed since we'd made Chris Reeve take flight at the falls to create one of the most famous scenes in film history.

It was fun watching *Superman* again at a special Comic-Con screening and participating in a Q & A session for a room of enthusiastic fans. After all these years, I was surprised that people still had so much interest in the Superman films, especially the first two. I could have kept talking and answering questions for hours, but I had to clear out to make room for Darth Vader himself, David Prowse, who had his own Q & A scheduled to follow mine.

I enjoyed talking to fans, young and old, who took the time to say hello and tell me how much they appreciated the work I'd done over the years. Some were interested in hearing about *X-Men*, while others remembered the work I'd done on *The Rocky Horror Picture Show*. The experience brought back a lot of great memories.

Comic Con had arranged to have an original cape from *Superman II* put on display next to my booth. In fact, it was the cape that I'd given to my friend Bob Thiel from Modern Crane during production of the film. Unfortunately, Bob had passed away shortly before the convention, but some of Bob's family had arranged for it to be displayed at Comic Con so fans could have their picture taken with it.

I'm happy to see that the special-effects bug has been passed down to the next generation of the family. My nephews Chris, Neil, Paul and Ian, along with their sister Gail, all work in special effects and have made the last name "Corbould" synonymous with technical excellence in the film industry. I've had the pleasure of shepherding some of their first experiences in the movie business as early as the first *Superman*.

The Corboulds are at the top of their game in a very competitive industry and they regularly work with legendary filmmakers like Steven Spielberg, Ridley Scott and Christopher Nolan. Neil won the Academy Award for Best Visual Effects in 2001 for his work on *Gladiator*, while Chris won his own Oscar in 2010 for *Inception*. In 2014, Neil won another Oscar for his work on *Gravity*.

Chris embarked on a journey to a galaxy far, far away as the special-effects supervisor on the highly anticipated *Star Wars: The Force Awakens*, and he was also appointed Officer of the Order of the British Empire (OBE) in 2014 for his contributions to the British film industry.

In 2006, Neil was hired as special-effects supervisor on *Superman Returns*, which was directed by Bryan Singer. Neil called me one day from the set of the film, which was being shot in Australia.

"We can't get the cape to flap quite right," he said. "Just *how* did you make it work all those years ago?"

Some philosophers have described time as a circle that inevitably loops back on itself. Maybe there's some truth to that.

Right before the opening of *Superman Returns*, I received an unexpected phone call from the Warner Bros. marketing department. They remembered how I'd projected the Superman emblem onto the falls to promote *Superman II*, and they wanted me to do the same for *Superman Returns*. It was only the second time in history that anybody had been allowed to project anything onto the falls other than the regular illumination, and I was at the helm both times.

Time seemed to circle back on itself again in 2012, when my nephews Chris and Ian both worked on Disney's epic *John Carter*. The film was based on my favorite book as a kid, Edgar Rice Burrough's *A Princess of Mars*. Even sixty years after first reading it, the story still resonates with me as a work of staggering imagination. I credit that book for jumpstarting my passion for science fiction and fantasy, ultimately leading to my career in cinema.

Although seeing the adventures of John Carter on the big screen was something of a dream come true, I was a bit hesitant to watch the film because I didn't want to be disappointed. Ever since reading the Carter books as a young boy, I had a very specific image in my mind of how the various creatures of Barsoom should appear. Luckily, I wasn't disappointed when I finally saw the film. Certain details were different than I had imagined, but it was a well-made movie and I'm proud of the amazing work that Chris and Ian did on the film. Even though it wasn't the box-office hit Disney was hoping for, at least it introduced the story of John Carter to a new generation of moviegoers.

My life has taken a lot of unexpected twists and turns since the days of reading those pulpy sci-fi tales as a boy. I've been fortunate enough to help Superman achieve liftoff and make the world believe that a man can fly. I've been lucky enough to take a magical journey with the King of Pop himself, Michael Jackson. I've been able to use my mind, heart and soul in making the impossible a reality on the silver screen for audiences around the world.

I'll always cherish the first time I saw those old black-and-white serials in the theater as a kid, and I can only hope that my work has inspired others as I was inspired by those who came before me.

As I sit with Colleen by my side, looking out over beautiful Lake Erie, I realize how lucky I am. But the adventure is far from over.

In April 2016, Colleen and I traveled to Florence, Italy, where I was presented with a Nemoland Legend Award from the prestigious Nemo Academy of Digital Arts. The award is presented "in recognition of those artists who have made history in the world of entertainment." I was deeply honored to receive the award for my body of work, and I am humbled at the notion that I've made a significant contribution to the world of cinema.

I can't wait to see what the next chapter brings. Whatever happens, I'm sure it will be more than super.

Accepting my Nemoland Legend Award.

With my amazing wife Colleen.

SELECTED WORKS

Director

Home Beyond the Sun (TV Movie)	2004
Superboy (TV Series) • "The Alien Solution" • "The Fixer" • "Bringing Down the House" • "Countdown to Nowhere" • "Back to Oblivion"	1988
Moonwalker ("Smooth Criminal" episode)	1988
The Kingdom Chums: Little David's Adventure (TV Movie, Co-directed with Bernard Deyriès)	1986
ABC Weekend Specials (TV Series) • "Pippi Longstocking"	1985

Special Effects

Shoot 'Em Up (Special-Effects Coordinator)	2007
Zoom (Special-Effects Coordinator)	2006
The Pacifier (Special-Effects Coordinator)	2005
Bulletproof Monk (Special-Effects Consultant)	2003
K-19: The Widowmaker (Special-Effects Coordinator)	2002
Get Over It (Special-Effects Coordinator)	2001
Driven (Special-Effects Coordinator)	2001
X-Men (Special-Effects Coordinator)	2000
Bride of Chucky (Special-Effects Coordinator)	1998
Sesame Street Presents: Follow That Bird (Special-Effects Director)	1985
Superman III (Director of Special Effects and Miniatures)	1983
The Wars (Special Effects)	1983
Curtains (Director of Special Effects: Act I)	1983
Class of 1984 (Special Effects)	1982
The Incubus (Special-Effects Director)	1982

Condorman (Special-Effects Supervisor)	1981
Superman II (Director of Special Effects)	1981
Saturn 3 (Special Effects)	1980
Superman (Creative Supervisor and Director of Special Effects)	1978
The Ritz (Special Effects)	1976
Lisztomania (Special Effects)	1975
The Rocky Horror Picture Show (Special Effects)	1975
Tommy (Special-Effects Supervisor)	1975
Alice's Adventures in Wonderland (Special-Effects Technician)	1972
The Ruling Class (Special-Effects Technician - Uncredited)	1972
200 Motels (Special Effects)	1971
Murphy's War (Special Effects - Uncredited)	1971
Moon Zero Two (Special-Effects Assistant)	1969
Battle of Britain (Junior Assistant: Glen Robinson - Uncredited)	1969
Inspector Clouseau (Special-Effects Supervisor)	1968

About the Authors

Colin Chilvers is a celebrated special-effects artist and filmmaker who won an Academy Award and a BAFTA Award for his work as Creative Supervisor and Director of Special Effects on *Superman: The Movie*. After launching his film career working in the art department of *2001: A Space Odyssey*, he worked on the special effects of such films as *Battle of Britain*, *Inspector Clouseau*, *Tommy*, *The Rocky Horror Picture Show*, *X-Men* and *K-19: The Widowmaker*.

Colin is also a director of commercials, episodic television and music videos. The 42-minute-long "Smooth Criminal," which he directed for Michael Jackson, garnered critical acclaim as the most ambitious music video ever produced.

Colin currently resides in Ontario, Canada.

Aaron Lam is a filmmaker, journalist and author in Canada. He has produced documentaries for Canadian television and he co-directed the documentary *The Shaw Festival: Behind the Curtain* for PBS. Aaron was the Managing Editor of the magazines *Business $ense* and *ENGINUITY*, and he wrote *The Fake-Chicken Kung Fu Fighting Blues*, a novel for young readers.

Aaron is also an avid collector of movie props, storyboards and concept art. Known for his knowledge of science-fiction film history, he has moderated panels with Academy-Award-winning filmmakers at The Hamilton Film Festival and the historic Zoetic Theatre in Hamilton, Ontario.

Index

CPSIA information can be obtained
at www.ICGtesting.com
Printed in the USA
JSHW020230190120
3678JS00001BA/47